GOVERNMENTS
AND
HIGHER EDUCATION –
the Legitimacy of
Intervention

Higher Education Group
The Ontario Institute for Studies
in Education

1987

The Higher Education Group
The Ontario Institute for Studies in Education
252 Bloor Street West, 9th Floor
Toronto, Ontario
1987

ISBN 0-7744-9801-3

Preface

This publication includes some of the invited addresses and research papers presented at the second conference on higher education, sponsored by the Higher Education Group of the Ontario Institute for Studies in Education. The theme of the conference, which was held in Toronto on October 23 and 24, 1986, was Governments and Higher Education - the Legitimacy of Intervention. The department was extremely gratified with the response to its call for papers. By crowding the program with concurrent sessions we were able to accommodate the six invited addresses (those of Harry Arthurs, Blair Neatby, Frank Newman, Maurice Kogan, Grant Harman and Kenneth Rea) and thirty-eight of the large number of submitted brief reports.

An international panel of judges (Dr. Grant Harman of Australia, Dr. Don Adams of the U.S. and Dr. Mary Corcoran of the U.S.) recommended which of the submitted papers to accept for publication. Unfortunately, space permitted the inclusion of only thirteen. The criteria for acceptance were (1) quality of the writing and originality of the material of the paper, and (2) appropriateness for the three sub-categories by geographical area - Canadian content, foreign other than U.S., and United States. The judges felt that the quality of many rejected papers was high, too high to discard them entirely.

Since there is a paucity of published material on Canadian higher education, seventeen of the rejected papers were submitted to the third assessor, Dr. Mary Corcoran, Professor Emeritus of Higher Education and Educational Psychology, University of Minnesota, to advise on the publication of a second book. Eleven of these will appear in a forthcoming Readings in Canadian Higher Education, volume I. They were chosen on the basis of (1) quality of writing and originality of material, and (2) centrality to the theme of government intervention.

It should be noted, therefore, that the organization of both these publications differs from that of the conference in which they appeared. For the conference the papers and addresses were grouped into sessions dealing with intervention as demonstrated by historical papers, economic interventions, interventions which affected programs and curricula, etc.

The purpose of the second conference was similar to that of the first one held in 1984: to bring together to discuss issues in higher education, focused on a common theme, those academics and gradute students whose field is the study of institutions and systems of higher education, the administrators who manage and speak for these institutions, and the officials of buffer bodies and governments who influence or make policies regulating them.

I would like to take this opportunity to acknowledge the excellent work of my secretary, Mary Lynn Ste. Marie, who did the word processing and copy editing for the book.

Editor
Cicely Watson
Chairman
Higher Education Group

Table of Contents

Keynote Address

The Question of Legitimacy

by

Harry W. Arthurs[1]

I am both flattered and intimidated by the invitation to deliver the keynote address at this conference. On the one hand, I positively revel in the notion that the several dozen distinguished speakers scheduled for the next two days will be feverishly re-writing their remarks as my "keynote" serves as a kind of tuning fork for the conference, establishing a perfect pitch against which they must modulate their views. On the other, paradoxically, I am keenly aware that my freedom of speech is circumscribed. I feel an obligation to the conference organizers to accept the inner logic of the topic they have asked me to discuss.

One might almost use my own ambivalence about my role as keynote speaker as a metaphor for the very question I am supposed to be addressing: the question of the legitimacy of government intervention in higher education.

Intellectuals, and especially those intellectuals who have organized themselves into powerful institutions such as universities, are in a sense the keynote speakers of society. We influence society in many subtle ways, but we do not stand entirely aloof from, or indifferent to, its assumptions and expectations. We record and preserve knowledge. We create, demolish and recreate knowledge. We even aspire to show how knowledge can be usefully applied in science and technology, human relations, the economy and all the other dimensions of modern society. Nor are we concerned with knowledge alone: wisdom, moral values, aesthetic sensibilities are all grist for our mill.

And how do we address this crucially important agenda? Not merely by teaching and scholarly research, as these activities are traditionally understood. We preach. We practice what we preach. We exhort and condemn. We consult and lobby and -

---

[1]President, York University, Toronto, ON.

all else failing - we take out short-term leases in choice locations along the corridors of power.

Heady stuff, this, but there is another side of the story. We know our limits, limits which derive directly from the extent of our collective involvement in practical affairs. We accept that we have obligations to society which are implicit in the important keynote role we have assumed. We have to justify ourselves in some way, and show that we are worthy of the work we have chosen to assign to ourselves. At our best, we do this by *ipse dixit*: "it is a hallmark of any great society that it supports its universities". At our worst, we stoop to conquer: "universities train the knowledge workers upon which modern economies depend, and provide the innovative thrust which is necessary for survival in an increasingly competitive world".

Here, in a few bold strokes - not to say over-worked cliches - I have attempted to sketch the background against which I hope now to explore the issue of government intervention and its legitimacy. The most salient feature of this background is that by our own choice, universities are both in and of society, implicated in its agenda and appealing to its predominant values.

Let me postpone for a moment the difficult question of what we mean by "government intervention", and turn instead to the even more difficult question of what we mean by "legitimacy". The term has many meanings, and is indeed itself the source of considerable dispute amongst social scientists. I do not intend to rehearse that dispute in full, but its essential core is an empirical one.

It is conventionally argued that governmental action is "legitimate" if it is understood to conform to the fundamental norms of a society. Sometimes those norms are procedural, sometimes substantive; but the perception that fundamental norms have been respected is thought to be what induces people to acquiesce willingly in official action which they might not otherwise support.

Some critics are agnostic about "legitimacy" on empirical grounds. They ask for evidence that respect or obedience are indeed generated by appeals to legitimacy. Others express

4

more active hostility to the whole notion of legitimacy. Legitimacy, they contend, expresses no intrinsic or anterior validity; the norms by which legitimacy is measured are as vulnerable to challenge as the derivative conduct which is being evaluated; appeals to legitimacy are mere expedient attempts to mystify, and thus to disarm opposition.

Given these very different points of view, it is no surprise that "legitimacy" is an intellectual commodity which comes in many shapes and sizes, each expressing in itself a set of assumptions about the nature of social behaviour, and a critical evaluative perspective.

For example, consider what we might call "formal legitimacy". We might say that government intervention is legitimate whenever it is taken in a manner which respects formal legal norms. If government intervention is accomplished through regulations or orders-in-council, they must be authorized by an empowering statute. If it is accomplished through legislation, the enacting legislature must be constitutionally competent to pass the statute. If it is accomplished through the articulation of a new judicial doctrine, that doctrine must stand scrutiny in the highest courts, and survive subsequent legislative attempts to revise it. But if intervention meets all of these tests, it is formally legitimate - regardless of our views about its wisdom or utility.

However, I did not escape into presidential freedom from twenty-five years of bondage in the law just to come here to deliver an elementary lesson in legality. If the formal legitimacy or legality of some particular act of intervention is what concerns you, I suggest that you seek counsel from a real lawyer who would likely enjoy talking about it.

Formal legitimacy or legalism - is itself an ideology. It assumes that regularity, order, constitutionality are themselves ultimate goods - regardless of whose regularity, order, or constitutionality is being respected. It expresses itself in such empirically problematic propositions as "we have a government of laws and not of men", in the idolatrous worship of the Charter of Rights and of its legal acolytes, and in disdain for the political process as an unpromising and unsavoury means for resolving important social controversies.

It follows from what I have said that legalism does not have much to tell us about government intervention. This does not mean that people will - or should - forbear from going to law as a way of attacking government action. The Charter especially tempts us to buy tickets in a litigious lottery which offers a large jackpot of legal rights. But do not overestimate your chances; the courts will not lightly strike down government action; governments which are found to have acted illegally often find other, juridically fool-proof, ways of achieving their objectives; and in the dustbin of recent history you will find many abandoned projects and dashed hopes of social movements which exhibited a naive faith in legalism.

Legalism has its counterpart in what might be called conventionism: a belief that we are indeed ruled by an unwritten constitution based on conventions which define the legitimacy of behaviour. Cabinet government, the party system and judicial independence are often "legitimated" by reference to such conventions. Indeed, the unwritten constitution seems to have recently acquired new importance as a legitimating device. In 1982, the Supreme Court of Canada found illegitimate - as a violation of convention - the unilateral attempt by our federal government to patriate the Canadian constitution.

But conventions no more resolve arguments over "legitimacy" than do laws; they are at best a rhetorical device which is used to discredit innovation on the grounds that it is inconsistent with past practice.

Suppose we wanted to object to recent government policies designed to lure universities into closer relations with the corporate sector. Obviously, there are lots of arguments one could deploy on both sides of the issue. But to argue that government has not conventionally intervened in university affairs in this particular way before, and that its intervention is therefore illegitimate, strikes me as a particularly weak argument.

Indeed, it is not only weak, but it may be ahistorical as well, as arguments from convention so often are: upon close examination, conventions which we thought to be ancient and unambiguous turn out to be neither.

Finally, the appeal to convention as a legitimating device is unlikely to satisfy people who are convinced that the conventional behaviour was fundamentally wrong, who believe that the present circumstances are not encompassed by the convention, or who argue that conventions must necessarily evolve as times change.

Thus, the argument that government intervention of a particular kind is illegitimate because it is unprecedented should not - and often does not - carry much weight, except with those who are convinced already that nothing should be done for the first time, or that the thing being done is in and of itself wrong, regardless of how it was done or by whom.

Let me offer a third example of how particular meanings of "legitimacy" are used to advance particular social assumptions. It is sometimes argued that the test of legitimacy is whether conduct is in accordance with a society's "fundamental" beliefs or values. Thus, conformity to liberal-democratic values is the test of "legitimacy" in our society, while no doubt conformity to "God's will" or some sectarian version thereof makes government action "legitimate" in theocratic societies.

What is so problematic in this approach to legitimacy is not just the notion that certain values are "fundamental", but the difficulty of trying to move sure-footedly from what is fundamental to what is operational in any given situation. In effect, the fundamental will require elaboration and adumbration, and debate over the propriety of the action in question may well be obscured by debate over the intriguing question of what is or is not "fundamental". In such a situation, the notion of legitimacy will be purely conclusory: the sorting out of what is fundamental will be dictated by the desire to reach a particular conclusion on what is legitimate.

To translate this last concern into our own context, one has only to try to imagine how the limits of academic freedom are defined in any society. In our own, for example, almost everyone would acknowledge that such freedom does not extend past the point at which it contradicts the fundamental tenets of liberal democracy and seeks to impose closure on intellectual enquiry. But where does this get us? If we analogize intellectual enquiry to "free speech", we might conclude that it is legitimate to permit racists to speak on our campuses; if we regard intellectual enquiry as requiring fundamental respect for the dignity of all participants in the learning process, we might reach a contrary conclusion about who may legitimately speak.

By now, I suspect, you will have heard more than you care to about the notion of "legitimacy". At least you will have heard enough, I hope, to make you sympathetic to the notion that the term does not serve us very well as an analytical tool for evaluating government intervention in the higher education sector.

I have now demolished half of my assigned topic, and stand convicted by my own standards as a poor excuse for a keynote speaker. You will therefore not be surprised to learn that I now mean to demolish the other half. Just what is meant by "government intervention"?

This is a question with some point in an historical era which has witnessed officially sponsored mass murder and selective assassination of intellectuals, book-burnings, closure of universities, McCarthyism and other forms of thought control, and a host of minor brutalities visited upon the community of scholars by governments of the left, right and putative centre.

Only a few of the less extreme forms of government intervention have been experienced by the universities of the democratic west. Often these have been stoutly resisted, sometimes endured silently, and occasionally - and to our discredit - connived in and even welcomed by elements of the university community. But at least we know second-hand what governments can do when they set their minds to the destruction of universities.

It is not government intervention in this sense that we have come here to consider. Rather we are looking at a much more subtle process, one which is not intended to destroy universities or even to impair the freedom of enquiry which is central to their existence. Government intervention, as we use the term, connotes attempts by the democratic state to persuade universities to adopt a course of conduct which is, or seems to be, consistent with their historic mission of research and teaching.

For example, government may try to ensure that specific groups - say professional or business interests or poor people or minorities - benefit from university activities. Government may try to enlarge or restrict access to university studies on grounds of equity or economy. Or government may try to impose upon universities institutional arrangements which achieve closer integration or greater competition, more democracy or less inefficiency.

In none of these situations is government consciously seeking to impose limits in the classroom, laboratory or library which are obviously and unequivocally repressive or restrictive. Yet all of them may be - and have been - stigmatized as illegitimate forms of government intervention.

Please understand the limits of the point I am making. In any of these situations, government can fairly be criticized for its choice of priorities, its lack of understanding of the effects of its action, or its choice of inappropriate techniques to achieve otherwise attractive goals. Government, God knows, is not always benign, clever or far-seeing. But the same can be said of all of us, without putting in question our fundamental integrity or the legitimacy of our actions.

I am going to suggest that the extremity of our reaction to government intervention springs from three different sources within the university community. First, it is an historically-informed defensive reaction against the terrible extremities of government intervention which others have suffered, and we have largely escaped. Second, it demonstrates our human-enough reluctance to change our ways, even when we know we ought to accept the implications of fair criticism or the burdens of new responsibilities. Third, it reveals our acute embarrassment at having actively sought and gratefully accepted government intervention so often that we can no longer find any rational grounds for resisting it.

It is this latter point that I wish to address. We have become habituated to "government intervention" in its most seductive form: subvention. We crave subvention: financial support through direct operating grants, land grants and capital grants, research contracts, students aid, tax credits and other fiscal measures by which governments effectively sustain almost all public and private universities around the world. We live or die by subvention. And it is subvention - that most insidious and necessary of interventions - which has lowered the threshhold of our capacity to say "no" rationally to government, and has led us to rely excessively upon "legitimacy" as the rhetoric of choice in what ought to be a serious debate over political and educational values.

Let me try to explain how and why subvention makes it particularly tempting for government to intervene in our affairs, and particularly difficult for us to refuse. Subvention implies that - however reluctantly, however inadequately - government is committed to higher education as a public good. Viewed as a public good, it benefits its immediate consumers, such as students and faculty members, but also many other constituencies. Merely to list these constituencies is to understand the source of government's temptation and our difficulty: parents who aspire to have their children educated, so that they can advance socially and economically; private and public sector employers who require a supply of literate, numerate and trained recruits; knowledge industries which directly consume the research output of universities, and the broader public which receives the benefit of advances in science, social science, and humanistic scholarship; university faculty and staff and employees of businesses which serve and supply universities, and the communities whose economy depends on the local employment opportunities they create; and the large numbers of graduates whose life chances - in the fullest sense - have been enhanced by a university education.

From government's perspective, then, a "legitimate" higher education policy speaks not only to the concerns of the academic community but also to the interests and wishes of these other constituencies. And thus our difficulty as well: if we wish to enhance our claims upon public resources, we must try to demonstrate that what is good for us is also good for many other people. Nor do we fail to convince ourselves of this: most of us genuinely regard scholarship and education not just as ends in themselves, but as important contributions to humanity and society.

Given this convergence of academic and government perspectives, how can we refuse in principle to link academic and other objectives more closely?

Down the slippery slope we go. Support for medical education and research is justified as part of a larger strategy designed to protect public health and alleviate the effects of illness. Major expenditures on business or engineering schools, it is hoped, will promote economic development. Bilingual higher education is meant to improve the social and economic status of our francophone minority. Even liberal education is seen to serve broad social objectives: the training and enfranchisement of the productive citizens of a modern industrial democracy.

Each of these positions, translated into government policy, can be disputed, especially at the level of detail. But few of us would argue that it is illegitimate for government to pursue them simply because other considerations are made to intrude upon initiatives which originate within the universities themselves.

I certainly do not mean to suggest that all of the constituencies I have identified are treated with equal solicitude by government. As a rule of thumb, the more concentrated and powerful the constituency, the greater its claim upon a significant share of educational expenditures: health and economics before social justice and general enfranchisement. But the legitimacy of intervention *per se* is assumed, and the only issues worth discussing are "how?", "how much?" and "on whose behalf?".

Let me now step back a pace, in order to ask the hard question: If we object in principle to intervention by subvention, what are we to do about it? Does anyone really propose that we should offer to strike some sort of reverse Faustian bargain in which we return what we have gained from our association with government, and in exchange recover our souls?

This is not a realistic or attractive option for most of us. We accept that it is legitimate for government to intrude upon other autonomies in order to advance broad public interests. Most of us, I imagine, are prepared to ban extra billing by doctors, insist that children be educated until they reach school leaving age, and require that broadcasters meet Canadian content rules. Few of us would recommend dismantling medicare, the public school system or the CBC, despite the risks of government intervention. In truth, we object neither to subvention nor to the government intervention which it necessarily implies.

Let me test my hypothesis. By enacting laws of general application, government has intervened to constrain the autonomy and infringe the interests of universities: employment equity is expensive and may be seen to clash with meritocratic hiring practices; copyright gets in the way of unlimited photocopying which is so convenient for teaching and research; safety rules designed for industrial contexts may be inappropriate in university laboratories; and the application of the Criminal Code to student misbehaviour may be viewed as extreme overreaction.

Yet, I suggest, in none of these instances would we argue that it is "illegitimate" for government to disregard our autonomy and interests - even if it is neither wise nor fair to do so.

This brings me to a crucial point. Arguments about the legitimacy of government intervention are often no more than disagreements about the wisdom or fairness of government policy. It is not intervention, *per se*, which agitates us, so much as the result of intervention in the particular instance. Yet knowing that full well, we still tend to cast our objection in terms of protecting our "autonomy" against illegitimate government initiatives. Why do we do so?

Sometimes our rhetoric is adopted for tactical reasons. It may mobilize the support of those who are neutral on any given issue, but inclined to mistrust government and defend universities. And complaints about legitimacy up the emotional ante: government intervention is made to appear as fundamentally oppressive and anti-democratic, rather than as merely wrong-headed.

Sometimes, however, our rhetorical opposition to government intervention is, in peculiar ways, highly principled.

12

On the one hand, there is a position I might uncharitably describe as mediaevalist. Nurtured on the notion that universities are one of the longest-lasting and most adaptable institutions in the western world, its proponents emphasize the autonomy which they have historically claimed if not always enjoyed. The guild tradition, they believe, has metamorphosed into freedom of enquiry, collegial governance, peer review, and all that we hold to be most valuable in the modern university.

How far this mediaevalist perspective is to be pursued remains unclear. I imagine that its proponents do not favour professions of faith or enforced celibacy for faculty members, although there may be some lingering affection for immunity from civil process and the election of university members to the House of Commons. But at the point at which historical references claim to be more than metaphorical, they cease to be entitled to good-natured deference, and demand instead close analysis. This they seldom survive.

There is a second principled position, espoused by members of the Society of Shakers of the Unseen Hand. Caught up in the general ecstacy of enthusiasm for the market as the arbiter of all public or social decisions, they resolutely mistrust all forms of government intervention, except those which are intended to produce optimal market conditions. In the realm of higher education, they are fortified in their faith by the happy coincidence that we all subscribe to "the marketplace of ideas" as the locus of unfettered intellectual enquiry.

But once again, metaphor is no substitute for analysis. No more than in the debate over other social or economic policies is the free market position in higher education detached from a keen sense of where present and future advantage would lie if deregulation were adopted, and government were indeed to revert to its role as the holder of the ring, rather than active advocate of the common good. No less than in these other spheres of debate are quantification and econometric analysis ultimately incapable of providing the complex, qualitative analysis which ought to drive public decision-making.

And there is a third principled position which I might call the platonic position. Its advocates posit the existence of ideal-types: a university is a place of learning; faculty members live to serve knowledge and their students; students come to university to discover and attain their full intellectual capacities. These are all ideal-types in which I believe, or would like to believe. From this platonic perspective, every act of government intervention which does not immediately, explicitly and exclusively fortify the ideal is illegitimate, out of keeping with the essence of universities, and an affront to the natural order of the universe.

Would that it were so, and would that I - as a creature which does not exist in the platonic lexicon: there are no ideal presidents - did not have to bear the sad tidings to my colleagues that life is just not like that. Universities, as I have already suggested, serve a multiplicity of needs and wants; some faculty members some of the time do exhibit characteristics which are found more often amongst other groups of mortals: they are nasty, self-seeking or lazy; and even as passionate a pedagogue as myself has occasionally noticed some divergence between the way I would like to find my students and their actual self-presentation.

In light of my agnosticism, then, I cannot find it in my heart to denounce government intervention as lacking in legitimacy for the sole reason that it stems from mixed motives or is intended to produce results which do not reinforce the platonic ideal of the university.

Let me now remind you of my argument so far. I have argued that the concept of legitimacy is by no means a clear one. I have suggested that government intervention is inevitable once we accept the basic premise of government funding. And I have tried, perhaps without success, to persuade you that such intervention is by no means wrong in principle.

But at the same time I should like to remind you of what I have not argued. I have most emphatically not said any of the following:

- that all government intervention is automatically a good thing;

- that the present policies of Canadian governments in the higher education sector are good for universities, much less good for the country as a whole;

- that it is impossible to define a set of principles upon which to mount coherent and cogent criticism of government intervention in any given case, or over a period of time.

To the contrary: I believe that it is not only possible but essential that we define those principles, and ensure that government intervention which offends them is challenged vigorously and effectively. And lying behind the principles must be - as there does not yet seem to be - a well-grounded and carefully articulated vision of the role of the university in this country at this moment in its history. Such a vision may be informed by platonic ideal-types, may be expressed in language rich in historical association and emotive power. But it must above all respond to what we are, who we are and where we are.

These are the issues which are authentic and important - not the hollow rhetoric of "legitimacy" or a reflexively hostile reaction to all forms of "government intervention".

What I am proposing is a prospectus for intellectual work, but it is also a program of practical political action. Here are the main lines of analysis:

- what practical steps can be taken to ensure that the central academic project of free enquiry is not only immune from government intervention, but actively and adequately supported by the state?

- what are the limits of reciprocal behaviour which the state is entitled to demand of the university, as the price of its protection and support?

- by what means can the multiple internal and external constituencies and many purposes of higher education be harmonized?

There are no definitive answers to these questions, and to even confront them is to commit ourselves to the grubby, tortuous and never-ending business of politics. But politics - in the broadest, nonpartisan sense - is where we must ultimately assert ourselves if we are to protect higher education from its enemies and save it from its friends.

Section I

The Historical Perspective

by

H. Blair Neatby[1]

This paper starts from the assumption that both governments and universities behave consistently with what they believe to be their best interests. Politicians and academics may be - and often have been - wrong about where their best interests lie, but we can sit in judgment later. Our immediate concern with the historical record is to understand when and why Governments of Canada and of Ontario decided to take a direct interest in higher education, and to understand when and why universities welcomed or resented this attention.

There are complications. Politicians are not always candid about their motives and may not even be clear in their own minds. Government policies are usually compromises. And in Canada we have a federal system in which both federal and provincial governments have left their mark on the university system. As for the universities, who knows who speaks for them? Administrators and faculty and students often have conflicting views about what is good for a university. Chronology is also important; over a relatively brief period of time, the interests of both governments and universities can change dramatically. The interaction of the evolving attitudes of politicians and academics has shaped the historical experience of Canadian universities.

For Canadians the debate is no longer over the pros and cons of private as opposed to public universities. Today Canadian universities are all publicly supported and will continue to be dependent on public support. For those who are convinced that he who pays the piper calls the tune, and that public funding somehow contradicts the fundamental values of a university, the battle is already lost. And the historical record does provide examples of government interference which most of us would find quite unacceptable. In the nineteenth century, for example, the provincial legislature at Queen's Park actually

[1]Professor of History, Carleton University, Ottawa, ON.

appointed professors to the chairs at the University of Toronto.[2] On the other hand, the extent to which governments have transferred funds to universities without demanding any accountability can also be astonishing. My own institution, Carleton College as it was in 1950, had no government charter at that time, and no bureaucrat had ever asked any questions about its programs and academic standards, and yet it received a provincial grant. The best interests of governments are not likely to be identical with the best interests of the universities but nor are they likely to be completely at odds. The universities to which we belong have been shaped by compromises to which both politicians and academics have contributed.

For government, universities are a means to an end. If the government's objective is economic growth and that growth seems tied to the exploitation of Canada's natural resources, a government that behaves rationally will make sure that there are enough forestry and mining engineers. If the focus shifts to advanced technology we would expect the government's interest in higher education to shift to scientific research and development. The changes are not likely to be dramatic - Canadian governments are not inclined to be reckless. They will still allow some funds to be spent on history, or even on Latin, as long as the universities respond to the current demand for engineers or for scientific research or whatever governments see as the priority of the day.

Governments are also responsive to popular attitudes which may be less defined than plans for resource development. If most Canadians believe that a university education is a good thing, if most Canadians are convinced that their universities are underfunded, politicians will notice. Governments, after all, are composed of citizens who are likely to share the attitudes of the majority. And politicians, whatever they may say, do study the latest Gallup polls and will be influenced by public opinion even if they do not completely agree.

---

[2] For the discussion of the relations between the University of Toronto and the Government of Ontario see E.A. Stewart, "The Role of the Provincial Government in the Development of the Universities of Ontario 1791-1964", unpublished Ph.D. thesis, University of Toronto, 1970.

Enough of these generalizations. How have politicians and academics responded in practice to evolving views of their own best interests? Let me begin with Canadian federal politicians. Federal intervention is of special interest because it is not obligatory; Ottawa has no constitutional responsibility and so its involvement in higher education can be directly linked to its own objectives. Section 93 of the British North America Act may say bluntly that provincial legislatures "may exclusively make laws in relation to education" but in this area our constitution has proved to be a very flexible instrument. Federal involvement has relied primarily on the spending power; that is, it has offered money and, as long as the provincial governments and the universities acquiesce, Section 93 has been irrelevant. Provincial governments have occasionally defended the constitution - Maurice Duplessis blocked federal grants to Quebec universities in the 1950's - but the other provinces have usually been willing to compromise their constitutional commitment for a price. When we study federal grants to universities we are dealing with political history, not constitutional history.

The first significant federal intervention dates back to the first World War when some politicians became aware of the connection between industrial development and research. German scientists before the war had contributed to Germany's preeminence in steel production and in textiles; during the war they had revolutionized the production of explosives. As early as 1915 a British White Paper, looking forward to the post-war world, had argued for the need to promote "scientific research with a view especially to its application to trade and industry"[3]. In Canada, the Minister of Trade and Commerce, Sir George Foster, used the same argument in Cabinet and persuaded his colleagues to appoint the Advisory Committee for Scientific and Industrial Research. The Advisory Committee, more commonly known as the National Research Council, was expected to coordinate and to conduct industrial research. It was not a high priority for the government during or after the war - railways and tariffs were still what federal politics was made of - and the NRC did not have any laboratories until the 1930s.

---

[3] Cd. 8005, 23 July 1915.

The National Research Council however was dominated by academics; of the original nine members, six were university men including the Chairman.[4] The federal funds they did administer went mainly to university scholarships and to university research. In 1917 the Chairman tried to justify these expenditures to a dubious Minister of Finance by arguing that "the Students and Fellows, as such, must not engage in studies for any University examination. They are to devote themselves during the tenure wholly to research, and, mainly, to research of industrial application".[5] But this emphasis on industrial research, if it ever existed, soon disappeared. The same Chairman was arguing two years later that universities should give training "not in industrial research but in pure and applied science which is held by all who have experience in research to be the best field in which to prepare students for a career in industrial research".[6] Within a few years even the lip-service to applied science was gone. Before there could be industrial research in Canada there had to be Canadian scientists, and to the academics on the Advisory Council this meant training in the fundamentals of science. The result was financial support for graduate students working with university scientists with established reputations. Scholarships and research grants were awarded by juries composed of academics; they were awarded only for study or research at Canadian universities. In 1928, H.M. Tory, then Chairman of NRC, could even boast to his Minister that "a large part of the research being carried on at Canadian Universities today has been made possible by the assistance of research grants to university professors and scholarships to university students recommended by their professors... We have been both anxious and ambitious that our universities

[4]Mel Thistle, The Inner Ring: The Early History of the National Research Council (Toronto: University of Toronto Press, 1966), pp. 9-10.

[5]A.B. Macallum to Sir Thomas White, 6 July 1917; quoted in Thistle, The Inner Ring, p. 23.

[6]A.B. Macallum, memorandum, 1919; quoted in Thistle, The Inner Ring, p. 57.

should lead the way in fundamental research."[7]

The government's initial objective had been industrial research but the academics on NRC had redirected the funds to support their own university research. In the process graduate studies and scientific research were given an impetus which altered the internal balance of the larger universities. To attribute this to government intervention, however, would be absurd. The federal government had provided funds but it had not imposed a research policy. University scientists had decided how the money was to be spent.

The second World War provides another example of the contacts between the federal government and Canadian universities. The government actively encouraged the training of engineers and scientists by offering financial support to the students and by ruling that no professional scientist or technician could leave the university for any other employment without its permission.[8] There is no record of any protest from the universities. Indeed, the universities themselves shared the overriding commitment to winning the war and were more than eager to cooperate. Military training became compulsory at many universities; at McGill two students who refused to participate in this training were suspended from the university by the Senate. Principal James of McGill and Principal Wallace of Queen's even suggested that students enrolled in the humanities and social sciences should lose their exemption from conscription.[9] The federal government showed more respect for arts students; it accepted university enrolment in all programs as being in the national interest. Instead of the recruitment of university contingents, which had been the pattern in the first World War, university students were

---

[7]H.M. Tory to James Malcolm, 29 February 1928; quoted in Thistle, The Inner Ring, p. 280.

[8]Stanley B. Frost, McGill University: For the Advancement of Learning, Vol. II, 1895-1971. (McGill-Queen's University Press, 1984), p. 220.

[9]Gwendoline Pilkington, Speaking with one voice: Universities in dialogue with Government. (Montreal: McGill University, 1983), pp. 28-29.

encouraged to continue their studies until graduation.[10]

With the end of the war, the federal government faced the probability of a post-war recession with high levels of unemployment among the veterans. One way of keeping some of the returning soldiers off the labour market was to pay them to go to university. This meant almost doubling university enrolment but the challenge was met by a remarkable collaboration between universities and government. The university administrators found makeshift classrooms and laboratories while the university professors accepted sharply increased teaching loads. The federal government, for its part, helped to make this possible by making a grant of $150 directly to the university for each veteran enrolled, as well as paying the student fees.

By the early 1950s most of the veterans had graduated. Instead of withdrawing gracefully from the provincial sphere of post-secondary education, however, the federal government over the next fifteen years intervened more directly than ever before. In 1957 it established the Canada Council with an endowment of fifty million dollars for the encouragement of the arts, and for research in the humanities and social sciences. Another fifty milion was provided to the universities for the construction of buildings related to the humanities and the social sciences. The federal government was now deliberately trying to influence university policy by allocating funds to a special sector of the institution. Even more tendentious, it was directing its funds to areas of higher education which directly impinge on social values and cultural identity. Spending money on science or even on health might have been tolerated by most provincial administrators but to fund the liberal arts was almost provocative. How do we account for this challenge to the sleeping dogs of provincial autonomy and French Canadian nationalism? And how do we account for the fact that even in Quebec the action of the Canada Council did not provoke a constitutional crisis?

---

[10]See James S. Thomson, Yesteryears at the University of Saskatchewan 1937-1949 (Saskatoon, Sask., 1969) for an account of the eagerness of Canadian universities to contribute to the war effort.

The explanation requires a shift in focus from domestic affairs to external relations. The Cold War is part of the story for, in the rhetoric of the era, democracy was being challenged by authoritarianism, and the free world had to meet the threat of the Communist world. The other concern was how Canada could survive in North America as the close neighbour of one of the superpowers, now that the British counterbalance could no longer be relied on. These two related problems led to a federal involvement in higher education in which the aims were never clearly stated and probably never clearly understood but which focused attention on the need to strengthen the humanities and the social sciences in Canada.

To many North Americans, Communism was an intimidating force because the enemy had a sense of mission, a commitment to a cause, and a willingness to make sacrifices, which somehow seemed lacking in what was called the free world. Democracies, so the argument ran, had forgotten that eternal vigilance was the price of liberty and had been seduced by material success. What was needed was a Great Awakening, a renewal of the democratic faith. In the United States President Truman's Commission on Higher Education, in a report entitled Higher Education for Democracy, saw the universities as advanced training units in this struggle for the minds and souls of the world. "Education for democratic living", it affirmed, "should become a primary aim of all classroom teaching and, more important, of every phase of campus life." Students should be given a liberal education with the first objective being "to develop for the regulation of one's personal and civic life a code of behaviour based on ethical principles consistent with democratic ideals".[11] In the United States this Cold War commitment to education for democracy had its darker side for it led to a witch hunt for the Communists and fellow-travellers who were indoctrinating the young. Loyalty oaths were imposed and tenured professors were dismissed. McCarthyism, as it was labelled, has been described as "the most devastating and demoralizing blow ever struck at American universities by their own government, state and

---

[11] Gail Kennedy, ed., Education for Democracy: The Debate over the Report. (London: Heath and Co., 1952), pp. 6, 23.

national".[12]   University administrators jettisoned academic liberty to prove the loyalty of their institutions, and even the American Association of University Professors showed a disturbing reluctance to defend its members.

Many Canadian educators also saw the link between higher education and the Cold War. It was no coincidence, for example, that Watson Kirkconnell, one of the most eminent academic Cold Warriors, ever eager to denounce the Communist schemers, was also one of the leading champions of the humanities in Canada and had championed them against what he saw as the betrayal by Cyril James and Stewart Wallace during the war.[13] But Canadians never fell prey to the excesses of McCarthyism. No governments in Canada demanded loyalty oaths for professors in publicly-supported universities. No universities dismissed professors on ideological grounds. But the Cold War did have some impact. Avowed Marxists were not being hired in those days and public expressions of radical opinions were certainly frowned on. Canadian democracy, however, did not demand the sacrifice of academic freedom.[14] We had the advantage of not being a superpower, of not feeling directly and solely responsible for the fate of the free world. But in Canada academic freedom was also protected by the Canadian ambivalence about the real threat to Canadian identity. Canadians could never focus their

[12]C. Vann Wood ward in The New York Review of Books, 25 October 1986, in his review of Ellen W. Schrecker, No Ivory Tower: McCarthyism and the Universities, (Oxford: Oxford Uunivrsity Press, 1986).

[13]Watson Kirkconnell, A Slice of Canada. (Toronto: University of Toronto Press, 1967), p. 316. For his advocacy of the humanities see his memorial to the NCCU in 1942 in *ibid*, pp. 237-9, and also Watson Kirkconnell and A.S.P. Wodehouse, The Humanities in Canada, (Ottawa: Humanities Research Council, 1947).

[14]For a balanced assessment of academic freedom at Queen's University after the war see Frederick W. Gibson, Queen's University Vol. II, 1917-1961, (McGill-Queen's University Press, 1983). Harry Crowe's political beliefs were doubtless a factor in his dismissal from United College but the ascribed reason was his lack of loyalty to the institution and not his disloyalty to the country; it is also noteworthy that the Canadian Association of University Teachers defended Crowe.

undivided attention on the Cold War because they also worried about the United States. In addition to the threat of Communism, there was the threat of the crude materialism associated with American society.

The Canadian equivalent of the President's Commission was the Royal Commission on the Arts, Letters and Sciences, better known as the Massey Commission, appointed in 1949. Brooke Claxton, who was mainly responsible for the appointment of the Commission,[15] was a committed Canadian nationalist who had earlier played a key role in establishing a public radio network in Canada and now wanted a Canadian television network to preserve us from American culture. Vincent Massey was his choice as Chairman of the Commission in part because Massey was an Anglophile for whom to be Canadian was to be profoundly British, and who had a patrician disdain for American popular culture. His distaste was shared by some of his fellow commissioners, especially Hilda Neatby, whose So Little for the Mind, denounced the nefarious influence of American progressive education on imitative Canadian educators.[16]

The Commission, which at first had not considered universities to be within their terms of reference, soon concluded that they were central to Canada's cultural survival. And within the universities it was the humanities which could save the day. The task of the humanist, they modestly affirmed, is "the exegesis and the preservation of all the elements which make of man a civilized being". The humanities had to be more than a gentlemanly or a ladylike veneer; "humanistic studies do not belong only to the faculty of liberal arts but should pervade the professional schools as well. They should permeate the entire

---

[15]For the origins of the Commission see J.L. Granatstein, Canada 1957-1967: The Years of Uncertainty and Innovation. (Toronto: McClelland and Stewart, 1986), Chapter 6, and Claude Bissell, The Imperial Canadian: Vincent Massey in Office. (Toronto: University of Toronto Press, 1986), Chapter 9.

[16]Bissell, The Imperial Canadian, p. 204, describes Neatby as "influential in the shaping and writing of the report".

university."[17] The federal government had a moral obligation to contribute to this great task. Otherwise, the Commissioners warned, "it denies its intellectual and moral purpose, the complete conception of the common good is lost, and Canada, as such, becomes a materialistic society".[18] Thus the crusade, as in the United States, was against materialism; in Canada, however, the humanities had to protect us against American as well as Russian materialism. The dangers were so diffuse that neither governments nor public opinion had a clear definition of what was disloyal or un-Canadian.

Canadian university spokesmen had no problem with the recommendations of the Massey Commission. Most Canadian university presidents still were humanists who, quite apart from the pressures of the Cold War and the fears of American influence, were often concerned about the expansion of scientific research and the growth of professional schools at the expense of the liberal arts. They welcomed the recommendation for a Canada Council and organized national conferences to support the proposal.[19] There was also the understandable eagerness to have another donor, in addition to the provincial governments. There was certainly no fear of the intrusion of government in the sensitive area of human values. If this was seduction, they welcomed it. Nor is there any reason to think that they ever regretted being seduced.

But the involvement of the federal government went far beyond specific support for the humanities and social sciences. Beginning in 1951 the federal government began making annual grants directly to Canadian universities. The grant in that year could have been interpreted as a pragmatic response to the financial crisis faced by Canadian universities with the end of federal grants for the veteran students; the seven million dollar grant providentially equalled the money which had come

---

[17] Report of the Royal Commission on the Arts. Letters and Sciences. (Ottawa: Queen's Printer, 1951), pp. 159, 137.

[18] Ibid., p. 8.

[19] Pilkington, Speaking with One Voice, pp. 70, 94.

to the universities because of the veterans. These annual grants not only continued but increased, until by 1966 they totalled almost one hundred millions.[20] There were also expanding grants to NRC which could be justified by precedent and by the links between scientific research and the national economy. The newly created Defence Research Board was directly related to a federal responsibility. Even the new Medical Research Council could be linked to national health or to the health industry. But the annual federal grants to universities met none of these criteria; they were not tied to research and they were not directed to any specific aspect of higher education. This expansion of the role of the federal government is all the more surprising, given the political context, because Maurice Duplessis denounced this encroachment on the provincial sphere and refused to allow the Quebec universities to benefit from the federal largesse. Louis St. Laurent had a well-earned reputation for respecting constitutional niceties and provincial rights. What had persuaded him to take this uncharacteristic step? And why had succeeding administrations increased the grants?

The explanation is linked to the commitment to economic growth, and the assumption that "highly qualified manpower", to use the jargon of the day, was a major factor in economic growth. Canada, it was believed, needed to increase its supply of professional, technical and managerial skills. A study for the Economic Council of Canada in 1965 even promised that government investment in university education would produce dividends in the range of fifteen or even twenty percent, far higher than any return from an investment in physical facilities.[21] Little attention was paid to the subject matter or the discipline. Economists assumed a direct correlation between the level of education and the level of economic productivity. The federal grant thus was justified as a

---

[20] John B. Macdonald *et al.*, Special Study #7, The Role of the Federal Government in Support of Research in Canadian Universities. (Ottawa: Queen's Printer, 1969), p. 92.

[21] J.R. Podoluk, Earning and Education, (Ottawa: D.B.S., 1965). See also Economic Council of Canada, Second Annual Review, (Ottawa: Queen's Printer, 1965).

contribution to economic growth - an area in which the federal government believed it had a legitimate responsibility. The unilateral approach to the constitution, however, became less and less acceptable to the provincial governments, which were equally committed to economic growth but which had concluded by the 1960's that they should plan their provincial economies. A compromise was reached in 1967 when the federal grants to universities were replaced by federal grants to provincial governments to cover half the costs of post-secondary education. This was still consistent with the assumptions about economic growth. Federal funds were still being directed to higher education and so to increased productivity; the inclusion of post-secondary technical and vocational training was a logical extension of this policy.

Canadian universities welcomed federal funding. The National Council of Canadian Universities and its successor, the Association of Universities and Colleges of Canada, representing the university administrations, and the Canadian Association of University Teachers disagreed on many things but they both petitioned the federal government regularly to increase its university grants. In 1962 a CAUT committee favored federal support in the form of a percentage of university operating costs although conceding regretfully that "as a practical matter, however, it is unlikely that the federal contribution could exceed that of the provincial government".[22] The Bladen Commission on University Financing, sponsored by the AUCC, insisted that the federal government should share the responsibility for financing higher education, although "in a form which avoids any invasion of the provincial right, and obligation, to direct and control such education". Federal funds were more important than any constitutional niceties.[23] Universities clearly preferred two paymasters because having two patrons would mean more money and would contribute to university autonomy.

---

[22]CAUT, Bulletin, September, 1962.

[23]Report of Commission to the AUCC, Financing Higher Education in Canada. (Toronto: University of Toronto Press, 1965), p. 67.

By the 1970s, however, the federal government had changed its mind. Part of the problem was the spiralling costs associated with the extraordinary expansion of post-secondary education, stimulated at least in part by federal payments covering half of the operating costs. The federal transfer payments increased at a rate of twenty percent per year until 1972, when the federal government limited the annual increase to fifteen percent. But there was more to it than that. The federal government was no longer convinced that all forms of post-secondary education contributed to economic growth, and believed that its money would be more wisely spent if it could be allocated to specific areas or activities. It was no secret that the federal government would have been delighted to opt out of support for university teaching and take over full responsibility for university research, if this had been feasible. In the meantime it tried to cut its losses in 1977 by replacing its post-secondary grants with what was euphemistically called the "Established Programs Financing".[24] The federal government under this program transferred a total of tax points and cash grants which was tied to the GNP rather than the costs of post-secondary education. After some twenty-five years, the federal government had dropped its policy of trying to foster economic growth by contributing to the general operating costs of Canadian universities.

The federal government still does not know what its relations with universities should be. The emphasis is still on economic growth but economists no longer agree on how this can be achieved. Canada, it is assumed, is engaged in a highly competitive scientific and technological race. What is needed is a research and development policy which will give Canada a competitive advantage. The Senate Special Committee on Science policy (the Lamontagne Committee) outlined some of the basic assumptions. Scientific merit could no longer be the sole criterion for research grants; the federal government should only invest in those projects which promised to have practical application and which related in some way to Canadian resources. It was also assumed that a much higher

---

[24]For a brief summary of the federal grants for post-secondary education see Peter M. Leslie, Canadian Universities 1980 and Beyond. (Ottawa: Association of Universities and Colleges of Canada, 1980), pp. 148-159.

proportion of federal aid should be devoted to development rather than to research. The federal government was easily converted. The difficulty was to devise a science policy which would guide the federal government in allocating funds to research and development. The federal government established a number of advisory bodies, including a Research Council, a Science Secretariat, and a ministry of Science and Technology, but without resolving its problem.[25] There was no shortage of advice or of candidates for research and development funds, but there has been no consensus on priorities. Without priorities there is no science policy.

Canadian universities, for all their association of direct federal grants with university autonomy, quickly adjusted to the system of federal grants to the provinces to meet half the costs of post-secondary education. Their fears for their autonomy were eased by the increased revenues which the new arrangement produced. In Ontario the universities with religious affiliations were hard hit because they had been receiving federal grants but now the federal funds would be channelled through the province and, under provincial regulations, they would get nothing. In most cases the response was almost immediate. These universities promptly "deconfessionalized" and got their money. The "Established Programs Financing" was a much more serious blow to the universities because, in effect, it meant the end of federal contributions to their operating costs. Indeed, university administrators and academics are not yet reconciled to the new situation. They regularly calculate what portion of the federal transfer would have been attributed to post-secondary education under the previous arrangement and vociferously protest if the provincial contributions do not match this sum.[26] They are wasting their time. Operating revenues now come out of the provincial budgets and have done so since 1977.

---

[25]See Louise Dandurand, "The Nature of the Politicization of Basic Science in Canada: NRC's role 1945-1976", unpublished Ph.D. dissertation, University of Toronto, 1982.

[26]For a recent example, see the CAUT Bulletin, October, 1986, pp.10-11.

University spokesmen have contributed little to the formulation of a federal policy on research and development. Academics have found it easy to agree that more money is needed for research and their demands for increased federal funding have often relied on the argument that Canada must be at the frontier of advanced science and technology in order to be competitive. But there has been no consensus on priorities. Some insist on the primary importance of fundamental research. Scientific breakthroughs are unpredictable, the argument runs, and so the money should go to the best scientists and the best projects, as determined by other scientists. Even the attempts by the federal government to orient research towards sectors of special interest to Canada - such as the Strategic Grants for Canadian Studies or for research on aging, administered by the Social Sciences and Humanities Research Council - have been denounced as unwise and somehow illegitimate. Federal officials see this as self-serving. Academics appear to be asking for more money but insisting that they must be trusted to decide how the money is to be spent. And indeed they are.

My role as an historian fortunately absolves me from predicting the future. A pattern, however, does seem to be emerging. The federal government has opted out of contributing to the operating revenues of Canadian universities. It is interested in funding scientific and technological research, and possibly even research in the social sciences if there is a possibility of an economic pay-off. Its grants to the research councils will doubtless continue, although the recent freeze with the sop of matching funds for private donations is an indication of their low priority. It would prefer to negotiate research projects, and whether this is done through the universities or directly with research groups does not matter. It should matter to the universities. Much of the research can and will be done by academics and their graduate students, often relying on university facilities. If the universities want to benefit they will certainly need to charge overhead costs. From the administrators' point of view they will also want to charge for the time spent on these projects by their staff. Academics prefer to moonlight and it is not yet certain that universities can do anything about it. More important, however, is the recognition that scientific research in Canada must be a combination of curiosity-oriented research and mission-oriented research, and that it is in the interests of both governments and universities to concede the legitimacy of both approaches.

Relations between universities and provincial governments are more complex. Canadian universities are provincial institutions. There is no national university and there will be no national university; nor is there any private university which is not regulated by provincial bureaucrats. Provincial governments are the paymasters, and universities are more and more being integrated into provincial university systems. Here again both governments and universities have their own interests and their own objectives, and government policies are compromises, shaped in part by the universities. For the historian it is not always easy to trace the development of these policies; the compromises were often arrived at through private discussions with no public record of the negotiations. Indeed, for the first half of the twentieth century differences of opinion between provincial governments and Boards of Governors almost never became common knowledge, and university administrators and academics may have been unhappy but they rarely expressed their sentiments in public. From the outside at least it was a picture of blissful harmony.

The harmony was more than a matter of appearances. Provincial governments and university authorities were in basic agreement on the function of universities and on how they could best achieve their objectives. Universities trained the children of the provincial elites; they served as a finishing school for their daughters and prepared their sons for admission to the liberal professions. These social functions were understood by governments and by university officials; there were no major confrontations over admissions, over course content or over student discipline because both groups shared the same social values. Cabinet ministers and members of the Boards of Governors might belong to different parties but they were all men of substance with similar views of the social order. University presidents were the chief executives of the Boards. The professors were subordinates; if they criticized the president or if they publicly defied social conventions they were vulnerable. For example, when President Murray of Saskatchewan fired four of his professors in 1919 for being disloyal to him, the provincial government gave him their full support. And when Mitchell Hepburn wanted Frank Underhill dismissed, Canon Cody was ready to oblige and was only deterred because some members of the Board demurred.[27]

For half a century the consensus on the role of the universities made overt government intervention unnecessary. Departments of Education administered elementary and secondary schools but they had nothing to do with higher education. Universities were rarely even mentioned in provincial legislatures. Provincial governments did provide annual grants to meet the deficits of the public universities but even these grants were not a matter of public debate. The procedures were surprisingly informal. The university president, with the support of his Board, would submit a request directly to the premier who, presumably with the consent of his Minister of Finance, would then decide the size of the annual grant, and there the matter would rest until the next year. Presidents would not protest publicly and legislators would not ask questions. As J.A. Corry once put it, the university of that time:

> ... rested in a backwater, out of the mainstream of life and action, little exposed to "the roar of bargain and battle". It touched directly only the lives of the tiny fraction of the young who became its students, roused the interest, and sometimes the concern, of their parents. In those who wanted to be its students and couldn't, it aroused yearnings but not opposition or criticism.[28]

And so universities were left undisturbed because they were doing what was expected of them with only modest demands on the public treasury.

---

[27]For Murray see D.R. Murray and R.A. Murray, The Prairie Builder: Walter Murray of Saskatchewan, (NuWest Press, 1984), Chapter 7; for Hepburn see M. Horne, The League for Social Reconstruction, (Toronto: University of Toronto Press, 1980), Chapter 10. It could be argued that the consensus between the government and the Board broke down because Hepburn did not share the values of the traditional elite.

[28]J.A. Corry, Farewell the Ivory Tower. (McGill-Queen's University Press, 1970), pp. 102-3.

The disruption came after the second World War, when both universities and governments changed their minds about the social purpose of higher education. For a brief interlude universities were seen as central to economic growth, to social change, and to improving the quality of life. Those of us who were academics in the 1960s found ourselves moving from the backwater to the forefront of social action, and we revelled in our unaccustomed prestige and our soaring incomes. It was an unprecedented era when old universities were renewed and new universities were built and when higher education took precedence over health or welfare or highways in provincial budgets.

Academics sensed sooner than politicians or university administrators that times were changing. They had accepted the low status and the penny-pinching of the pre-war years and had loyally coped with the constraints of wartime and the crowding by the veterans. But then, at a time of declining enrolments, and when university administrators and politicians were talking of getting back to normal, the university professors behaved in a quite uncharacteristic manner. Many of the ringleaders were social scientists, scholars with research degrees imbued with the social value of research. They did not think of themselves as college teachers but as university professors; as professionals they equated their status with that of lawyers and doctors. They formed faculty associations and demanded higher salaries and improvements in their working conditions, all of which showed a rising estimate of their own self-worth. The demands were modest enough, but for university professors even modest demands were a radical development. The immediate results were even more modest than the demands. But over the next decade, when other Canadians began to look to the universities as crucial institutions for social change, professors, often to their own surprise, found themselves treated with extraordinary respect. In part it was because spiralling enrolment increased the demand for academics. Salaries doubled, and professors were given single offices, telephones, and more secretarial assistance. There was more to it than the demand for teachers. Indeed, staff-student ratios actually declined, and the average level of academic qualifications of the faculty actually improved - in sharp contrast to the pattern just after the war when the veterans had appeared on campus.

36

In the 1960s universities were competing for a combination of researcher-teacher and the concern for research made a difference. Research funds, travel grants and sabbaticals became an important part of the pay package. The new status also led to changes in university government. Senates grew more powerful and academics were admitted to Boards of Governors; presidents, deans and chairmen received term appointments, chosen by search committees which included faculty members. By the end of the 1960s professors had a status and a prestige which their predecessors had never dreamed of.

The new benefits and privileges came surprisingly easily because the provincial governments had been converted to the social significance of universities. The literature might suggest that this was a recognition of the importance of research and development or of highly qualified manpower in a competitive world. Certainly this was what government advisors were saying.[29] Even politicians included them in their armory of arguments. But it is not certain that these were decisive in persuading governments to double their expenditures on universities and then to double them again. I can speak with some assurance about Ontario, having looked at the records of the Advisory Committee on University Affairs.[30] For the crucial years of the early 60's this Committee guided the government. Indeed, with Leslie Frost as its leading figure, it almost was the government as far as university policy was concerned. But Leslie Frost did not talk about advanced technology in a post-industrial world. He was more impressed by the projections of university enrolment doubling within a decade. As a Conservative he was worried about the political consequences if in ten years the universities had no room for these students. Parents would not be pleased and would surely blame the government. The wise politician would make sure

---

[29]Every province had a royal commission or task force on higher education in these years of expansion. Advanced research and graduate studies were always included in the justification for increased provincial support.

[30]See Paul Axelrod, Scholars and Dollars: Politics, Economics and the Universities of Ontario 1945-1980 (Toronto: University of Toronto Press, 1982) for the complicated history of this committee.

that there was room. And so the CUA took the initiative. It called in the university presidents and offered incentives for expansion. It also welcomed community initiatives to found new universities and, especially in the case of York, it encouraged the planners to raise their sights to meet the expected need. Thus in Ontario the effective spur for university expansion seems to have been the commitment to university accessibility. The pattern varied from province to province but in each case the highest priority seems to have been given to providing places.

Universities, however, could also influence the pattern of higher education. Governments might be worried about numbers but Boards of Governors and university presidents often had other priorities. The established universities wanted to improve their academic reputations. For them, the government's generosity was an opportunity to expand libraries, improve laboratory facilities and appoint prestigious scholars. As practical men they knew what the governments wanted and would pay for, but they also knew that expansion, if carefully planned, could contribute to their own objectives as well. Professors hired to teach undergraduates could be selected on the basis of their publications and their potential as research directors. Formula financing reflected the governments' emphasis on accessibility; the weighted formulas, usually weighted very much in favour of professional and doctoral programs, reflected academic priorities. In the heady years of affluence, university expansion could meet the differing priorities of governments, of university administrators and even of professors.

In more recent years the choices have been more difficult. Governments were shocked by the increasing proportion of young people going on to university and by the spiralling costs of open-ended formulas. One obvious option was to limit accessibility, to restrict admission only to the better students. Provincial governments, however, shied away from this option, fearful of the outcry from angered parents. An alternative was to restrict the more costly programs. In most provinces governments did regulate the establishment of additional professional schools and of new doctoral programs. But there were narrow limits to what governments dared to do. They could prevent the creation of new faculties of education or of law, for example, but community pressure made it almost impossible to close down any existing faculties. It proved to be even more difficult to control the costs of graduate studies. Governments were often convinced that significant savings in faculty salaries and library or laboratory costs could be made by eliminating some doctoral programs. This "rationalization", as it is still euphemistically called, met with a stubborn and an impressively effective resistance from universities. The leading university in the province might aspire to be the center of graduate studies but other universities were determined to keep what they had and to keep their options open for the future. In Ontario the Committee of University Presidents forestalled the government by elaborate ACAP (Advisory Committee on Academic Planning) studies, discipline by discipline. The academic evaluators applied academic criteria and, not surprisingly, found most of the existing programs were academically sound and that even new programs were academically justifiable. After some years of this approach to "rationalization" the frustrated provincial government pointed out that the result had been a net increase in doctoral programs.

Another approach was the commission or task force where public-spirited citizens and hard-headed businessmen could advise the government on where to apply the axe. But here the tradition of university autonomy warded off almost every assault. If the province had too many faculties of engineering or of architecture, which one should go? Neither commissions nor governments have shown the courage to make what is seen as an academic judgment. Universities have not volunteered. Thus university administrators, supported by the faculty, have been able to frustrate the provincial governments' efforts to impose structured and more hierarchial provincial university systems.

Governments have not been helpless. They have wanted to limit the costs of higher education and to some extent they have succeeded. The expenditures on education have declined by comparison with expenditures on health or welfare. Financial constraint has been imposed by limiting the total university budget, usually by limiting the formula increases. As a solution this satisfied nobody. University professors find themselves negotiating salaries with universities which have severely limited budgets. University administrators must cut costs across the board with almost no room for discretion or flexibility. Provincial governments have controlled their expenditures but are not able to eliminate what they regard as wasteful programs or direct funds to new areas. If this continues it will eventually frustrate the legitimate aims and expectations of all of these groups.

In the meantime, however, the present impasse serves as the most recent illustration of my thesis that neither governments nor university administrators nor faculty can determine university policy on their own, and that in the past and the present, and presumably in the future, any decisions affecting higher education will represent compromises between a number of interest groups.

Politics and Its Limits on Intermediaries and Un

by

Lee Southern[1]

This paper begins with a discussion on an ab
level of the public interest in Canadian higher e
serves as the context for government-intermedi_ _.versity
relations. It describes the current centralizing trends in the
relations and examines the operational behaviour of these
organizations from a political viewpoint. The requirements of
political behaviour are defined and applied to higher education,
in particular to intermediaries. The paper concludes with the
suggestion that, contrary to the opinion of many, politics acts
as a protector of higher education.

The Public Interest and Higher Education in Canada

On an abstract level no responsible person would deny that
provincial governments have a legitimate interest - both in the
reasonable and the legal senses - in Canadian higher
education. According to Robbins, public interest in
universities is reasonable because

> ...it is unlikely that separate consideration by
> independent institutions of their own affairs in their
> own circumstances will always result in a pattern
> that is comprehensive and appropriate in relation to
> the needs of society.[2]

Briefly stated, the needs of society which constitute the
substance of the public interest in higher education include the

---

[1]Secretary to the Council, Universities Council of British Columbia,
Vancouver, BC. (The Council was abolished by the BC Government, March 31,
1987.)

[2]Baron Lionel Charles Robbins, Higher Education Revisited. (London:
MacMillan, 1980), p. 13.

41

ing.[3]:

- The liberal education of selected young adults is a fundamental public objective of university education. The manner of this education may be more important than the subject content. Its aim is to implant in students a lifelong desire for learning, the power of objective analysis and critical examination of data, opinions and values, so that they are better citizens able to discover their own mental powers and limitations.

- The continuing education of adults seeking university level instruction for their own personal growth and satisfaction is a corollary extension to the provision of a liberal education.

- Professional training is a complementary public educational objective to liberal education. As well, universities are called upon to provide professional development programs to enable employed adults to meet their career advancement needs and to cope successfully with the rapid pace of technological change.

- The intellectual activities of research for the purposes of advancing knowledge and understanding, and the satisfaction of creative curiosity, must be a permanent major objective of university work. As part of the research continuum, the universities must include people skilled in the use, as well as the acquisition, of knowledge who are prepared to apply their skill to research tasks of direct benefit to society.

---

[3]This description of the public interest in higher education has been extracted with modification from a University Council of British Columbia planning document, Facing Tomorrow's Needs in Higher Education: British Columbia University Education into the 1990's, (Vancouver: UCBC, January 1986).

• The intellectual activity of scholarship must be a signature characteristic of university work if it is to preserve cultural heritage, to re-examine past values and to consider the contemporary application and relevance of such values.

While the foregoing wording might be varied, essentially, it is a statement which confirms that the universities share with government a public interest in higher education.

As a consequence of providing public funding to higher education, the provincial government's interest is lawful when it seeks to ensure that universities have clear and appropriate objectives and that optimal value is obtained for the public monies allocated to them. Moreover, on a legal level, in Canada, the public universities operate on the basis of provincial statute and, accordingly, possess prescribed functions and enabling powers. The provincial governments have formal powers in the field which, in large degree, they have circumspectly proscribed in certain areas pertaining to the academic operations of the institutions. Therefore, while recognizing the statutory prerogative of provincial government to alter its relations with universities, it can nonetheless be said that there is a sharing of formal power. In addition, some provincial governments have delegated powers to intermediary bodies.

The establishment of intermediary bodies has been a recognition that an arms-length relationship between government and universities is desirable. It is also recognized, however, that with public funding comes responsibility for public financial accountability. The notion of a buffer then arises, and one common form has been the interposition of an intermediary body between the government and the universities on the following rationale:

> The argument is that universities should be shielded from bureaucratic control and political interference because of what they do. The main activities of universities are teaching, research and public interest. The argument that those who perform these activities should be shielded from bureaucratic control rests on the fact that these

activities can only be done by professional academics who have mastered a complex body of knowledge through extensive formal training and apprenticeship. The complexity of the work and the high degree of specialization means that their work can be neither directly supervised nor effectively regulated by conventional hierarchial controls; instead, control comes from professional norms and peer controls. Attempts to apply conventional hierarchial administrative techniques can be dysfunctional in that they tend to drive out competent professionals causing those who remain to become discouraged or to take collective action to vent their frustration.

The argument that those who perform the activities should be shielded from political interference rests on the fact that the activities of universities involve ideas and, to quote Sibley,

"...the university, at its best, seeks to hold in balance two equally important forces, on which all progress depends: orthodoxy and dissent. It cannot succeed in this task except in the presence of a reasonable, though far from absolute, autonomy."

Together, or separately, these two arguments form the case for a buffer between universities and the governments which subsidize them. However, these arguments do not form the case that the buffer need be an intermediary body. The buffer role can be provided by means of lay governing boards and statutory safeguards concerning hiring, promotion, and discharge of academic staff. The case for an intermediary body rests on the need for coordination and planning within multi-university systems. More precisely, the case for an intermediary body must rest on its performance of these functions. All relevant things considered, an intermediary body must produce better results than alternative buffer arrangements.[4]

The creation of such bodies with statutory powers increases the sharing of legal power, albeit in unequal proportions, in government-university relations in Canada.

In summary: It is submitted that provincial government-university relations in Canada are characterized by agreement-in-principle on:

- the scope of the general objectives or public interest in higher education;

- the need for some degree of financial accountability for the use of public funds appropriated to higher education;

- the potential usefulness of buffer arrangements often involving intermediary bodies; and

- the sharing of legal powers.

Let us now shift our focus to current trends at the operational level of these relations.

Current Trends in Government-University Relations

In the past, the operational exercise of government authority over universities tended to be *ad hoc* and limited to particular matters whereas today it has expanded in scope and is sustained in nature. In effect, higher education is now considered by government to be an instrument of policy. Until recently such an approach was more accepted in the European university than the North American. But its occurrence is becoming increasingly commonplace in Canada, although its legitimacy is being questioned. Hence one supposes the *raison d'etre* and topicality of the theme for this conference.

---

[4]Kenneth Strand, <u>A Review of the Role of Intermediary Bodies</u>. (Vancouver: UCBC, January, 1984), p. 11.

Governments of western countries are acting directly in academic areas. In France this year the minister for higher education (with faculty support) revoked a Ph.D. awarded by the University of Nantes. In the United Kingdom, the Secretary of State for Education and Science has indicated to the Vice-Chancellors that his preference is for all new academic appointments be made without tenure. His ministry has requested "action plans" from the universities showing evidence of progress in the following areas: program selectivity and rationalization, academic standards and staff appraisal, as well as areas which have indirect impact on academic decisions such s financial management and monitoring, performance indicators, and pay and structure of the faculty. The University Grants Committee, (a venerable forerunner of the Canadian higher education intermediaries, largely composed of university academics) has constructed a ranking of university research strengths by subject to serve as the basis for differential resource allocation. In Canada, the block grant principle is being eroded in several provinces as governments increasingly make designated program grants usually under the euphemism of "excellence funding". Clearly, there is a trend in government towards strengthening external controls over universities and, in some cases, intermediaries in higher education are following the same line.

The consensus of the government and universities on the abstract and legal levels discussed in the previous section breaks down on the operational level. It is at this level that the issue is joined: who is to exert effective influence on specific outcomes of higher education? This is the major issue underlying the conference theme. The role of the intermediary in influencing the outcomes in higher education is the focus for the remainder of this paper.

I submit that successful politicians exert effective influence on the outcomes in higher education because the relations between government and university are essentially political. The explanation for this contention is contained in the definition of politics and the description of the requirements for its practice which follow.

46

The Political Nature of Organizational Behaviour in Higher Education

The operational features of politics involve: (1) conflicting interests and differing views as to specific objectives, (2) disbursed ability to effect outcomes, resulting in the need to form coalitions to achieve objectives, and (3) by so doing often requiring compromises on the objectives. Such is the stuff of politics.

The question for higher education is: How is it that conflicting operational views occur when governments and universities share general objectives within a consensual abstract and legal framework? There are three possible explanations. First, conflicts occur when the issues raised have no single correct answer. Higher education abounds in such issues. For example:

- in addressing the general objectives of higher education, what constitutes the specific curriculum of a liberal education? What priorities and balance ought a university to strike between general and professional education, between undergraduate and graduate levels, between academic directions originating within the university and ones originating within government?

- in assessing the financial requirements of higher education Bowen points out that

    ... Because higher education is conducted at so many different levels of expenditure and with so many different allocations of resources, however, there is no precise need that can be objectively defined and defended.[5]

---

[5]Howard R. Bowen, <u>The Costs of Higher Education</u>. (San Francisco: Jossey-Bass Publishers, 1980), p. 16.

- in developing a procedure for public financial accountability there is no agreed upon convention but rather a multiplicity of government schemes for fiscal scrutiny, often changing even within jurisdictions from year to year.

Second, operational conflicts occur when participants have differing intellectual and institutional perspectives. For example, a faculty member's principal loyalty may be to his academic discipline, a university president's duty to his institution, and a minister of the Crown's to the cabinet, his party and the electorate. Nor should it be omitted that academics, bureaucrats and elected officials alike take actions "aimed not only at the discharge of duty but also at the satisfaction of passion, appetite and unreflecting habit".[6]

Third, operational differences are inherent in any relations in which effective influence on outcomes is distributed differentially. For example: as noted earlier, the statutory powers vary unequally between government, universities and intermediaries; the salience of higher education is greater for some governments than others; the abilities of some university presidents to persuade ministers and *vice versa* is greater than others.

The impact of these conflicting conditions which permeate government-university relations causes pressure for the use of bargaining and coalitions to reach compromise and consensus, that is, politics. Finally, men differ in motivation and about what should be done. Men and women share power in government and university organizations. Their behaviour is political by necessity, in order to get anything done. In varying degrees this political phenomenon applies in the making of an academic appointment by faculty; in the development of a university's institutional academic plan; in the allocation of funds to different groups within the university; in the allocation of public funds among individual institutions by an intermediary; and in the appropriation of a level of funding for higher education by a government.

---

[6]Henry Fairlie, The Life of Politics. (London: Methuen & Co. Ltd., 1968), p. 22.

The simple theses of this paper are that (1) the behaviour of both those in government and those in higher education is political, and (2) those who understand political processes, possess and apply political skills stand a better chance of realizing their objectives than those who do not behave in this manner. The corollary is that for an intermediary to be effective in government-university relations, it must become effective politically. This is ironic because the traditional view of these bodies was that they should be objective and aloof from politics. As Strand noted above, the case for the utility of a higher education intermediary lies in its ability to produce results in the areas of coordination and planning within a multi-university system. It is suggested that such results can only be achieved through the application of political means. Conversely, if an intermediary fails to operate politically it will be either ignored or eliminated.

While simple in concept, the idea that men, especially "university men", operate on a political basis is not usually publicly acknowledged. Political operations have a pejorative connotation, antithetical to the notion of academic objectivity and rationality. Objectivity and other concepts held to be the desirable means of inquiry are common expectations of universities and their members. That a university president should admit to the pursuit of political ends - that is, to effect compromises, by political means through bargaining - does not enhance the image of the scholar. Privately, however, academics, bureaucrats, appointed and elected officials, all players in higher education, will confess to, and often boast of, their successful political manoeuvers. And frequently they complain that the failure of their efforts is due to the "political" intervention of others. This double irony only serves to illustrate the nature of man's ambition and the ubiquity of political processes. If Princeton's Woodrow Wilson really did believe that open covenants could be openly arrived at (an academic approach to the solution of problems), it might well account for his failure to lead influential men into the League of Nations and ensure its survival. Open inquiry and complete disclosure of information are not part of the political process.

Political Requirements for a Higher Education Intermediary

What does it mean for an intermediary to operate politically? It involves forming a view of what needs to be done based on actual conditions and the collective motivation and interest of the members. That in itself is a political operation, in the sense that there is not one correct "image" of conditions, motivations and interests and, therefore, there will not be one "correct" solution to the problem of what to strive for and what compromise to accept. Rather, it will be a view based on only some of the principles, interests and appetites of the intermediary members as applied to such questions as: How should the development of higher education be planned and coordinated? How much consideration should be given to individual universities' aspirations? How much public/government interests? The degree to which each intermediary member possesses the will and ability to influence outcomes will determine the degree to which the intermediary's original agenda becomes compromised. An influential and strong-minded chairman, for example, may have his individually conceived agenda carried without amendment.

Once having adopted the agenda, the intermediary as a collective (guided by its most influential members since all groups are governed by elites), will move to the next step. That is to develop strategy and tactics to achieve the agenda objectives, a task that cannot be achieved simply by appeal to the universities to come and reason together. Politics requires that there be analysis of the following four factors[7]:

1. Who plays? Parties whose interests and actions can have an influential effect on decisions and actions have to be identified. These include not only senior players, that is, institutions' senior administrators and governing boards, and

---

[7]For a comprehensive and detailed application of a political model of organizational behaviour see Graham T. Allison (Director of the Kennedy School of Government at Harvard University) Essence of Decision, (Boston: Little Brown and Company, 1971). This paper draws on his methodology.

government's bureaucratic and elected officials, but also representatives of the informal influence structures.

2. What influences each participant's views and what "interests" do they represent?

3. What is each participant's influence on outcomes?

4. What is the game? How are the participants' views and influence combined to yield decisions and actions?

Based upon such an analysis, the intermediary must adapt its preferred outcome to the conditions determined in the analysis and formulate its strategy and tactics to achieve a modified outcome. The implementation stage follows and requires the exercise of the political skills of manoeuvre, management and persuasion rather than the making of "vainglorious declarations of policy or principle".[8] That persuasion must prevail over fiat results from the reality that

the world... is a world of scarcity and... all the resources... are limited, both material resources of wealth and unmaterial ones of time and political support... All these resources have alternative uses

and,

it is the politicians' acknowledgement that he must be ready to accommodate other wills and other desires than his own.[9]

Accordingly, in these circumstances the intermediary must carry out four political tasks:

----

[8]Fairlie, The Life of Politics, p. 20.

[9]Ibid., p. 22.

1. *reconcile conflicting interests and formulate a policy which if not approved will, at least for the time being, be agreed to by the government and universities.* In the long run, the intermediary body must gain the confidence and support from both sides of its partnership for it has no public base of authority and cannot function effectively without them.

2. *maintain public interest in issues in higher education.* This task has two dimensions. In its role as advocate for higher education, the intermediary may increase the salience of this sector for government, thereby enhancing the prospects for sustained government financial support by maintaining public interest. Conversely, in its role as servant of the public, it must protect the public interest by ensuring that the universities attend to the general objectives of that interest.

3. *act as a catalyst on the views of government and the universities as*

> an adjuster of interests and ideas... to search for the point of contact between different and sometimes opposing ideas, the common ground which alone can make concerted action possible.[10]

An intermediary, as a relatively independent third party, can serve to broker conflicting objectives of governments and universities, thereby possibly avoiding potentially undesirable increased government control over universities resulting from impasse.

4. *link informed thinking on higher education and public opinion - an educational function.* An

---

[10]*Ibid.*, p. 24.

intermediary can facilitate the sophistication of public interest in higher education by disseminating the thinking of knowledgeable and respected educators.

Conclusion: Politics as Protection in Higher Education

Two conditions invariably arise when men organize to accomplish an objective: first, differences will arise over the objectives and how to reach them; second, the ability to get one's way will be limited in some degree by the support available from others. Universities, governments and their intermediaries are not exceptions. Politics, the effective use of influence to achieve objectives, is the operational dynamic.

It is the contention of this paper that if intermediaries are to be effective in facilitating an appropriate arm's length relationship between government and universities they cannot operate solely on principles or pleas for cooperation; they must be active players in a political process. These bodies must navigate by carefully drawn maps based on accurate perceptions of the converging interests of the governments and universities.

Government intervention in higher education, as this paper suggests, is controlled by the operation of political processes which place inherent limits on the effective influence of all parties on the outcomes. Despite public statements, by governments, intermediaries and universities alike, of commitment to a rationally planned coordinated system of higher education such an objective is not achievable unless both the government and the institutions perceive actual outcomes as being beneficial to their individual and varied interests. To develop a working coalition of these interests is a political task of great sensitivity and complexity for the intermediary. However, although provincial governments hold the upper hand in terms of legal power to intervene in higher education, this very political complexity serves to make their effective intervention difficult. Hence politics can protect university autonomy.

In this regard, Carswell, retired secretary of the United Kingdom University Grants Committee, has recently written:

> The obvious directions from which the autonomy [of a university] can be threatened are rarely the dangerous ones, or rather they only become dangerous if other political circumstances unconnected with the universities have cleared access to them. Naked political influence over appointments, courses, admissions, if attempted by authority in its own name, can usually be headed off or exposed, and, although in my experience such attempts have occurred, they have been rare and uniformly unsuccessful. Private influence by persons in power, exerted directly on a university or on individuals in it, is another matter. Such persons inevitably have their own affiliations in the university world, and that world knows well enough how to deal with such approaches. It is not and cannot be isolated and insulated from the worlds of politics, business, the professions or the trade unions. How could it be and remain a university world? Autonomy includes the right to accept influence just as much as to resist outside authority.[11]

In higher education there have been many "authority interventions" - the popes and princes in mediaeval times, ministry and treasury board analysts of today. Throughout, scholars have played a protagonist role; all have had to be politicians. The game of influence remains constant. The number of players has increased, so there has been a related increase in the number of interests and operational objectives. To the extent that these new influences have been effective, universities have changed their forms and functions through time and across geographic locations. The interposition of intermediaries in higher education, if their members are disposed to delimit government's and their own management role in university activities, can aid in the cooperative accomplishment of the agreed general objectives of higher

---

[11]John Carswell, Government and the Universities in Britain. (London: Cambridge University Press, 1985), p. 151.

education. In the past, universities have successfully acquired large scale public and private funding with few strings attached. As Sibley has noted, Canadian intermediaries have aided them in this endeavour.[12] In a world where power is diffused it always helps to have allies.

This diffusion of power must be addressed because no one office is in sole possession of all truth. No university president, intermediary chairman or minister of the Crown should have a completely effective influence on outcomes in higher education. What at bottom protects us all is the political process in which

> ... the essence of any responsible official's task is to persuade other players that his version of what needs to be done is what their own appraisal of their own responsibilities requires them to do in their own interests.[13]

The acceptable limits of politics are determined by principle, honour and duty but that is the subject of another paper.

---

[12]W.M. Sibley, The Role of Intermediary Bodies in Postsecondary Education. (Paper presented to C.M.E.C. Conference, Toronto, 1982), p. 8.

[13]Allison, Essence of Decision, p. 177.

State Control of Degree Granting: The Establishment of a Public Monopoly in Canada

by

Michael L. Skolnik[1]

The fundamental instance of government intervention in the university is at the stage of conception. Should government disallow the union of intellectual resources with the institutional authority to grant degrees, issues related to subsequent intervention do not arise.

A central issue in the study of government intervention in academe, thus, involves the exercise of state control of the authority to grant degrees. The stance of the state on this matter may be viewed along a continuum. At one extreme, the state may regard the institutional authority to grant degrees as a natural right which may be exercised by voluntary associations of its citizens and place no restrictions on organizations which would wish to award degrees. At the other extreme, the right to award degrees may be regarded as a privilege to be granted only at the pleasure of the appropriate civil authority. Between these two extremes, there may be varying degrees of severity of the conditions imposed upon those organizations seeking to grant degrees.

The purpose of this paper is to examine the rationale for state control of degree granting and the conventions, practices, and regulations surrounding degree granting which have evolved in Canada. The paper focuses particularly upon the experience of Ontario, the province which has the most detailed statutory regulations in Canada pertaining to degree granting. Reference will be made also to recent legislation in Alberta and concerns expressed about the subject in British Columbia. As well, the Canadian experience will be compared to that of the

---

[1]Professor, Higher Education Group, OISE, Toronto, ON.

United States. The paper will conclude with comments on the implications of prevailing Canadian practices with respect to the broader issues of government intervention in academe.

First, however, it is necessary to consider briefly the nature of degrees.

What is a Degree?

A great variety of educational institutions offer a great variety of programs of study, upon the completion of which the student is awarded a document attesting to the satisfactory completion of the program of study. In some instances, this document is called a degree, in others a diploma, certificate, or other designation. In the case of some programs for which a degree is awarded, it may be possible in other institutions to find programs which, on the surface at least, bear a considerable resemblance to the degree program, but which earn the graduate some other designation. It also has happened that course work which at one time in an institution earned credit for some other designation, after a change in the status of the institution, was rewarded by the conferral of a degree.

The foregoing observations suggest that attempting to define a degree in terms of particular academic content may be quite difficult. In fact, there is extraordinary variation in the content which various institutions deem necessary for the conferral of a degree. The numerous attempts of institutions and agencies to produce a standard definition of the learning achievement signified by the term, degree, have proven futile.[2]

Not surprisingly, the International Encyclopedia of Higher Education follows a somewhat different approach to offering a

---

[2]For a summary of such attempts, see Phyllis Keller, Getting at the Core (Cambridge: Harvard University Press, 1982).

definition of the term, degree: it defines a degree as a designation awarded by a university attesting that its recipient has completed a particular course of study.[3] The same source defines a university as an institution possessing certain attributes, one of which is the authority to grant degrees. While this circularity may be distressing to one who would wish for a more intellectually satisfying conception of something so central to academe as a degree, it does point to one central truth about degrees. The definition of a degree is not only highly subjective, it is also inherently political. What constitutes a degree is determined through the reconciliation of the opinions of the duly constituted agents within the institution which awards it; and if they, in turn, derive their status from some higher authority, then indirectly, but ultimately, through the reconciliation of the opinions of the relevant actors on some higher stage.

Archetypical Source of Authority

Whether the modern university has truly evolved from an archetypical community of scholars, or is essentially a relatively new type of social institution is something which I will leave to others to ponder. For an autonomous community of scholars to certify that a neophyte had attained sufficient mastery to become a peer member of the community certainly would not have required the imprimatur of an agent external to

---

[3]Asa S. Knowles, ed., The International Encyclopedia of Higher Education, 10 vols. (San Francisco: Jossey-Bass, 1977), 1:342a. Actually, the Encyclopedia defines a degree as a title conferred by a university or a college. The definition concerns the context wherein the terms, college and university, have quite similar meanings in terms of institutional status, but with university connoting greater institutional breadth than college. As noted in UNESCO's World Guide to Higher Education: A Comparative Survey of Systems, Degrees, and Qualifications, 2d ed. (New York: Unipub, 1982), p. 43, while the terms were at one time "almost synonymous," at present in Canada, college "refers to an institution which offers postsecondary courses for transfer to a university, or courses which are occupationally oriented, or both."

the community.[4] It would appear that the practice of seeking the imprimatur of a sovereign or bishop was motivated by considerations of gaining status, respect, financial assistance, security of life and property, or the stamp of patriotism or moral rectitude - not because such invocation was a necessary condition of conducting the affairs of the community. Only with the rise of the modern state, the widespread appreciation of the monopoly rents which could accrue to the holders of degrees, and institutionalization of the state's role in policing the marketplace did government control of degree granting become an issue in some jurisdictions.

The Rationale for State Control of Degree Granting

The control of degree granting by the state is a form of social regulation, and, as such, it would appear that the literature on regulation, as it has developed in the disciplines of Economics, Political Science, and Public Administration would provide the most useful frame of reference for considering the rationale for state control of degree granting. A qualification of this observation is that the regulation literature has a distinct focus on economic behaviour,[5] and depending upon how narrowly one conceptualizes "economic", one may feel varying degrees of discomfort in applying to higher education concepts which have their roots in the study of the production and exchange of goods and services. Yet, the regulation literature provides an extremely broad framework for examining the behaviour of organizations which obtain and transform resources; it has

---

[4]Nathan Schachner concurs with this view in The Mediaeval Universities (New York: A.S. Barnes, 1938), pp. 44-45, noting that the early centres, like Paris, Bologna, Salerno, and Oxford "sprang spontaneously into being without adventitious aid from Pope or Emperor," but that later, "Pope and Emperor and King viewed these astonishing growths with interest, each pondering how best to turn these phenomena to his own advantage." In The Community of Scholars (New York: Random House, 1962), p. 26, Paul Goodman cites Rashdall's view that prior to the idea of a sovereign Leviathan, masters did indeed conduct the inception of new masters "on their own responsibility," adding, with deference to Rousseau, that "apparently the university was born free and everywhere it is in chains."

[5]Robert D. Cairns, Rationales for Regulation, Economic Council of Canada Technical Report No. 2 (Ottawa: Economic Council of Canada, 1980), p. 2.

been applied to sectors which produce public goods; and it offers a well developed framework for the study of situations where licensing is central to public policy debate. Whatever other outcomes they have, institutions which grant degrees ration a commodity which has an economic value - degrees - and this rationing function invokes questions which the literature on regulation has been developed, in part, to address.

At the highest level of abstraction, there are three categories of rationale for government regulation: efficiency, which usually pertains to correcting market failure; distribution; and social and cultural objectives. The regulation literature has been heavily influenced by scholars from the United States who have been preoccupied with efficiency and distribution concerns, whereas in Canada social and cultural objectives have provided a relatively more important motive for regulation.[6]

Natural Monopoly and Destructive Competition

The dominant efficiency rationale in the classical literature on regulation is that of natural monopoly. A natural monopoly is said to exist when the total costs of production in a sector are lowest at all levels of output if there is only one producer, i.e. there are continuously and substantially declining marginal costs. Traditionally, public policy in the case of natural monopolies has been to restrict competition and to regulate the price, output, and sometimes other behaviour of the monopolist.

It is now widely recognized that there are few natural monopolies.[7] Research on economies of scale in higher education has demonstrated that the minimum efficient size of a university or college is relatively small, and that beyond a scale that is substantially smaller than the normal market

---

[6]*Ibid.*, p. 3.

[7]Economic Council of Canada, Responsible Regulation: An Interim Report (Ottawa: Ministry of Supply and Services Canada, 1979), p. 46.

size, diseconomies of scale set in.[8] Natural monopoly, then, is not normally a strong rationale for regulation in higher education.

Such research findings, notwithstanding, the popular notion (or perhaps, myth) that there are significant economies of scale in higher education has had, and continues to have, a substantial impact on policymaking.[9] The assumption that there were considerable economies of scale in the provision of university studies was at the foundation of the policy in Western Canada of concentrating resources in a single provincial university, a policy since modified slightly to allow for a few additional institutions in each province as the population grew.[10]

While a literal interpretation of natural monopoly, with its analogy to natural gas or hydroelectric energy distribution where there may be room for only one supplier, is inappropriate for higher education, a weaker version appears to hold sway in many quarters: namely, that to ensure efficient operation of each institution, the number of universities must be strictly limited.

This view that the market can easily become overcrowded, gives rise to a fear not just of inefficient scale of operation, but that in attempting to expand to a more efficient scale, or merely to remain viable, organizations will engage in "destructive competition", wherein the quality of goods and services produced deteriorates as suppliers cut costs, or excessive sums are spent on advertising as competitors try to

---

[8]See, for example, Howard R. Bowen, The Costs of Higher Education (San Francisco: Jossey-Bass, 1980), pp. 192-196, and Carnegie Commission on Higher Education, The More Effective Use of Resources: An Imperative for Higher Education (New York: McGraw-Hill, 1972).

[9]"Small is Vulnerable", The Times Higher Education Supplement (London), 7 February 1986, p. 28.

[10]Robin S. Harris, A History of Higher Education in Canada 1663-1960 (Toronto: University of Toronto Press, 1976), pp. 224-26.

lure customers from one another. Where destructive competition is thought likely to be more than a temporary condition, in response to a temporary business downturn, restriction on entry is one obvious way of trying to prevent such maladies.[11] On the other hand, the less draconian approach of imposing standards on service, quality, financial responsibility and the like may be a more appropriate strategy. In choosing among these approaches, it is necessary to consider whether producers would in fact debase standards in their competitive struggle; and to determine whether the benefits which might be secured by limiting entry are greater than those which freer competition brings, as well as the feasibility of effectively monitoring standards.[12]

It is not easy to demonstrate any particular propositions regarding the virtue of those who run universities, the benefits of institutional differentiation and competition among universities, or the effectiveness of mechanisms for ensuring academic standards. There is thus a division of opinion between academic conservatives and liberals regarding the advisability of limiting the number of degree granting institutions in order to prevent the maladies associated with destructive competition. Americans, being more ideologically committed to the market than Canadians, have tended to tout the benefits of pluralism and competition in higher education. They have developed a system of higher education characterized by ease of entry and great diversity, but also by perennial concerns about possible dilution of academic

---

[11]The desire to strictly limit the number of universities in Western Canada predates the inclusion of some of these provinces in the Confederation. Harris, p. 224, cites a statement of the Premier of the Territories, who was also Minister of Education, in 1903, urging that the West avoid "evils which by reason of competing institutions had been experienced in the Eastern Provinces". It is not clear whether the evils referred to were inefficient dispersion of resources or practices of destructive competition, but these two concepts are closely related.

[12]Alfred E. Kahn, The Economics of Regulation: Principles and Institutions, 2 vols. (New York: John Wiley, 1971), 2:178.

standards.[13] By contrast, Canadian higher education has been marked by stringent controls on entry, limited diversity, and, except during the recent period of funding constraint, confidence that standards were being maintained.[14]

Externalities

A third form of market failure which may justify government intervention is the existence of externalities. Externalities exist when there is a divergence between the net benefits which accrue to the private decision makers contemplating a particular decision and the net benefits to others who are not a party to the decision, most generally to society as a whole. Negative externalities, such as environmental pollution, have provided a powerful rationale for restrictive regulation, while positive externalities have often been seen as a justification for public subsidization or for forcing private decision makers to do things which they might not otherwise do, like getting vaccinated.

It has generally been accepted that education has substantial positive externalities, and these have provided much of the justification for compulsory schooling and subsidization of education at all levels. The existence of substantial positive externalities in higher education, which Bowen[15] has estimated, could hardly be seen to justify restricting the number of institutions; rather, these would provide a rationale for facilitating accessibility, through ease of institutional entry and other means.

---

[13]Harold Orlans, "The End of a Monopoly? On Accrediting and Eligibility", Change 12 (February-March 1980), pp. 32-37.

[14]See Peter Leslie, Canadian Universities 1980 and Beyond: Enrolment, Structural Change, and Finance, AUCC Policy Study No. 3 (Ottawa: Association of Universities and Colleges of Canada, 1980), and Michael L. Skolnik, "Diversity in Higher Education: The Canadian Case", Higher Education in Europe II, 2 (1986): 19-32.

[15]Howard R. Bowen, Investment in Learning (San Francisco: Jossey-Bass, 1980).

Inadequate Information

For a market to work effectively, decision makers must have adequate information to make rational decisions in the light of their values and preferences. In a world of increasing specialization and complex technologies, the information required for intelligent decision making for many goods and services cannot be summed up in their immediately observable properties.[16] Where information is inadequate, there are two principal approaches which government can take to remedying the situation: it can require suppliers to provide adequate information, or it can establish licensing regulations wherein only those suppliers who meet certain standards are allowed to operate.

Accreditation mechanisms, as they have developed in North America, represent a voluntary initiative of producers themselves to address the problem of inadequate information. Accreditation is a process in which institutions consent to periodic review by an external agency which determines whether the institution (or program in question) does, or does not, meet certain standards. Although technically voluntary, in many situations the consequences of failure to attain accreditation are such as to make accreditation for all practical purposes compulsory. Accreditation evolved in the United States as an appropriate non-governmental accompaniment of a system characterized by a tradition of "virtually free and untrammeled operation" by private degree granting institutions within the states.[17] In the more governmentally controlled environment of higher education in Canada, accreditation has not evolved to the extent to which it has in the U.S. and institutional - as opposed to program - accreditation is uncommon in Canada.

---

[16] Economic Council of Canada, Responsible Regulation, p. 48.

[17] Postsecondary Education Convening Authority, Approachehs to State Licensing of Private Degree Granting Institutions: The Airlie Conference Report (Washington, D.C.: Institute for Educational Leadership, George Washington University, November 1975), p. 8.

Concerns about the adequacy of accreditation procedures in the U.S. have led numerous states to establish licensing mechanisms for higher education institutions in recent years. Licensing legislation applies only to private institutions, as the "founding, funding, and regulation of public institutions is the usual responsibility of a state governing or coordinating board".[18] As of Summer 1986, eight states had no licensing legislation at all, and among the others there was great variation with respect to procedure, criteria, and rigour.[19] Licensing regulations in the United States generally involve the imposition of relatively modest conditions on institutions which seek to grant degrees, and it is doubtful that they work any more stringently than accreditation to restrict the number of degree granting institutions.

Regulation as an Instrument of Distribution

Regulation often has distributional effects and is frequently sought by those whose behaviour is to be regulated in order to constrain the speed with which the free market redistributes rewards.[20] Thus, one should not be surprised to see those who have the greatest stake in existing degree granting institutions calling for stringent controls on the entry of other institutions into this market.

Regulation may also be used to redistribute benefits to consumers, as for example, when a transport regulatory agency grants a license for a profitable route on the condition that the licensee also agrees to service an unprofitable route.[21] Within higher education, analogous distributional objectives might be the extension of access to client groups with special needs, i.e.

---

[18]*Ibid.*, p. 3.

[19]Richard M. Millard, President of the Council on Postsecondary Accreditation, Washington, D.C., private communication, 29 July 1986.

[20]Bruce Owen and Ronald Braeutigam, The Regulation Game: Strategic Use of the Administrative Process (Cambridge, Mass.: Ballinger, 1978), p. 26.

[21]Economic Council of Canada, Responsible Regulation, p. 51.

those in remote regions, those not able to conform to traditional scheduling patterns, or those not meeting conventional admission standards but nevertheless demonstrating academic potential. In a higher education system characterized by easy entry, new institutions may appear on the scene to meet these needs. Where this avenue is restricted by entry controls, regulation may be a useful tool for ensuring that those institutions which enjoy the monopoly property right that is the authority to grant degrees direct their resources to meeting such needs.

Regulation to Achieve Social and Cultural Objectives

In its study of regulation in Canada, the Economic Council of Canada noted that since Confederation, "successive Canadian Governments have used their taxing, spending, and regulatory powers to create a national consciousness or sense of identity that is maintained even at some costs to its citizens".[22] While the major thrust of such regulatory initiatives has been in communications and transportation, education is also an area of particular relevance for regulation aimed at protecting national or regional cultures, as evidenced by the various policies of recent Quebec Governments in this respect. Consistent with approaches taken in the communications sector, one might expect regulations which would, for reasons of cultural identity, restrict the Canadian operations of foreign based educational institutions, or impose "Canadian content" requirements on them. The goal of creating a common culture, notwithstanding, Canadians have been quite tolerant of private elementary and secondary schools which embrace a variety of religious, ethnic, and social values. Paradoxically, as we will see in the next section, they have not been so tolerant at the postsecondary degree level where the potential role of educational institutions in transmitting a common culture is a good deal less than it is for the elementary and secondary schools.

---

[22]*Ibid.*, p. 52.

Regulation of Degree Granting in Canada

In contrast to the United States where traditionally little attempt was made to limit the number of degree granting institutions, Canadian higher education has been characterized by policies of stringently limiting the number of degree granting institutions. Whereas in the United States either no state authority is needed to grant degrees or such authority is exercised by a licensing commission, in Canada, the granting of the authority to award degrees has been a prerogative of provincial legislatures. In this respect, practices in Canada differ also from those in the United Kingdom where no legislative approval (or license) is required for an institution to grant degrees.[23] As such, obtaining the authority to grant degrees in Canada has involved an intensely political process.

With respect to the control of degree granting in Canada, the similarities among the provinces are much greater than the differences. In no province can an indigenous institution grant degrees without an act of the provincial legislature, and in contrast to the United States where half the degree granting institutions are private there are only a few private degree granting institutions in Canada.[24] Also, except for Nova Scotia, the number of degree granting institutions in Canada is substantially fewer on a per capita basis than in the United States. Yet, there are some differences in the regulation of degree granting among the provinces. For example, while most

---

[23]"The Phony War",The Times Higher Education Supplement (London), 23 August 1985, p. 10.

[24]Despite the frequency of their use, the terms, private and public, as applied to institutions of higher education, are rarely defined. While the authoritative Carnegie Commission classification of institutions, as well as statistical publications of the U.S. Office of Education, distinguish in tables between private and public institutions, neither source defines the basis of that

provinces prohibit local operations of foreign institutions, Ontario has detailed regulations through which such institutions may be given approval. One province, Alberta, has recently enacted legislation for the accreditation of private colleges for degree granting.

Accreditation of Private Colleges in Alberta

After decades of unsuccessful and frequently contentious attempts by private religious colleges to gain the right to grant baccalaureates in arts and sciences, the Private Colleges Accreditation Board was established by legislation in 1984, with the power to make recommendations to the Minister of Advanced Education with respect to the approval of baccalaureates that may be offered by private colleges.[25] Of the twenty private colleges in Alberta, of which eighteen have a religious affiliation, one had received approval to grant degrees in some programs as of 1985.

---

distinction. In a random sampling which I made of twenty-five books on the structure and/or governance of higher education, none defined private or public even though all employ both terms liberally. In its glossary, the International Encyclopedia of Higher Education (vol. 1, p. 489a) defines a private institution as one which is "supported primarily from tuition, fees, endowment income, and donations", adding that while some tax funds may be received, these "have little or no influence on policies and operations." By contrast, a public institution is funded primarily by government. In Volume 6 "Legal Aspects of Higher Education" by Jacob C. Diemert, (p. 2470), the Encyclopedia notes that with few exceptions, the privateinstitution is incorporated under a state's nonprofit corporation law, while a public institution is established by a state constitution or legislative statute. By either of these definitions, all but a few of the degree granting institutions in Canada are public; and the Degree Granting Act in Ontario expressly prohibits private degree granting institutions under the second definition, while policy since the early 1960s (which is presently under review) is to disallow them under the first definition.

[25]Private Colleges Accreditation Board, Annual Report 1984-85 (Edmonton, Alberta, 1985), p. 1.

One constraint in the new procedures which may significantly limit the extension of degree granting is the stipulation that "normally" a private college must first have an agreement of affiliation with a public university for the program for which it seeks to grant degrees.[26] Given that the university community did not endorse the Government's decision to expand the number of degree granting institutions,[27] the affiliation requirement is likely to prove a weighty restriction indeed. This placing of an existing university in what some would regard as a conflict of interest situation has been challenged in other jurisdictions. For example, in North Carolina, where a similar requirement exists, the lawyer for a private institution which was refused approval by the University of North Carolina complained that this was like having Macy's judge Gimbel's.[28] It is perhaps a permissible digression to note that Gimbel's has been forced to close its main store, but that the lawsuit against the State of North Carolina was successful (though there were numerous other considerations in the judgment).[29]

Loopholes in British Columbia

Legislation in British Columbia appears to prohibit the granting of secular degrees (i.e. those other than for

---

[26]*Ibid.*, p. 19.

[27]Minister's Task Force on Policy for Private Colleges, Toward a Comprehensive Policy for Private Colleges in Alberta: A Report to the Minister of Advanced Education and Manpower (August 1982), p. 14.

[28]Orlans, p. 36.

[29]North Carolina General Assembly, Memorandum to Members of Legislative Research Commission Committee on Higher Education Regulation (Raleigh, N.C.: General Assembly Legislative Services Office, 28 December 1983).

certification of clergy) by any institution other than those authorized in the Universities Act. However, concern has been voiced recently by spokespersons for the public universities over "the growing number of postsecondary degree granting institutions that fall outside the purview of the Act".[30]

After Trinity Western University obtained degree granting status through a private member's bill in the legislature, over the opposition of the Universities Council of British Columbia, Council expressed alarm that the incident will be regarded "as a precedent by a number of other private universities which consider themselves to be in a somewhat similar position".[31] Council observed that in the private member's bill route to degree status, there is no requirement for prior academic evaluation, or even for formal advice from Council on the suitability of the private institution being considered for degree status.

In the same advisory memorandum which dealt with indigenous private institutions in the Province, Council also expressed concern about American universities offering degree programs in British Columbia. While the British Columbia legislation is not as clear as that in Ontario regarding the local operations of foreign institutions, apparently these off-campus programs fall outside the Universities Act.[32] The most visible such institution, City University of Washington, offers non-traditional programs in Vancouver. It has been criticized by

---

[30]Michelle Morissette, "Variety of Postsecondary Education Institutions Concerns B.C. Officials", CAUT Bulletin 32 (November 1985): 9.

[31]Universities Council of British Columbia, The Accreditation of Degree Granting Private Institutions in B.C.: Proposed Procedural Guidelines, An Advisory Memorandum to the Minister of Universities, Sciences, and Communications (January, 1986), p. 1.

[32]Ibid., p. 4; also Morissette.

representatives of British Columbia universities for its admission standards and for its non-traditional programming. British Columbia universities do not recognize its degrees, although its degrees are recognized by almost all American universities and some Canadian universities, including McGill. The Executive Director of Universities for the B.C. Government has defended City's right to operate in the Province, noting that it "is obviously serving a need that is not being met at other universities".[33] To date the Government of British Columbia has not acted on the calls from the university community to strengthen the legislation and/or administration regarding local private institutions and off-campus programs of American universities in the Province, and representatives of the universities fear an uncontrolled expansion of degree granting activities from both sources.

Regulation of Degree Granting in Ontario

Faced with similar issues as British Columbia, the Ontario Government moved in 1983 to establish the most comprehensive legislation and supporting regulations on degree granting in Canada. The stated purposes of the 1983 Degree Granting Act (Chapter 36, Statutes of Ontario), are threefold: (a) to regulate the operation of out-of-province degree granting institutions in Ontario; (b) to establish in law the tradition that no Ontario institutions can grant degrees without an act of the legislature; and (c) to provide enhanced protection against degree mills.[34]

Although representations had been made to the Government for a number of years regarding the need to address the three issues listed above, as is so often the case, it took a specific incident to bring these concerns to a head in the form of new legislation. That incident was the Government's inability under previous legislation to restrict the degree granting activities in Ontario of the Northland Open University, an

---

[33]Morissette.

[34]Ontario, An Act to Regulate the Granting of Degrees: Policy Compendium (Toronto: Ministry of Colleges and Universities, April 1983), p. 1.

institution which derives its corporate status from letters patent issued by the Government of Canada but which was not authorized to grant degrees by an act of any legislative body in Canada.[35]

With respect to private institutions in Ontario, many of the same issues have arisen as in Alberta and British Columbia, the chief difference being that it has been a stated policy of the Ontario Government since the early 1960's that no new degree granting institutions will be permitted, because the province already has "a sufficient number of degree granting institutions".[36] Since passage of the 1983 Act, one private Church affiliated institution has succeeded in obtaining the authority, over Government opposition, to grant a secular Master's Degree, through a private member's bill. This degree is recognized by almost all major universities in the world, except for a few in Ontario, and a high proportion of its graduates go on to do doctorates, so it is unlikely that standards were an issue. Most likely, Government opposition to the institution reflected the absence in Ontario of any tradition of private or specialized degree granting institutions and

---

[35]*Ibid.*, p. 5. It is of interest that a case that was in many ways similar to that of the Northland Open University occurred in Ontario more than fifty years earlier. Frontier College, an institution which brought education to the logging, mining, and railroad camps, was offering degree programs in Ontario on the strength of a federal charter. Netto Kefentse ("Universities and Labour Education in Ontario: A Study of Cooperation between Unions and Universities" [M.A. dissertation, University of Toronto, 1975] pp. 26-35) notes that the prospect of Frontier College awarding degrees "caught the ire" of the Ontario universities, and the Province sought to prevent Frontier from granting degrees in Ontario. Legal advice provided to the Government indicated both that the Province had the constitutional jurisdiction to enact legislation which would prohibit Frontier from granting degrees, and that legislation was the most effective instrument for curtailing Frontier's degree activities. In the event, a political solution was found which involved Frontier giving up its degree aspirations across the country, and not until a similar case arose a half century later did Ontario enact the type of legislation which was recommended in the 1930s.

[36]Ontario, Granting of Degrees, p. 5.

72

Government concern that ultimately it would have to provide funding if the institution attained degree granting status - though in Alberta and Quebec, even private colleges which do not grant degrees are eligible for government funding.

Presently, the policy on non-extension of degree granting is being reviewed by the Government. In its brief on the subject, the institution referred to above argues that "at present, institutions of higher education that depart from the majority cultural model are ... treated as unwelcome intruders", and it urges a tolerance of private degree granting institutions which is appropriate for a pluralistic society.[37] The institution reports also that the advice of a previous Government that it seek to offer its program through affiliation with an existing university, rather than granting its own degrees, proved ineffective as the existing universities were unreceptive.[38]

The aspect of the Ontario legislation for which there is detailed regulation and which has received the most attention is that which relates to the Ontario operations of out-of-province institutions, particularly institutions operating from the United States. To be eligible for Ministerial Consent, an American institution must be accredited by an appropriate U.S. accreditation agency; and the Minister may require the U.S. accreditation agency to visit the Ontario site and certify that the Ontario program meets the same standards as the program in the home jurisdiction.[39]

A major issue in developing the regulations was whether to rely upon U.S. accreditation to ensure standards, or to subject

---

[37] Institute for Christian Studies, Brief to the Ontario Council on University Affairs on Government Policy Concerning the Establishment of New Free-Standing Secular Degree Granting Institutions (Toronto: 1 July 1986), p. 9.

[38] Ibid., pp. 7-8.

[39] Ontario, Policy Statement Re the Granting of Ministerial Consents as Authorized by the Degree Granting Act, Chapter 36, Statutes of Ontario, 1983 (Toronto: Ministry of Colleges and Universities, November 1985).

the American programs, most of which are at the graduate level, to the same review process as applies to the graduate programs of Ontario universities. That review is conducted under the auspices of the Council of Ontario Universities, a voluntary association of the universities. Council had urged the Government to subject all graduate programs in the province to the same review process. However, the Government demurred, noting that the out-of-province institutions were not members of the association which would be conducting the review; were not eligible for the Ontario funding which was provided for programs which received satisfactory appraisals; and that the out-of-province institutions should not purport to be offering, necessarily, programs of equivalent standards to those of Ontario universities. In the matter of standards, thus, the Ontario Government accepted U.S. accreditation for American institutions, and the existence of a charter by an act of the Parliament of Canada or a provincial legislature, regardless of whether there is any accreditation or external program review, for institutions based in other provinces of Canada.[40] In short, the Ontario regulations countenance the possibility of a variety of different standards for out-of-province institutions operating in Ontario.

In addition to the above requirements, the out-of-province institution must satisfy conditions pertaining to student demand, adequacy of library facilities, and societal need. The first two conditions have not proved an obstacle, since institutions are not likely to apply for permits for programs for which there is insufficient student demand, and library resources may be provided through arrangements with provincial universities or on-line access to the home institution. The main emphasis in the documentation by the Ontario Council on University Affairs (OCUA), which has the formal responsibility for advising the Minister on applications from out-of-province institutions, has been on assessing societal need.

---

[40]In addition, out-of-province Canadian institutions must be members of the Association of Universities and Colleges of Canada. However, membership in AUCC does not imply that particular standards in academic programs are being met.

Thus far, judging from OCUA's first such Advisory Memorandum in 1986,[41] the concept of societal need - for the operationalizing of which, apparently, OCUA has been given little guidance from the Ministry - has been taken to mean that the program in question is not likely to be provided by an Ontario university. There has been little discussion of other possible interpretations of societal need, e.g. labour market demand for graduates of the program or intrinsic worth of the program, concepts which are understandably difficult to apply.

Expressed in another, perhaps more provocative, way, societal need appears to have been operationalized as protecting the market for Ontario universities. Within the United States, state regulatory agencies have had to tread warily in this respect because there is a precedent for considering educational activities under the definition of "commerce" within the Interstate Commerce Clause of the U.S. Constitution and such an interpretation of societal need might be deemed unconstitutional.[42] While possibly a similar interpretation could be upheld with respect to the Canadian Constitution relative to programs of out-of-province Canadian institutions, national constitutions would not apply to extra-national operations of educational institutions. Whether the protection of domestic educational institutions from foreign competition would contravene international trade agreements is another matter, as is the relevance of control of degree granting to free trade talks between Canada and the United States.

In practice, the application of the societal need criterion is difficult because Ontario universities have the latent capability to offer a variety of programs which they are not

---

[41]Ontario Council on University Affairs, Advisory Memorandum 86-I: Ministerial Consents Pursuant to the Degree Granting Act, 1983 (Toronto: OCUA, May 1986).

[42]Orlans, p. 36.

presently offering. Relatively easy cases arise in those instances where the program in question is highly specialized and not likely to be of interest to an Ontario university. A case in point is the Master of Science in Manufacturing Management offered by the General Motors Institute of Michigan to GM employees on GM premises in Oshawa, Ontario which was recently approved on the grounds that no Ontario university was in a position to offer the same program.[43]

The largest, and possibly most troublesome area to adjudicate, has been the Master of Education programs. In some cases, American universities have applied to offer these programs in communities not served by Ontario universities. The Government, then, is faced with the problem of determining whether to deny the application on the basis that an Ontario university states that it could, in principle, serve the particular community, or require more concrete evidence of the Ontario university's presence in the community.

However, the most intractable issues with respect to M.Ed. programs of American universities in Ontario have been ones of standards. Many of the American programs have lower minimum admission requirements. There is also criticism of some aspects of their non-traditional programming approaches in comparison to those of Ontario universities. Unfortunately, there is little documentation of these issues, but in the extensive interviews which I have conducted among staff and students in the American programs it has been clear to me that much of the appeal of the American programs to Ontario

[43]OCUA, Advisory Memorandum, p. 9.

residents lies in these features.[44] Leslie has noted that there is a much wider range of standards among American universities, and I have noted elsewhere that non-traditional approaches to university education are not well developed in Canada.[45] Thus, by and large, the presence of American programs in Ontario offers residents of the Province opportunities which they might not otherwise obtain from Ontario universities: for some, the sheer opportunity to pursue a graduate degree when they have been judged unacceptable in relation to academic admission requirements of Ontario universities; for others, non-traditional approaches to scheduling, residence requirements, curriculum and the like.

To a considerable extent, the adjudication of applications from American institutions to offer programs in Ontario revolves

---

[44]As Chairman of the Admissions Committee for M.Ed. programs in Community College Studies in the only Ontario university to have such a program, I have had a considerable involvement with students who are trying to decide between our program and those of American universities. Generally, admission to our program requires a mid-B average in the last year of a relevant Bachelor's program, while some of the American universities, I am told, accept a C average. Further our program does not accept the undergraduate status of all foreign universities, e.g., some American universities are not recognized for admission purposes. No student whom I have interviewed, who was admissible to our program, has chosen to enrol in an American university program in Ontario. In that sense the programs might be said not to be in competition with one another. Given the substantial professional development needs of Ontario community colleges (see Michael L. Skolnik, Brian Sharples and William Marcotte, Survival or Excellence? The Report of the Instructional Assignment Review Committee [Toronto: Ontario Ministry of Colleges and Universities, July 1985]), my impression is that the programs of American universities are performing a valuable service for Ontario education, and I have no hesitation in giving guest lectures in those programs when asked to do so. The issue continues to generate much heat within the Ontario university community though, and there are those who remain skeptical of the appropriateness of allowing institutions to operate with potentially lower academic standards from those of Ontario universities. Perhaps one of the chief effects of the availability of the programs of American universities has been that they serve as an escape valve for pressure which might otherwise build up regarding the need for a review of the appropriateness of current admissions and related policies for graduate studies in Ontario universities.

[45]Leslie, p. 61, and Skolnik, "Diversity", p. 28.

about value judgments concerning what constitutes appropriate admission standards and program requirements. In spite of whatever differences academics, civil servants, and politicians may have concerning government intervention in academe, my sense is that most would agree that admission standards and curriculum are not appropriate realms for government intervention. Yet, through the process of giving Ministerial Consents for American institutions to operate in Ontario, the Ontario Government may be forced to take a stand on the appropriateness of various educational philosophies and approaches for its residents. Should the Government decide, in its handling of Ministerial Consents, that greater diversity of admission standards and programming approaches is in the interests of higher education in Ontario, then it is not too great a step for it to encourage the public university system which the Government has established and finances to itself address these needs rather than relying upon foreigners to do it. The new regulations governing the programs of American institutions in Ontario could thus have a steering effect quite out of proportion to the quantitative significance of these programs in Ontario higher education.

I shall conclude this section on regulation of degree granting in Ontario by noting two somewhat paradoxical aspects of current public policy, both of which Ontario shares to varying degrees with other provinces. The first is to suggest that the act of granting degrees is apparently deemed of such special significance that, unlike the provision of almost all other goods or services, an act of the legislature is required to provide this particular service. Even for enterprises in fields where life and death may hang in the balance - hospitals, airlines, or the handling of toxic waste, for example - authority for granting approval is delegated by the legislature to a licensing or regulatory agency. In neither the United States, the United Kingdom, or Australia - the only other countries which I have examined - is an act of the legislature required to permit an institution to grant degrees.

Second, I can find no other realm of enterprise in which a political jurisdiction prohibits its own residents from producing goods or services whilst at the same time has a formal mechanism for approving applications of foreign corporations to provide those goods or services. Such a policy might make sense if the goods or services in question have considerable negative externalities, such as the disposal of noxious waste, but higher education is generally deemed to have positive externalities. In the realm of culture, the impact of such a double standard might be mitigated somewhat by imposing Canadian content requirements on the foreign corporations, but there are no such requirements in the present regulations, even for programs where appreciation of relevant Canadian institutions would be of great importance, such as educational administration programs.[46]

One can conclude only that the act of granting degrees is deemed by Canadians to carry with it certain symbolic, or even mystical, connotations, which like the creation of money - and a degree is a form of currency - warrant unique treatment in human affairs.

Concluding Comments

In this concluding section, I would like to attempt to draw some inferences, from the discussion of policy and practice, regarding the role which the various possible rationales for regulation outlined earlier have played in the control of degree granting in Canada; and to indicate some implications for government intervention in the affairs of universities of what I believe to have been the dominant rationale with respect to the regulation of degree granting. It is, of course, no easy matter to determine a government's rationale for most policies, as spokespersons for government usually are less explicit about the rationale for their actions than the student of their actions would wish. Also, the formulation of policy is often the outcome of a process of compromise among conflicting interests. As such, no simple statement of rationale can adequately summarize the complex interactions which precede in the

---

[46]While grants are available for the development of Canadian Studies and Canadian instructional materials, this is not the same as having requirements for Canadian content in the curriculum to which all students are exposed. In fact, even the grants program for Canadian Studies has come under strong attack from some academics. For example, see David J. Bercuson, Robert Bothwell, and J.L. Granatstein, The Great Brain Robbery: Canada's Universities on the Road to Ruin (Toronto: McClelland & Stewart, 1984).

observed actions.[47]

These caveats notwithstanding, there is reasonably compelling support for the proposition that the dominant rationale in regulation of degree granting in Ontario has been that of protecting a monopoly for the public university system as it had evolved by the mid 1960s. The oft repeated statement that no new degree granting institutions would be allowed because the Province already had a sufficient number of such institutions, points to this interpretation, as does the particular emphasis, in giving Ministerial Consents, upon approving only those programs of out-of-province institutions which do not compete with programs of Ontario universities.

With respect to indigenous private institutions, the absolute prohibition on degree granting status precluded the possibility that standards might become a relevant issue. In regard to out-of-province institutions, the fact that no review is required for programs of Canadian institutions, and that U.S. accreditation - with all the criticisms which have been made of that mechanism - is accepted for programs of American institutions, poses serious obstacles to making the case that protection of standards has been a major consideration in the development of regulatory policy in regard to degree granting in Ontario. Moreover, given that in all likelihood, the number of private institutions which would wish to offer degrees in Ontario is relatively small, it is difficult to conclude that realistic fears of destructive competition lie at the heart of the Ontario approach to regulation of degree granting. That universities might perform a vital function in transmitting and protecting a common cultural identity is indisputable, but that this factor has had much to do with the policy on degree granting is another matter. Not only has the Government not imposed any Canadian content curriculum requirements on Ontario universities, but neither has it imposed such requirements upon foreign institutions operating in Ontario.

---

[47]David Easton, A Framework for Political Analysis (Englewood Cliffs, N.J.: Prentice-Hall, 1965).

The dominance of the natural monopoly rationale which we find in Ontario would seem to apply, as well, to the rest of the country, but the evidence is more difficult to marshall, because the corresponding legislation and regulations are less detailed elsewhere and the accompanying policy statements are less explicit. Also, there are some indicators that other rationales have played a modestly greater role, relative to that of natural monopoly, in some provinces. While historically, the view of the university as a natural monopoly was the cornerstone of regulatory policy in the Western provinces, the establishment of a mechanism for accrediting private colleges in Alberta indicates a weakening of obeisance to that particular view of the university, and an elevation of concern about standards which is associated with the rationale for regulation that emphasizes inadequacy of information. However, the requirement for a private college to have an affiliation with a public university suggests a continuation of homage to the idea of a monopoly status for the public universities - though a more generous interpretation of this requirement could acknowledge also the relevant expertise which the universities have for the task of assessing the quality of programming in smaller, sometimes newer, private institutions. The recent tolerance shown by the Government of British Columbia toward both local private degree granting institutions and programs of non-traditional institutions from the United States demonstrates the first major crack in the traditional Canadian predilection toward viewing the university as a public monopoly, as well as an unprecedented receptivity toward allowing the free market to operate in higher education.

The Nova Scotia university system, with its extensive diversity even by U.S. standards, confounds any attempt to characterize Canadian higher education as a whole as reflecting a natural monopoly orientation toward postsecondary degree education, and indicates as well the difficulties of making any generalizations which will stand up across the country. Respecting religious and regional loyalties, Nova Scotia, with a population less than one-third of Toronto's, supports a system which includes a dozen independent degree granting institutions.[48] All the degree granting institutions in Nova

---

[48]Nova Scotia, Report of the Royal Commission on Post-Secondary Education (Halifax: Government of Nova Scotia, 1985).

Scotia have come into the public fold and hence are a direct burden on the public purse, and needless to say, the Province, like its sister provinces, tends not to allow any new private degree granting institutions.

The only province where cultural identity has been a major factor in regulatory policy in education is Quebec, but in higher education this has been manifested largely through ensuring an adequate system of Francophone degree granting institutions, not through restricting other institutions. Unfortunately, in preparing this paper I have not been able to find much documentation of Quebec policies toward degree granting, but interviews with educators in that province have suggested that Quebec may be the most lenient of Canadian provinces with respect to regulation of degree granting, including permitting the Canadian institution, referred to earlier, which was denied the right to operate a degree program in Ontario the right to operate in Quebec.

Thus far, no mention has been of those arguments for regulation which were referred to earlier under the heading of "distribution". These consist not so much of arguments in favour of restricting entry, but of regulating the behaviour of those organizations which are permitted to serve a particular market. The control of tuition levels in those institutions which have been given the monopoly privilege to grant degrees is an illustration of regulation to serve distributional objectives. The example of transport regulatory agencies directing transport companies which have been awarded monopoly privileges to service clients whom they might not otherwise service was noted earlier, where it was observed that the analogy in higher education might be to direct universities which have been given a monopoly to service clients whose needs at present are being met mainly by American universities.

The latter example points to the principal implication of our analysis which is relevant to the larger issue of government intervention in academe. Within a free market paradigm of higher education, the state might - arguably, given the imperfections in most markets - defer to market forces to meet the various educational needs which may arise. However, where postsecondary degree education has been treated as a public monopoly, that option, whatever its practical limitations, is not available. Thus, a greater role for government direction may be warranted where the university system is a de facto public monopoly.

Holding a publicly granted monopoly in the market is in many ways an enviable position. It is also a position of considerable, and justifiable, vulnerability to state intervention. As possessors of such a monopoly privilege, Canadian universities, in at least all but a few provinces, have no legitimate recourse but to accede to government interpretations of the public good in higher education. Like other monopolists, they should hope that government will exercise prudence, wisdom, and restraint in its intervention, but in the last analysis, they have no basis for challenging intervention.

Graduate Studies in Ontario: The Role of the Universities and the Role of Government

by

L.A.K. Watt[1]

Introduction

The development of graduate studies in the Ontario universities over the past 20 years provides a unique example of the interaction between universities and a provincial government operating either directly or through its appointed advisory body. This paper traces the historical development of this interaction, shows how it affected the development of graduate studies in the province and finally speculates on what problems the Ontario universities are likely to face in the future.

The Structure of the System

There are fifteen provincially supported universities in the province of Ontario; at the present time all offer graduate work at the master's level and ten offer programs at the doctoral level in at least some disciplines. The universities are members of the Ontario Council on Graduate Studies (OCGS) and are represented on that Council by the academic administrative officer responsible for graduate studies, usually the Dean of Graduate Studies. The OCGS, in turn, is an affiliate of the Council of Ontario Universities (formerly the Committee of Presidents), a somewhat larger body including, in addition to the fifteen provincially supported universities, other institutions which offer only undergraduate programs. The institutions are represented on the COU by their executive heads and an academic colleague normally chosen by the Senate or governing body.

---

[1]Past Executive Vice-Chairman, Ontario Council on Graduate Studies; Acting Dean of Graduate Studies, University of Waterloo, Waterloo, ON.

The government ministry responsible for post-secondary education in the Province of Ontario is the Ministry of Colleges and Universities (MCU). Throughout the 20-year period which this paper deals with, the government has received advice on the development of the universities from an intermediary body, the members of which are appointed by government. At the present time the advisory body is the Ontario Council on University Affairs (OCUA) which came into existence in 1974. Its predecessor was the Committee on University Affairs.

Direct government intervention in university affairs in Ontario is rare, but intervention through actions of the advisory body has been common. This paper examines the role that the universities, the government's advisory body and the government have played in the development of graduate studies in Ontario over the last 20 years.

The Concern About Quality

During the late 1950s and early 1960s enrolment in graduate studies in the Ontario universities, as elsewhere in Canada, grew at a rapid rate. Not only was graduate enrolment rising in existing programs, but new programs were being introduced by the old institutions and the new universities. In 1965, as a result of concerns arising from this rapid growth in graduate enrolment and the high cost of graduate education, the Committee of Presidents of the Universities of Ontario, in collaboration with the Committee on University Affairs and the provincial government, established a commission under the Chairmanship of Dr. J.W.T. Spinks, then President of the University of Saskatchewan, to study the development of graduate studies in Ontario universities. The Spinks Report was submitted to the Committee on University Affairs and the universities in 1966. One of its recommendations was that the government establish a Provincial University of Ontario modelled after the New York and California State systems. This University of Ontario would have semi-autonomous campuses at each of the then fourteen provincially assisted universities in the province, but it would be administered centrally by a Board of Regents and an Academic Senate. The universities and the government rejected this proposal, but the presidents recognized that something must be done to ensure greater coordination among the universities in the development of graduate studies.

Accordingly, in 1966 the Committee of Presidents established the Ontario Council on Graduate Studies to provide advice on how graduate studies in the province should be developed. The most immediate concern of the OCGS was the academic quality of the new programs. Therefore, as one of its first acts, it established an Appraisals Committee which would be responsible for appraising all proposals for new graduate programs to ensure that they were of adequate academic quality. One of the first examples of university/government cooperation occurred at this time as the government agreed that it would not provide funding for any new graduate program until it had received a favourable appraisal. The universities, for their part, undertook to submit all new programs for appraisal before they were implemented and not to implement any program which did not receive a favourable appraisal. This provision, whereby all new programs are submitted for what is now called a standard appraisal before being implemented, is still in existence. Receiving a favourable appraisal is still a necessary condition for a new program to be eligible for government funding.

During the first five years of its operation the Appraisals Committee dealt with 97 submissions for new program approval. Of these 41 were for Ph.D. programs and 56 for master's programs. In the following years the rate of growth in new programs, particularly at the doctoral level, declined significantly. During the next five-year period only 13 new doctoral programs were submitted for appraisal.

The appraisals system has ensured that new graduate programs meet rigorous standards of academic quality. It has also had a profound impact within the universities. Virtually all Ontario universities have introduced their own internal quality controls in order to screen out weak programs before they are sent for external appraisal. Since only the programs that have gone through this internal process are submitted to the Appraisals Committee, very few proposals fail. Concerns about the quality of new programs had been met. However, other concerns were emerging.

A Concern for Planning

By the early 1970s, the Government of Ontario had begun to question the need for continuing growth in costly graduate enrolment. In particular, the number of doctoral graduates had expanded significantly since the mid 1960s. At the same time, university hiring of new faculty members was slowing down, so academic positions were less readily available to the graduating Ph.D.s. This slowdown in the academic job market and the continuing increase in the graduation rate for Ph.D.s led to fears that there would be a considerable oversupply of doctoral graduates and many unemployed Ph.D.s. These fears subsequently proved to be largely groundless, but at the time they were very real in the minds of government ministers responsible for funding graduate programs. Moreover, their fears were fueled by projections emanating from Statistics Canada which projected graduation rates to the end of the 1970s and failed to look at what was happening to enrolment. It was clear from an examination of enrolment trends that the number of Ph.D.'s graduating would drop off by the mid 1970s, since by 1970 enrolment had already begun to level off and in some disciplines had actually declined.

Arguments based on enrolment trends, however, failed to convince the Ontario government. It decided that something must be done to halt what it saw as runaway growth in graduate enrolment and in doctoral enrolment in particular which, if left unchecked, would impose an unbearable financial burden on the taxpayers. Accordingly, in 1971 the government introduced a moratorium on the funding of all new graduate programs. This situation was, of course, unacceptable, particularly to the new universities, since it meant that the graduate enterprise would be frozen in the configuration that existed at that time. A healthy graduate enterprise must be free to respond to new developments by introducing new programs and expanding existing ones as new fields of study and research open up.

As a result the universities, acting through the OCGS and the COU, entered into discussion with the Committee on University Affairs, the government's advisory body, on ways to get around the "freeze". What emerged was an agreement on the part of the universities acting collectively through the COU and the OCGS to establish an Advisory Committee on Academic Planning (ACAP) which would carry out a series of discipline planning assessments. The ACAP would examine all of the graduate programs offered in the province in a particular discipline, discipline by discipline, over a period of years until it had covered all the disciplines in which graduate work was offered. The objective of this planning exercise was to rationalize the development of graduate work in each discipline. The final outcome of the discipline planning assessment would be a COU report setting out the recommendations to universities which would constitute the development plan for the discipline. The universities agreed to be bound by these recommendations; the government, agreed to lift the embargo on funding new programs in a discipline once the COU plan for that discipline had been approved, and agreed to fund all new programs in the discipline which were deemed by ACAP to be consistent with the provisions of the COU plan.

In conducting these planning assessments ACAP was responsible directly to COU, although it was a committee of OCGS. The role of the OCGS in the planning assessments, therefore, became a secondary one. The final decision on what recommendations emerged rested with the COU, that is, with the university presidents and academic colleagues, not with the graduate deans. This arrangement led to a good deal of tension within the university community. The first planning assessments were completed in 1973. By 1976 ACAP had completed assessments in 22 disciplines. The government, true to its word, removed the embargo on each discipline as the COU plan was approved. In those disciplines new programs could then go forward as soon as they had passed a standard appraisal and been judged by ACAP to be consistent with the COU plan. The universities, for their part, accepted the outcome of the ACAP assessments, but with much more reluctance than they had accepted appraisals. A few of the ACAP assessments generated real hostility. Nevertheless, despite the objections raised against the ACAP exercise the impact of the planning assessments on the Ontario university system was, on the whole, a positive one. It forced universities to examine programs that had been in existence for a number of years and, in several cases, led to programs being sharply curtailed, although very few were actually closed.

The exercise also led to the development of much more inter-university cooperation than had previously existed and resulted in the emergence of truly joint programs. The first such joint program was offered through the Guelph/Waterloo centre for graduate work in Chemistry. Since then several have been established where proximity makes it possible, in particular at Carleton University and the University of Ottawa and the Universities of Guelph and Waterloo. The net result of these joint endeavors is a smaller number of programs offering a stronger and broader range of activities in the disciplines involved. It is doubtful if these joint efforts would have emerged without the pressures brought about by the ACAP planning assessments that identified areas in which such collaboration could result in stronger programs.

The Beginnings of OCUA Intervention

By the mid 1970s the government's buffer body, now the Ontario Council on University Affairs (OCUA), considered that the ACAP planning exercise was not working properly. It was OCUA's view that a successful planning mechanism should lead to the closing down of some graduate programs and a rationalization of the graduate offerings across the system. The universities countered this by pointing out that expansion in the system had slowed down drastically and it was totally unrealistic to expect a significant number of program closures as long as their quality was satisfactory. While the system looked at as a whole may not have needed all of the graduate programs in certain disciplines, the universities argued that the programs were needed if they were to become complete universities. The OCUA, however, was not impressed. On the assumption that one of the difficulties in closing programs probably arose from Ontario's enrolment-driven university funding formula (which counted students in various categories, assigning funding weights to the programs), in 1976 OCUA announced a three-year suspension of the formula. During this period enrolment growth would not generate any additional revenue for a university but, equally, enrolment decline would not result in any revenue loss. It was OCUA's expectation that universities would thereby be encouraged to reduce enrolment in certain programs and indeed even close programs. This did not happen for the simple reason that the formula suspension was known to be temporary. At the end of the three-year period the universities would almost certainly be back under an enrolment sensitive funding formula. Thus, if they did cut back on enrolment, eventually they would be financially penalized. This is precisely what happened. In 1978 OCUA announced that, beginning with the 1979-80 academic year, funding would once again be on an enrolment sensitive formula although heavy damping factors had now been introduced which would decrease the benefit of increased enrolment and also limit the penalty for decreased enrolment. The government's advisory body had taken the first steps towards a much more active role in graduate program planning.

Quinquennial Planning - Direct OCUA Intervention

Early in 1978 OCUA formally introduced the concept it called "quinquennial planning", giving notice that henceforth it intended to play a much more active role in planning the development of the graduate enterprise in Ontario. In an advisory memorandum to the Minister of Colleges and Universities issued in March of 1978, OCUA announced its objectives for the first quinquennium, the period running from 1979-80 through 1983-84. They were:

- recognition and protection of outstanding doctoral programs;

- support of good quality graduate programs;

- elimination of graduate programs of unsatisfactory quality;

- prevention of further duplication of graduate programs;

- recognition of high quality graduate programs in new fields of study for which there is a genuine need; and

- maintenance of a satisfactory amount of scholarship and research activity in the university system.

Council's advisory memorandum went on to establish four criteria for funding new graduate programs during the first quinquennium through which it expected to achieve the objectives above. These funding criteria were:

- evidence of need in Ontario and Canada to be provided by ACAP and endorsed by COU;

- certification from ACAP through COU that no similar program in the field proposed is available in Ontario (in exceptional circumstances Council may be willing to entertain a recommendation from ACAP through COU for funding a master's program where there is a similar program in Ontario but where there is also strong evidence of regional importance and student demand);

- certification from ACAP through COU that the proposed program has passed a rigorous appraisal and at the time of appraisal was not found to require improvements; and

- certification from the institution that admissions to the program commence prior to its being proposed for funding consideration.

These objectives and recommendations for funding of new programs were accepted by the Minister and came into effect for all programs introduced into the system in the first quinquennium.

The universities supported the OCUA objectives and, with one exception, accepted the funding criteria. On the surface at least little had changed.

Of course, the third criterion, that the program must have passed a rigorous appraisal, was nothing new. Nor, in effect, were the first two, since ACAP, in deciding whether a new program was consistent with the COU plan, had been taking into consideration evidence of need in Ontario and Canada, and the extent to which the proposed new program duplicated existing ones. However, ACAP had always been careful to define what it called "undesirable", duplication recognizing that any new program in an established discipline would, to some extent, inevitably duplicate existing programs. What ACAP felt was important was the extent to which the new program provided a graduate level educational opportunity not available elsewhere in the province. The fourth criterion was also related to one which ACAP had commonly used, namely student demand. However, it went beyond what had previously been required. It insisted that universities actually admit students to the program prior to applying for funding approval. This criterion placed the universities in a difficult dilemma. Unless they admitted students to the program they could not apply for funding; on the other hand, if they admitted students and then were denied funding they would find themselves committed to enrol students in a program for which they would receive no provincial funding. Despite university objections OCUA refused to change this provision.

These, then, were the four funding criteria put forward by OCUA in its advisory memorandum issued to the universities in March, 1978. As the universities applied for funding for new programs, however, it soon became evident that there was an unwritten fifth criterion: that the program be consistent with the aims, objectives and existing strengths of the institution wishing to offer it.

Moreover, COU was asked to advise OCUA as to whether or not the proposed programs met this fifth criterion. The COU was unwilling to do so. It argued that, given its particular mandate and method of operating, it was not the appropriate body to decide whether or not a program was consistent with a given institution's aims, objectives and existing strengths. In the light of this refusal no proposed new programs were funded for several years.

What was important about the introduction of the funding criteria for the first quinquennium was not the nature of the criteria, which were similar in substance to those that ACAP had been using all along, but the fact that for the first time the government's intermediary body, OCUA, was playing an active role in decisions on the funding of graduate programs. Prior to this, OCUA had accepted the advice of the universities acting collectively through COU with respect to whether or not a program met the necessary criteria for funding. Now, while asking for advice and recommendations from ACAP through COU, OCUA began increasingly to disregard that advice in arriving at its own decisions. Indeed the OCUA established its own Academic Advisory Committee (AAC) to provide it with the kind of expert advice that the ACAP had provided to OCGS and COU. Up to this time the Ontario universities, acting collectively through COU, had been largely able to prevent direct intervention by government, or the government's advisory body, by accepting some limitations on their individual autonomy for the collective good. By the early 1980s, however, it was clear that collective action by the universities was no longer adequate to prevent the intervention of OCUA in the planning process. This raised the question of the role of ACAP and COU in the planning process.

The End of the ACAP Era - Introduction of Periodic Appraisals

Recognizing that changes were occurring, COU in September 1979 established a special committee to review graduate program planning. This committee issued a discussion paper in June 1980 and a final report in March 1981. The discussion paper, among other things, explored a number of alternative approaches to the problems of graduate planning. In the final report the Committee accepted that the universities were not able to "effectively deal with the review of program proposals according to a set of planning criteria which it has not established itself". Instead the Committee recommended that COU concentrate on the role the universities could perform best - the appraisal of the quality of graduate programs - and leave the planning to OCUA. To give substance to this view, the committee recommended the introduction of a program of periodic appraisals under which every graduate program in the Ontario university system would be subject to a review by the Appraisals Committee over a five-year period. (After a more realistic assessment of the workload involved the period was extended to seven years.) The program was approved by OCGS and COU to begin in 1982.

Periodic appraisals identify programs in four categories: (1) those that are of good quality and are expected to maintain that quality at least until the next review; (2) those that are of good quality at the time of the review but for which problems are anticipated within the next few years because of pending retirements of senior scholars or significant program reorganization; (3) those that the Committee considers require minor improvement to become of good quality; and finally, (4) those that the Committee considers to be so weak academically that major improvements would be required to bring them up to an acceptable quality. They must be closed and cease admitting students for at least two years, after which they can be re-opened only if they pass a standard appraisal as a new program.

At first OCUA accepted this division of roles, but gradually it began to raise doubts about the degree of rigor of the appraisals being conducted. And the universities began to fear that OCUA, having taken firm control of the planning process, might wish also to get involved in the academic appraisals. Such a move would represent the ultimate step in the intervention into the operation of the universities' graduate programs by the government's advisory body. To prevent this the universities, acting through OCGS and COU, agreed in the fall of 1985 to have a team of independent assessors examine the appraisals process. Accordingly, a committee of three people in whom both the OCUA and the universities had confidence was commissioned to carry out an exhaustive study. This committee, which reported in April 1986, concluded that the appraisals process "produces reliable and credible judgments of the academic quality of existing and proposed graduate programs in Ontario". The report was accepted by OCUA and in August, 1986 was accepted by the Minister of Colleges and Universities. The outcome of this study has firmly established the division of roles: the universities acting collectively through the OCGS and the COU are responsible for certifying academic quality; the government's buffer body is responsible for judging the eligibility of programs for funding on the basis of planning criteria.

The Second Quinquennium

The first quinquennium ended in the academic year 1984-85. In March 1984 the universities were informed through the issuance of another OCUA advisory memorandum what the funding criteria would be for new graduate programs in the second quinquennium. These were:

- that the program has passed a rigorous academic appraisal as certified by the COU and at the time of the appraisal was not found to require improvements;

- that there is evidence of societal need and student demand for the program in Ontario and/or Canada;

- that the proposed program does not duplicate an existing program in Ontario unless the institution proposing the new program demonstrates to Council's satisfaction that exceptional circumstances obtain such that Council should recommend the program for funding despite the duplication involved;

- that the program is consistent with the aims, objectives and existing strengths of the institution offering the program and is included in the institution's five-year plan; and

- that the program is deserving of funding even at a time of economic constraint.

The OCUA also established criteria for the continued funding of existing programs which, in effect, accept the periodic appraisals as the basis for establishing funding eligibility. Only programs that were considered to require major improvements would be ineligible.

These criteria were essentially no different from those used in the first quinquennium. The so-called fifth criterion of the first quinquennium had now been spelled out explicitly and there was the additional one that "the program is deserving of funding even at a time of economic constraint". The requirement that students be admitted to the program to demonstrate student demand was dropped.

As this paper is written we are two years into the second quinquennium. Based on the funding decisions made so far by the OCUA, it would appear that the situation has stabilized. Once again the universities, by acting in cooperation to introduce a program of periodic appraisals, were able to prevent any further intrusion into the operation of the university system by the government's advisory body. How long the situation will remain stabilized with the present division of power remains to be seen.

Looking to the Future

It is evident from this outline that the development of graduate studies in the province of Ontario over the last 20 years has involved a unique blend of collective action by the university community and an increasing degree of intervention by the government-appointed advisory body, culminating in the current situation, which allows the universities to determine the academic quality of new and continuing programs and the government-appointed body to determine which new programs are deserving of funding.

What lies ahead? There are a number of areas where further steps must be taken if the universities are to avoid further government intervention, either directly or through its advisory body. On the quality side, in my opinion, the system of periodic and standard appraisals is working well. I see no cause for concern as long as the universities live up to their commitment that only programs of good quality will be allowed to continue in the system. There will be pressure from some quarters to allow programs that require minor improvements to be given more and more time to make the specified improvements, thus allowing them to continue in the system. The universities must resist these pressures and close down programs that still do not meet the quality standards after a reasonable period of time.

At the same time I do not believe that the present situation that entirely removes universities from the system planning process can be sustained. It is already clear that the outcomes of the periodic appraisals provide evidence in some disciplines of areas in which university cooperation and planning will be necessary to provide for a rational development of programs. There are a number of disciplines in which several universities have programs that are all low in enrolment and require improvements to achieve a good level of quality. Such a situation cries out for cooperative action and consolidation of programs. At the present time the OCUA and its AAC have not been involved in this aspect of planning. It is clear, however, that unless the universities take action before too long the OCUA will be forced to.

The Ontario universities have faced nearly a decade of economic constraint. They almost certainly will have to face continued constraint for the foreseeable future. In such circumstances it makes eminently good sense for them to cooperate to conserve resources and to ensure that the system of universities offers an adequate spectrum of good quality graduate programs. To achieve this, certain institutions will have to cut back their graduate offerings in some areas and concentrate resources on programs of proven strength. At the present time I see no evidence that this is happening; quite the contrary, the universities seem to be scrambling to pour resources into programs that have been identified as weak and requiring improvement rather than husbanding those resources to build on the programs already identified as being of good quality. In some cases programs that have achieved international stature are being starved for funds while resources go to shore up weak and mediocre programs.

The periodic appraisals results provide the universities with information on which they can plan their future development, both individually and collectively, to build a system of strong graduate programs that will serve the province well. Whether the universities operating through the OCGS and the COU can face up to the kinds of decisions that will be required, if this is to come about, remains to be seen. If they cannot, then I predict that the government or the OCUA will intervene, whether it wishes to or not, to ensure that the strong programs remain strong and limited resources are spent wisely. The situation presents a challenge and an opportunity to the universities. The question is whether they will be able to meet it or whether, through inaction, they will invite further intervention by the government or its advisory body. The universities have risen to the challenge of quality control but that is not enough. They must also play a role in the long-range planning of the university system or others will plan it for them.

The Orderly Distribution of Opportunity in Ontario: A Comment on the Behaviour of Universities and Governments

by

John Holland

and

Saeed Quazi[1]

Admitting students to universities in Ontario is a well recorded, readily quantifiable, annually recurring phenomenon. This paper is concerned with the business of admissions as a service performed by the universities for the government of Ontario, with some aspects of the nature of university/government relationships that pertain to the rationing of opportunity, and with inhibitors operating on government propensities to intervene in the rationing functions of universities.[2]

It is appropriate to begin this commentary with a few observations about the public-finance context of higher education. In 1972, the colleges and universities of Ontario commanded 11.8 percent of Ontario Budget expenditures (excluding interest on provincial debt); in 1985, they commanded 7.4 percent. The decline in the relative magnitude of this category of public expenditure has been relentless and quite constant (see Table 1). It was accompanied by a comparably relentless erosion of real-dollar expenditures (in operating grants) per student after 1978 (see Table 2). These observations are only introduced to indicate that the rationing challenges facing the province and the universities are not likely to be ameliorated by making increased public funds

---

[1]Associate Professor, Higher Education Group, OISE; Project Director, Higher Education Group, OISE, Toronto, ON.

[2]This paper complements an earlier study by the authors, "Who Goes to Which Universities in Ontario?", paper presented at the Canadian Society for the Study of Higher Education Conference, Montreal, 27 May 1985.

available to universities, i.e., by making it feasible for the universities to expand their operations.

Ontario universities, by several measures, are operating at peak levels. Full-time first year enrolment in 1985-86, at about 37,051, had only been exceeded once (in 1983 at 37,925), and was 5.7 percent higher than in 1975. Total undergraduate enrolment, at about 162,400, was up about 16 percent over the decade. The estimated number of first degrees to be conferred in 1985-86 equalled the 1983 high of 39,430 and was 8 percent higher than the total of 1975 (see Table 3). First year enrolments had been about 22.2 percent of the age 18 population in 1975, they were 26.4 percent in 1985. We may change the emphases in the presentation of the numbers a bit and say that they represent a decade of constancy. Total undergraduate enrolments were about 18.7 percent of the 20-24 population in 1975, and about 19.8 percent of that population in 1985. First degrees (bachelor and professional, including post-degree professional diplomas) awarded in 1975-76 were equal to about 24.7 percent of the population aged 22; first degrees awarded in 1985-86 were equal to about 23.7 percent of the population aged 22.

There had been some fluctuations during the decade. First year enrolments, particularly, had changed. The levels in 1985-86, though only 5.7 percent above 1975, were about 10 percent higher than those of 1980-81, and represented a recovery of about six percentage points in the participation rate. Nevertheless, it is clear that the system now is notable for constancy of scale. This suggests a very stable rationing process at work. Each year about two-thirds of Grade 13 students apply to university, and about two-thirds of those are accepted and show up to register in September. That is, about 44 percent of Ontario Grade 13 students go to university the next year. But in 1973 about 71 percent of those who applied were accepted and registered, and in 1983 about 64 percent. So, constancy notwithstanding, the system is becoming a bit more selective (see Table 4).

These students go to one or another of the fifteen universities in Ontario. The universities can be ranked 1 to 15 by the percentage of their first-year students who have been given the accolade, Ontario Scholar, or by the average Grade 13 marks of the same students. The results are very nearly the same (rank-order correlation: .95 in 1983, see Table 5). They can also be ranked by the percentage of registrants who identified that institution as their first choice. This is a crude index of the exclusivity of institutions, and it is negatively correlated with the percent-of-scholars and average-grades indexes (rank order correlations: -.62 in both cases in 1983). For example, the university with the highest average student marks had the lowest ratio of registrants to applicants who identified that institution as their first choice. The one with the lowest average entering students' marks had the highest ratio of registrants to first choice applicants. This is only to say, of course, that exclusivity attracts well qualified applicants, but exclusivity means to exclude.

Exclusivity is itself an index of prestige. In the case of universities, its presence is usually demonstrated by a policy of resisting pressure to expand, i.e., refusing to accommodate to the demand for places. The attractions of exclusivity to desirable students allow the exclusive schools to exclude the more. The universities that grew least in numbers of first-year students in the years 1978-83 were, in 1983, the ones with the highest ratios of first-choice applicants to registrants, i.e., the ones best able to be more exclusive. The rank-order correlation between increase-in-registration those five years and demonstrated exclusivity in 1983 was -.66 (see Table 6). The universities with the highest ratios of applicants in 1983 to registrants in the year before were the ones able to exclude the largest portion of first-choice applicants in 1983 - not surprisingly. The rank-order correlation for this index of the attractiveness of exclusive institutions and this measure of exclusion at the next round of selection is .86.

There is, of course, something to be said for the attractions of exclusivity beyond noting that it allows for more exclusions. The varied propensities of Ontario universities to grow during the five years 1978 to 1983 is closely related to the variable that was their ability to attract prestigious students at the end of the period. Growth in first-year registrations over the period is correlated with the percent-scholars variable in 1983 at -.76 (see Table 7).

Speculation as to whether or not such a system of publicly funded universities can survive, and the difficulties of directing its evolution, motivate the comments which follow about governments and universities. This is, perhaps, the same thing as saying that the pages to follow address the question of why intervention by governments in the workings of universities is such a difficult, dangerous and thankless business.

The Chance Play of Winds and Clouds

Universities are creatures of the late middle-ages, invented as agencies of melioration in that brutish period. The reader who concedes to this assertion is probably not surprised to observe that, in our time universities claim certain privileges by right of virtue as well as precedent, and expect citizens to recognize an identity of their own and university interests. Nor is he likely to be dismayed by what is claimed by universities. The best apologists for university privileges, after all, usually confine their cases to cogent arguments that these institutions ought to have a monopoly on the granting of academic degrees, and, in connection with this, ought to be autonomous agents of society for determining who will study, what will be taught, and who will teach it.[3]

As conventional as it may be to claim that our universities are vestiges of the middle-ages which have, through the successive ages of the modern period, consistently performed some meliorative social functions, one can as well suppose that our universities have little or nothing to do with the centres of learning in pre-modern times. One can also suppose that

---

[3] This often paraphrased assertion of "four freedoms" (including "how it should be taught") is not usually footnoted. It seems to have come into modern currency from South Africa via Justice F. Frankfurter of the U.S. Supreme Court in a concurring opinion. See United States Reports, 354. (U.S. Government Printing Office, 1957), pp. 234-270. The Sweezy v. New Hampshire decision deals with the petitioners free exercise of the right to lecture and the justifications of the State's right to interfere in that exercise (p. 261). The Court ruled against the justifications of intervention and in favour of Sweezy's right to lecture. The four "essential freedoms of a university" are mentioned by Frankfurter only in quotation, from a statement of a conference of senior scholars from the University of Cape Town and the University of Witwatersrand (p. 263).

centres of learning by whatever name, in whatever time, have always been integral parts of a social arrangement, and not establishments more transcendent, universal or virtuous than the other organizations they did business with.

There does not exist a cogent frame-of-reference in history, law or logic, that apologists for university privileges can resort to in making a case for maintaining, instituting or exercising those privileges. If we confine ourselves to the usual standards of plausibility, about all we can say is that universities have the privileges they do because they have assumed them, and the assumption has not been effectively countered, or because they have been granted them by the state. Working back from that, we can say they have assumed the privileges they have because their officers perceived opportunities for institutional enhancement or aggrandizement and responded to them. We can say, too, that the state has granted them the privileges they have in order that the legislators might be freed from direct responsibility for some difficult rationing decisions.

With the exception of leading, a function with which it is closely associated, rationing is the most prestigious responsibility society gives to an individual. It is a high-status activity to serve on conscription boards and say who must serve and who need not, to serve on parole boards and say which convicts will be freed early and which will not, to serve on censor boards and say whose salacious films will be shown and whose will not, and even to serve on abortion committees and say which fetuses will be destroyed and which will not. Much of the prestige of being a teacher, lawyer, doctor or clergyman has to do with the rationing activities of the occupational role. There is more prestige, of course, in being a principal, a high court judge, a chief-of-surgery or a bishop. People in these prestigious offices both ration and preside. For an organization, though, there can be no distinction between a rationing role and a leadership role. When we speak of the leadership role of Harvard University, or of the Bank of Canada, we have in mind the attention we all pay to the rationing decisions they make and to the influence of those decisions on the discrimination practiced by others. Harvard would have little to ration, and not much influence had generations of corporation officers not assiduously made decisions in favour of corporate aggrandizement. And the

Bank of Canada would not make the grand decisions for rationing credit that it does,and not influence the behaviour of all of us the way it does, had it not been granted special privileges by Act of Parliament, in return for relieving Parliament of some odious rationing decisions.

Lon L. Fuller, the American legal philosopher, was much concerned with notions of justice pertinent to administrative law and contract adjudication, and his essays are fascinating treatments of the intellectual and normative bases of rationing. The essays that deal most directly with the form of social ordering that he called managerial direction made much use of Wittfogel's reasoning to the effect that a political-economic arrangement that requires a highly organized and differentiated work force producing a product (water) that is distributed administratively is inordinately conducive to despotism.[4] Fuller remarked that:

> ... over the world and through history, the most diverse rules have been applied to the allocation of irrigation water. ... first come, first served, to each according to his needs, to each according to the needs of society, to each according to the luck of the draw.

> The diversity of these rules is a tribute to human ingenuity. It may also be a tribute to the difficulty of the task human ingenuity sets for itself when, instead of leaving the distribution of moisture to the chance play of winds and clouds, it assumes the task itself.

> We no longer have any problem of explaining how a concentration of managerial skill enhances the power of a political ruler who is himself unlikely to know anything about irrigation engineering. ...it is understandable that (the distribution problems) should be referred to the Big Decider himself.

> ... It may be said of priests that in every society they are specialists in solving unsolvable problems.

---

[4]K.A. Wittfogel, Oriental Despotism. (New Haven: Yale University Press, 1957).

... If the function of magic in primitive society is indeed to serve as a kind of tranquilizer, as a means of reducing anxieties, then it is no mystery that the hydraulic ruler, as well as his subjects, should have need of it.[5]

In Ontario, water (mostly from public sources) is most often given away or sold at an administered price approximating the cost of delivery. But, of course, as Fuller well realized, there are other industries with highly organized and differentiated work forces producing products that must be administratively distributed. The justice system is one of these, and higher education is another. The most challenging rationing job performed in Ontario has nothing to do with water. It is the annually recurring task of directing some portion of the new cohort of young adults into universities, while directing a larger portion of them away from the universities, and then directing a part of the university students into the most sought after schools and faculties, and a larger part of them to other institutions and faculties. The system can only be said to be working well if most of the students admitted to the institutions and faculties they wanted believe they are there because they deserve to be, and if most of the students not admitted to university, and to the institution and faculty of their choice, believe they are not where they want to be because they don't deserve to be there. To bring this off to most people's satisfaction year after year, is a remarkable accomplishment. It is a job done by the universities, as a set of autonomous operations, competing for the same population of choice students. But the job is done for the state. If the universities cease to do the job, the Government will have to answer for allowing an orderly process of distributing status and economic opportunity to degenerate into one in which the distribution is left "to the chance play of winds and clouds," or it will have to assume the task itself, at least until some other institutional arrangement is invented.

---

[5]L.Fuller, "Irrigation and Tyranny," in The Principles of Social Order: Selected Essays of Lon L. Fuller, edited by K. Winston (Durham: Duke University Press, 1981), p. 208.

No such challenge as this confronted medieval governments, and no such task as this was presented to medieval universities. It has only become a function and service of Ontario universities in very recent decades. The universities could not do the job if they were not generously subsidized by the Government, if there did not exist a provincial system of secondary schools producing several streams of qualitatively differentiated school-leavers with uniform documentation on all students identified as likely to go to university, if there were not a system of awards for scholarship administered by the Ministry of Education, and if all the universities did not compete for the same students, for all the same accolades, and, more important, for priority of place on the same ordinal listing.

The general approach to selecting students in every university is to take applicants in order of their secondary school grades until as many places as the university wants to fill are filled. There is no evidence that this system maximizes the good that universities do for students or for society. It does allow each university to maximize its prestige, as that is reflected by the institution's competitive standing among the other universities. This is to say that each university may maximize its status in the same way that the Toronto Blue Jays may maximize their standing in the American League.

The objective of the Blue Jays is clear enough, so is that of every other team in the league. The objective of the league itself is maximum average earned revenues of all teams, which is determined by the curiosity, interest and amusement of fans. Earned revenues will vary some depending on which teams are in final contention for the pennant, but the important thing is that there be an order of all teams in the league, and that they compete for priority of place on the same ordinal scale. The competitive objective of each of the fifteen universities in Ontario is almost as clear as is that of teams in the American League.

Each university contends for priority of place, but the league has nothing to maximize. There is nothing comparable to the average earned revenue of all teams, nothing that reflects varying levels of curiosity, interest and amusement of fans. Beyond saying that the social want that is an orderly distribution of social and economic chances among young adults has been served, not much can be said for or against the annual competition, which is not based on a great deal of conjecture.

Serving social wants is the business of the state, not of universities. The universities perform a function for the state for which they are paid. The job is done more or less well, depending upon how generally accepted is the propriety of this way of distributing opportunity. For the distribution to be orderly, and the social want fulfilled, there must not be anything approaching general skepticism about the propriety of it all. This skepticism is best avoided if attention is never cast upon the eclectic, pragmatic, experimental tactics that each university resorts to in its competitive role, and which, collectively, are the tactics that the university system uses in performing its most important rationing task, the annual distribution of differentiated opportunities among a new cohort of young adults. Chances that the system will continue to work more or less as it has been for several decades are maximized if the illusion can be maintained that it has been working in more or less the same way for nigh on to a millennium and that universities know precisely what they are doing and how to go about it.

The truth of the matter, of course, is that nothing like Ontario as we know it ever existed anywhere in the world until a few decades ago. Government didn't do the things it has to make the universities the agencies for distributing opportunities that they now are until about thirty years ago, and the system has been operating, with anything like its present effect, only for about twenty years. Nobody knows whether or not the rationing behaviour of universities has done us any collective good. We don't even have a well articulated statement of what that good might be. Perhaps we would all be better off if access to the most sought after universities and programs were by lot, or, even, if we systematically sent the "worst" students to the "best" universities. All we can say for sure is that we (as we give effect to our wishes via political action) do not want everybody who applies to university to get there, we do not want all universities to be equally easy to get into, we do not want everybody who is bright and hard working and wants to be a lawyer, or a doctor, or a chartered accountant, to get into professional school. The universities as they are now constituted, and as they are now behaving, are effecting a pretty orderly distribution of opportunities every year, and the thing we do not want, a sudden and complete opening of all occupations to everybody who meets some set of occupationally relevant achievement and performance requirements that we are willing to specify, is being evaded.

But the proportion of new cohorts of young people who are becoming doctors, lawyers,engineers,economists and ethicists has already increased beyond the point at which a convincing case can be made that all aspirants with the especial requisite talents, and only those with especial requisite talents, are being admitted to the corresponding specialized studies. Universities, like Fabius Cunctator, may only be delaying for a while, a very important while, the advance of forces intent upon disrupting the arrangement of things we are accustomed to.

The universities have been the agencies for regulating the dissipation of learning-based monopolies. Monopolies, in this sense, are simply occupations in which wages reflect some differentials between actual hourly wages or piece-work rates of qualified workers and the wage rates that would prevail if no qualified workers were precluded from offering their services because they lack some university-granted credentials and no workers were unqualified because they were excluded from university.

Universities in Ontario might have expanded the places in law schools, medical schools, and in any and all schools and faculties, at twice the rate, or at half the rate that they did (these past five, ten, twenty or thirty years). Lawyers, doctors and the various occupational specialists who get all or part of their credentials at university benefited for the fact that universities did not increase the enrolments in their respective faculties more, and suffered for the fact that universities did not increase enrolments in those faculties less.

Government support of universities might have been more generous or less generous than it was, and this no doubt would have affected the propensity of universities to train more or fewer lawyers, doctors and graduates of every sort. But at any level of government generosity, it has been universities that made the decisions to accept and reject students. And, finally, every would-be freshman undergraduate either did or did not become a student because the least acceptable university to him did or did not admit him. Whether or not any given applicant has gotten to university has not been a decision of Government.

Persons for All Employments

New formulations of what the privileges of universities are and ought to be, and of the duties and utilities of universities, are never scarce. The most widely read of these, on this continent at any rate, come from newly elevated university presidents, or university presidents newly celebrated for one reason or another. If these presidents are somehow charismatic or newsworthy, their descriptions, conjectures and prescriptions are treated as factual and scholarly statements about the nature of universities, and as explanations of the privileges they enjoy. It takes some years, often some decades, before these writings are appreciated for what they tell us about the men and times that produced them, and about the social history of higher education. At about the same time, it becomes clear that they tell us very little about the nature of universities, and they are even less use to the understanding or rationalizing of the privileges of universities. Apparently, universities are episodic phenomena. To learn more and more about them, is not the same thing as learning something about their nature, about how they got to be the way they are, or why they develop as they do.

Reading and writing about universities would be very different from what it is if there were a frame of reference to use in rationalizing the privileges of universities. But if there were a frame of reference in history, law or logic, it would have to exist also in natural law. This is to say that there would have to exist some modern formulation of statements about the nature of man that would have an almost obvious connection with a set of propositions to this effect: the granting of degrees by universities to somebody (or everybody), under conditions set by the universities, fulfills a social want; essential to the fulfillment of that social want is rationing in the form of excluding some people, at any given time, from the good the universities have to give; professors and other university officers doing that rationing in the interest of their respective institutions will, thereby, effect the fulfillment of that social want; and, though the state exists to serve social wants, this one is better served by deputizing universities to do it than by a legislature taking direct responsibility for instructing its executive and bureaucracy to do it and monitoring their performance.

Nobody is about to undertake this formulation. Indeed, this is a time when natural law, if brought up at all by practical people, is rarely acknowledged explicitly as the heart-of-the-matter for cogently reasoned reforms, whether reforms of taxation, the justice system, financial intermediaries or higher education. Social critics in our time are well advised not to talk to us too directly or openly about human nature. But perhaps this has been heuristically sound for as long as philosophers have been writing about political reform. Swift never told us that we ought not to look to the very clever to fill the responsible positions in society. But Gulliver, in his candid way, explained to us that, quite naturally, in Lilliput, public affairs had to be managed by people without extraordinary gifts, and, as it naturally happens, it was well that the very clever were excluded:

> In chusing Persons for all Employments, they have more regard to good Morals than to great abilities; For, since Government is necessary to Mankind, they believe that the common Size of human Understandings, is fitted to some Station or other; and that Providence never intended to make the Management of public Affairs a Mystery, to be comprehended only by a few Persons of sublime Genius, of which there seldom are three born in an Age: But, they suppose Truth, Justice, Temperance, and the like, to be in every Man's Power; the Practice of which Virtues, assisted by Experience and a good Intention, would qualify any Man for the Service of his Country, except where a Course of Study is required. But they thought the Want of Moral Virtues was so far from being supplied by superior Endowments of the Mind, that Employments could never be put into such dangerous Hands as those of

Persons so qualified; and at least, that the Mistakes committed by Ignorance in a virtuous Disposition, would never be of such fatal Consequence to the Publick Weal, as the Practices of a Man, whose Inclinations led him to be corrupt, and had great Abilities to manage, to multiply, and defend his Corruptions.[6]

It was only something over 100 years after Gulliver's time that North Americans came to see the wisdom of Lilliput's approach to public affairs. By the middle of the nineteenth century, the Americans had already learned, and other industrializing societies were learning very rapidly, that there is not actually a nice distinction between public affairs and private affairs once the organizing propensities of citizens have been freed up, even their propensities for large, complicated enterprises that will long outlive their initiators. Indeed, the organizing principle of modern society is nothing more than the Lilliputian notion that ordinary people have to run public affairs. The strategy for letting them do this is the free granting by legislatures of corporation charters.

Charters for commercial and industrial undertakings are freely granted, and modern polities, especially the states of the United States of America, have even experimented boldly with unrestricted granting of charters for banks and universities. This mode of organizing things has brought about a change in the governing of modern states. Legislatures, of necessity, must deal ever more generally and ever less directly with the people who run our important enterprises for us. There are good philosophical reasons for governments to limit their own powers to intervene capriciously or particularistically in the running of things, universities included. But the practical reasons are even more impressive. These practical reasons for governments not interfering with the running of corporations explain the freedom from government interventions that our Ontario universities enjoy much more convincingly than do any notions about ancient traditions or even any claims about the virtues of scholars and universities and the benefits of academic freedom.

---

[6] J. Swift, Gulliver's Travels, edited by Paul Turner. (Oxford: Oxford University Press, 1971), p. 46.

What modern universities are, what they do, and what they are good for are much more intrinsically related to the history of economic organization in the West since the 1770s than to the exciting events of the late Middle Ages, of the Renaissance, of the Age of Discovery, or of the Age of Reason. Incidental to the American Revolution and the ensuing political hegemony of a mercantile-industrial class was the electing of state legislatures with unprecedented propensities to grant charters for commercial organizations. State legislatures accommodated groups of citizens applying for charters with such alacrity that the connotations of privilege associated with getting a charter were quickly diluted. For more than thirty years after the Revolution,and more than twenty years after the inauguration of government under the Constitution of 1789, however, each incorporation was still literally an act of a legislature exercising sovereignty. This experiment in the democratizing of entrepreneurial organization boded likely to monopolize legislative energies. If legislatures were to be freed-up for more exciting politics, charters had to be more stringently rationed or the process be routinized and bureaucratized.

In 1811, New York State enacted a general incorporation law enabling the secretary of state to grant charters. Henceforth, all applicants who met the requirements set down in the general legislation would be chartered by bureaucratic action. Even before this act, states were already in competition with one another to attract investment and business by making incorporation easier. But the mobilization of the bureaucracy in this inter-state competition marked the beginning of a new era. Inter-state and inter-community competition to attract businesses by passing legislation and administering regulations in ways businesses appreciate had begun. It was a departure in industrial policy that appealed to politicians under new realities of free-trade, meaning especially the freer movement of capital and labour across state boundaries.

Nothing in the written record of efforts to intellectualize the American Revolution and of the organizing of politics and the economy in the Federalist Period suggests that inter-community and inter-state competitions would take the forms and have the consequences that they did. It was by design that capital and labour were becoming freer, and in general this

111

probably worked to the advantage of the interests it was intended to serve. Certainly it worked to the interests of the families, corporations, towns and states that invested and speculated in new lands, in the infra-structure projects to serve them, and in the bonds and currencies of the Federal Government and the new banks. But, apparently, no interest group in fact wanted the states to lose control over corporations.

When it was clear that a liberal policy of incorporation in one state called for more liberal policies in other states, and ultimately for an abdication of state control over the numbers, sizes, natures and locations of corporations, those consequences were accepted, but not sought. The import of these observations is that when businesses or factors of production are free to move, they do move to the place of best advantage. The freer the world of trade is, the more certainly one jurisdiction must do what its neighbour does, when what the neighbour does is advantageous to the people, capital and enterprises both jurisdictions want.

Other states followed New York's lead in making incorporation a bureaucratic function. In 1844 incorporation in Britain ceased to be dependent upon a special grant by Crown or Parliament. The limited-liability chartered company with the property rights and some of the other rights-in-law of individuals soon became the usual mode for the organization of most kinds of enterprise in the modern, industrialized nations.

In many countries a university has status in law very much like other chartered companies. As new universities have appeared in large numbers in many jurisdictions in recent decades, universities have come both to resemble other corporations more, and to be thought of as resembling other corporations more.

It was in the states of the United States that corporation charters were first given to universities in large numbers, just as it was there that other corporations were first chartered in large numbers. The Ninth Edition of the Encyclopedia Britannica (1890), in the article on universities, noted that "the report of the commissioners of education for 1883-84 gives a list of no less than 370 degree-giving universities or colleges." The point was then made that nearly 90 percent of them had been established in the preceding thirty-five years. The article did not note, however, that some institutions chartered in those years never actually became campuses with professors and students. Some institutions that did actually operate for a time did not last long or were absorbed into other institutions.

Corporations and universities existed in great numbers in late nineteenth century America. Some of those corporations grew into the largest in the world. Most never amounted to much and many disappeared. Some of the universities never amounted to much either, but some of them grew into the biggest in the world, and some hired professors from the great universities of the world. Sometimes it was the money from those big American corporations that those big (or not so big) American universities used to hire those professors. In general, the state governments did not have a great deal to do with determining which universities would command huge fortunes and grow into rich and influential institutions.

The states, in effect, abdicated control over corporations by chartering so many. In large measure, they lost control over universities because they chartered so many. To some extent they lost control over universities because they lost control over corporations. Universities could turn to corporations, and to the men who owned or ran corporations, for financial help. Those corporations and those people could benefit the universities, and they could control them to varying degrees over varying periods of time. And, of course, they still can.

Of most importance to the future of American universities, and of universities of the Western World, were two aspects of the emerging character, or nature, of corporations in nineteenth century America. In 1816, still very early in the period of rapid proliferation of corporations, and actually before the rapid proliferation of universities, the State of New Hampshire unilaterally altered the charter of Dartmouth College, intending to make that private institution the state university. An effective majority of the college community resisted the reorganization of the college. In law, the reorganization was objected to by the officers of the corporation, the members of the Board of Trustees. The strategy of their case was based on the proposition that the sovereign state could not revoke a charter. Daniel Webster was an alumnus of the College and the College's lawyer in this case. He was also a very influential Federalist politician and perhaps the most effective lawyer in New England. Whatever the importance of the lawyer's eloquence, influence and genius, the case was decided in favour of the College (the Board) by the U.S. Supreme Court in 1819.

The Supreme Court did not recognize Dartmouth College as a special corporation. The State of New Hampshire had not the right to unilaterally revoke or change the charter of Dartmouth College because it was a chartered corporation, not because it was a chartered college. A charter is a binding contract between a corporation and the state, and cannot be unilaterally abrogated.[7]

The importance of this precedent, to the states of the United States and to all jurisdictions with related jurisprudential systems that were to experience the proliferation of corporations, is the greater for its place in time.

Corporations were to exist in numbers over which the states could not exercise effective direct control, and could not be unilaterally undone by the state. It followed that the rights of participants (investors) in corporations and the conduct of

---

[7]United States Reports, 17. Reports of Cases Argued and Adjudged in the Supreme Court, 1819, pp. 518-71. "And even if the king be founder, if he grants a charter incorporating trustees and governors, they are visitors, and the king cannot visit. A subsequent donation, or engrafted fellowship, falls under the same general visitational power, if not otherwise specifically provided. In New England, and perhaps throughout the United States, eleemosynary corporations have been generally established in the latter mode, that is, by incorporating governors or trustees, and vesting in them the right of visitation" (quoting from Webster's arguments before the Court, p. 551). "It may be public, that is general, in its uses and advantages; and the State may very laudably add contributions of its own to the funds: but it is still private in the tenure of the property, and in the right of administering the funds" (Webster. p. 568). "They [the trustees of Dartmouth] had, therefore as they contend, privileges, property, and immunities, within the true meaning of the bill of rights. They had rights, and still have them, which they can assert against the legislature, as well as against other wrongdoers" (Webster. p. 569.) "It results from this opinion, that the acts of the legislature of New Hampshire, are repugnant to the constitution of the United States. ... The judgement ot the State Court must, therefore, be reversed" (Chief Justice Marshall, decision. p. 654).

114

corporations as enterprises would depend upon the discretion of officers of the corporations. Corporations, then, were <u>by nature</u> potentially immortal and, of necessity, autonomous. These were to be the two important aspects of the emerging character of corporations. Universities, too, were <u>by nature</u> potentially immortal, and of necessity autonomous,and for these reasons the rights of participants (students, professors, benefactors) and the conduct of the universities as enterprises would depend upon the discretion of officers of the corporations. These were the men of affairs who so fascinated Thorstein Veblen, and to whose abilities, insights, illusions and vanities he attributed the character, the natural character, of American universities.[8]   The American experiences with this proliferation were to be repeated with varying degrees of intensity and similarity in other democratic-capitalistic jurisdictions, notably Canada.

The bureaucratization and democratization of charter granting, and the subsequent proliferation of commercial corporations is a familiar aspect of Canadian economic life. Perhaps less apparent is the propensity of Canadian provinces to charter universities.

<u>The World Almanac, 1980</u> affords a plausible approach to comparing the Canadian and American propensities to charter universities. <u>The Almanac</u> (using U.S. Office of Education sources), lists 1337 Senior Colleges in the United States as of spring, 1979.   "Senior College", apparently, allows the grouping of degree granting colleges and universities, but excludes the large class of institutions that qualify as community or junior colleges. <u>The Almanac</u> (using Statistics Canada sources) lists 51 colleges and universities in Canada for 1977-78. (The advantage of using the <u>Almanac's</u> numbers is that they allow us to say that a third party has determined which institutions, in each country, are and are not colleges

---

[8]T. Veblen, <u>The Higher Learning in America: A Memorandum on the Conduct of Universities by Business Men</u> (Stanford, Ca: Academic Reprints, 1954 {first published 1918}). Veblen's analysis of universities is usually recognized as flawed, his writings hardly seem prophetic, he likely did not describe things quite honestly. Nevertheless, his Chapter II, "the Governing Boards"' is probably the best - and most entertaining - explanation of why universities are run by business men that we are likely ever to read.

and universities for the purposes at hand.) By the _Almanac_ editors' reckoning, there were 26 times as many colleges or universities in the United States as there were in Canada at the end of the 1970s. Because there are about 9.5 times as many Americans as Canadians, we can say that there are about 2.7 times as many colleges and universities per American as per Canadian. And, because there are 19 universities in Ontario, as The Almanac chose to count them, and about 27 times as many Americans as Ontarians, we can say that there are 2.6 times as many colleges and universities per American as per Ontarian. By this estimate, then, it seems that there is what might be called a North American propensity to charter universities that sets us apart from European states, and the propensity is more pronounced in the U.S. than in Canada. The difference is not striking, however, and the differences are greater among the states and provinces than between the two countries. Nova Scotia, for example, has about twice the number of universities per capita as does the United States.

The propensity to charter institutions in large numbers is not an Americanism that has come lately to Canada. The World Almanac, 1929 counted 638 American colleges and universities ("Chief Colleges" was the term used) and 26 Canadian colleges and universities. Americans outnumbered Canadians about twelve to one then, so there were only about twice as many institutions per American fifty-seven years ago.

All of this is to say nothing about the right that is peculiar to universities, the right to grant degrees. It is this monopoly that makes universities what they are and raises questions about which other classes of corporations are appropriate analogues to employ in explaining the behaviour of universities and their relationships to government.

Economists and all students of business organizations have long been keenly interested in observations that oligopolistic firms do not always charge prices high enough to prevent an excess of demand in the markets they dominate. This is tantamount to saying that these firms engage in some kind of rationing behaviour at least part of the time. The phenomenon has commanded new attention in response to the oil panics of 1973 and 1979, including the attentions of economists with a historical bent.

Alan L. Olmstead and Paul Rhode in "Rationing without Government: The West Coast Gas Famine of 1920" (American Economic Review, December, 1985, pp. 1044-1051) tell the story of rationing by Standard Oil of California during the first large scale oil-shortage in the U.S. "Domestic consumption jumped 25 percent in 1920... driving the real price of crude to levels unmatched over the next fifty years. On the West coast, a separate oil market dominated by Standard Oil of California, crude's real price doubled during 1920." In April 1920, SoCal urged motorists to "buy as little gasoline as possible." The major companies "...jointly forged a rationing program for all California, designed to cut consumption by 15%." Olmstead and Rhode make the point that there is no definitive explanation for the behaviour (suppressing of prices) of the oil companies. Of more interest was the behaviour of the U.S. and California Governments. The possibility and threat of government investigations apparently affected corporate behaviour regarding pricing and rationing, but not in any very consistent way, and governments did not intervene directly or decisively, nor did they promulgate policy for intervention.

Olmstead and Rhode emphasize the behaviour of firms in their conclusion more than the behaviour of government agencies. The story they tell, however, suggests that governments were content with the apparent effects of their potential for intervention or reaction, but did not have a strategy for involvement. Clearly, there was no political advantage to either a government imposed rationing system or to a government motivated freeing of prices to rise faster than they were, or fast enough to eliminate excess demand. SoCal was administering a tolerable, if not quite orderly rationing system. Or we may say that SoCal was conducting an exercise in managerial direction, and governments were able to avoid direct responsibility for the associated inequities.

But most classes of corporations, oil companies included, allocate most of their goods and services via a price system, most of the time. And most rationing functions in our society are not the business of business corporations. The only category of corporations in this class that undertakes a rationing function as an essential part of the work the companies in it do is banks.

Banks ration credit. This is their major societal function. They work about as well as universities do as rationing systems. Most people believe that a person who is denied a loan by several banks is not credit worthy ... because the banks turn him down. If the banks lend somebody money, most of us consider him credit worthy, because the banks lend him the money. Of more import, most of us, when we, ourselves, are turned down for a loan, believe that we didn't deserve to get it, and when we are approved for a loan, believe that we did deserve it.

Of course, the person who is turned down for a loan this month may be invited into the same bank to borrow money next month. His credit worthiness, by definition, is much improved,but his assets, liabilities and behaviour are likely the same as before. Of more import, the bank's lendable funds have increased (relative to loan applications). It is also the case that the student who is turned down for computer science or law school this year may be welcomed as a student next year. Not because he or she has changed, but because the university's applications-to-places ratio has changed.

The Science of Intervention

The legal and safe way for governments to intervene in the affairs of banks is to do it in accord with *a priori* conventions of propriety and standard practice, regulations and legislation. New conditions, of course, can motivate new regulations and legislation that immediately impinge on the decisions bank officials make. It is important to emphasize, though, that when making banking laws, and laws pertaining to government relations with banks, governments have the organized disciplines of money-and-banking and macro economics to use as frames-of-reference in explicating ends and means, and in projecting the image of law-makers going about their business disinterestedly, objectively and wisely.

The important point is that money-and-banking is a science. Predictions and generalizations are based on consistent data series, many scholars acknowledge the utility of the same data, and use them in replications of and variations on one another's work. Moreover, the science is additive, to some extent new generalizations are based on, or complement older ones, and when new generalizations contradict older ones, the non-congruency is made explicit. Legislatures and regulators empowered by legislatures, have an *a priori* frame of reference to use in making legislation or regulations that give powers to banks, or place new constraints on their behaviour.

The point can be made that a scientific specialty as fluid as money-and-banking is only the stuff of pretentious casuistry, and it will always allow the pursuit of particular interest X as a concomitant of common good Y. But money-and-banking has itself been analyzed as means to ends. In our time, this can only mean to analyze its utility to policy to counter economic stagnation. This, in turn, presupposes a more inclusive science, macro economics.

> Every comprehensive "theory" of an economic state of society consists of two complementary but essentially distinct elements. There is, first, the theorist's view about the basic features of the state of society, about what is and what is not important in order to understand its life at a given time. Let us call this his vision.. And there is, second, the theorist's technique, an apparatus by which he conceptualizes his vision and which turns the latter into concrete propositions or "theories." (Joseph Schumpeter)

Schumpeter presented this *obiter dictum* on social science in his obituary essay on John Maynard Keynes for the American Economic Review (September, 1946, p. 268). More specifically, the context was Schumpeter's comments on the origin of the modern stagnation thesis in Keynes' writing. The purport of his observation on facts and theory, in that context, is that it may not be difficult to accept somebody's ideas of how facts fit together, but it may be very difficult to agree on the facts. This may be almost irrelevant to the business of governments and universities in Canada, but not quite.

Banks, as a class, claim to be about as old as universities. Their origins are almost as obscure, and their written histories too are very impressionistic and short on facts. Like universities, banks are more the products of industrial reorganization in the nineteenth century than products of more

119

ancient or more romantic times. Interestingly, though, when politicians and interest groups promote particular policies and legislation for the banking business, little is said about the antiquity and virtue of institutional privileges. Spokesmen for banking's special-interests can be as pretentious as spokesmen for university special-intersts, but theirs are not the pretentions of history, tradition and culture, theirs are the pretentions of science and rationality.

The proliferation of banking corporations is a fact of life in many industrialized nations in our time, though other nations have not adopted the American's profligacy in chartering banks to the same extent that they have in chartering industrial and commercial corporations, or even universities. The important point to make, however, is that banks and universities are corporations very much like trading and manufacturing companies, though they do have very special powers of creation. Universities grant degrees that they create, not from land, labour and capital, but by acts of will and by exercising a corporate privilege. And banks lend money that they create by will and privilege.

As soon as banks and universities in the United States existed in large numbers, they could not effectively be controlled by governments. If politicians were to be effective in directing their behaviour or their evolution, it would be increasingly important to do so by indirection and generalization.

When governments in Canada and other countries in similar stages of political and economic development turn their attentions to banks, it is possible to articulate policy propositions, and to criticize the same, in terms of some common perceptions and scientific notions about banks and the business climate, and even about banks and the grandest propositions politicians can formulate pertaining to our economic destiny. This is not to claim that the sciences of money-and-banking and macro economics came along first, then governments modified the practice of freely granting charters to banking corporations and leaving them largely outside the purview of regulation. But the opposite is not the case either. It seems that the logical frames-of-reference for reclaiming government control of banks and policies for doing that have developed together. Again the American case demonstrates the phenomenon most dramatically.

New York had not included banks among the businesses that the secretary of state was empowered to charter under the General Incorporation Law of 1811. In 1838, however, New York enacted a general incorporation law for banks. Other states, in the United States and elsewhere followed. Though, in most cases outside the United States, not to the same degree, even approximately. The three decades to follow were to see banks proliferate more rapidly than universities in the United States. But the situation would change for banks long before it would for universities.

Had the United States been a smaller country, and one with a very well-defined privileged class, the rationing of private advantage that accompanies the severe rationing of bank charters might have been a matter of discrete negotiations and interest-exchange among the members of that elite group, and a tolerable, orderly process. The United States was long past that stage of its social development, however. Had there been a general toleration of rationing according to the influence of individual interests, so many and various would the influential parties have been that had to be accommodated that no orderly process would have been possible. There was no choice, then, but to rationalize the granting of charters, and the distribution of privileges of expansion to already chartered banks, in accordance with the newly developing specialties of money-and-banking and macro economics.

If, in practice, this is casuistry and the rationalizations are constructed to see that influential interests are served, the opposition and critics have the same frames-of-reference to use, and the political costs of accommodating influential interests can be made intolerable. It was to correct anarchy of a sort, even if only a perception of anarchy, that the Federal Government gained control of banking that the states had given up. If the difficult rationing decisions that this control entailed could not be handled in an orderly manner, the effect would only be to exchange one sort of anarchy for another. There were only two courses open to the United States Government, to socialize banks and direct upon itself all the odium attendant upon the rationing of credit, or to find bases in logic and science for the rationing of the privileges to do banking and to expand banking operations.

The history of experiments in chartering banks, and of government interventions in the business of banking in Canada is particular, but not so very different from the same history in the United States, the facts that Canada has a branch-banking as opposed to a unit-banking arrangement notwithstanding. In Canada, banks are run by bankers, it is they who ration credit, and this is done in an orderly way. Intervention in this business by Government is criticized and defended by arguments that refer to principles in a body of scientific literature. Legislation or regulation to change the structure of the banking business in the Prairies, for example, will be argued about as being or not being in accord with the canons of money-and-banking. Influences by Government on the Bank of Canada, and the behaviour of the Bank itself, are criticized and defended with reference to concepts from macro economics and what those notions imply about the effects of the Bank's behaviour on employment rates, interest rates, price levels and foreign exchange rates. The agreement on principles, theories and on what are appropriate intellectual sources, are notable. The arguments are mainly about facts, facts "about basic features of the state of society."

The academic specialties we call money and banking and macro economics are what they are. One may have any opinion of their worth as disciplines, but the fact remains that they are policy sciences par excellence. Without them, governments could not intervene in the orderly rationing process maintained by bankers without exposing themselves to charges of capricious interference in the business of corporations, serving special interests, or fostering anarchy. It would be as reckless, unsatisfying and dangerous to intervene in the banking business as to interfere with the internal decisions of universities.

There is no science that pertains to relating corporate behaviour to social consequences for universities as money-and-banking purports to do for banks. Even less is there a set-of-ideas on which there is some notable agreement that they explain how facts about universities, and government policies regarding them, fit together. We can expect little in the way of agreement on facts "about basic features of the state of society" that university behaviour - and government policy for universities - should be concerned about. And if there were such agreement, we would not have a scientific-frame-of-reference to show us how those facts fit together. Under these conditions, it is probably to the advantage of all concerned that the illusions be maintained that universities are vestiges of older times, times about which we have more romantic notions than well documented knowledge, and that the people who run them and work in them have some especial knowledge of how what they do is a service to humanity.

TABLE 1
Ontario Provincial Expenditures
1972-1983

($ million)

Year	Total Expenditures (1)	Total Expenditures less Interest (2)	Expenditures for Colleges and Univers. (3)	3 ÷ 1 as a % (4)	3 ÷ 2 as a % (5)
1972	6,412	6,008	706	11.0	11.8
1973	7,223	6,698	784	10.9	11.7
1974	8,722	8,133	878	10.1	10.8
1975	10,490	9,765	1,019	9.7	10.4
1976	11,743	10,853	1,158	9.9	10.7
1977	12,920	11,887	1,257	9.7	10.6
1978	13,913	12,683	1,372	9.9	10.8
1979	15,346	13,938	1,446	9.4	10.4
1980	17,273	15,678	1,542	8.9	9.8
1981	20,415	18,577	1,677	8.2	9.0
1982	22,943	20,825	1,885	8.2	9.1
1983	24,947	22,412	2,014	8.1	8.9
1984	26,898	23,976	1,804	6.7	7.5
1985 (interim)	29,316	26,065	1,930	6.6	7.4
1986 (planned)	31,492	27,917	2,069	6.5	7.4

(1) Total budgetary expenditures.
(2) Total budgetary expenditures less interest on provincial debt.
(3) Total budgetary expenditures of Ministry of Colleges and Universities.

Source: *Ontario Budget,* Table C-3, 1972-1986.

TABLE 2
Total and Per-Student Operating Grants

	Colleges			Universities		
	Total ($1,000)	Per Student Current$[1]	Per Student 1981$[2]	Total ($1,000)	Per Student Current$[1]	Per Student 1981$[2]
1974-75	—	—	—	467,137	2,690	5,095
1975-76	—	—	—	575,249	2,913	4,980
1976-77	—	—	—	658,663	3,265	5,190
1977-78	—	—	—	703,262	3,669	5,404
1978-79	270,505	3,135	4,242	743,450	4,002	5,415
1979-80	292,719	3,123	3,869	780,889	4,140	5,130
1980-81	311,207	2,985	3,357	848,101	4,273	4,807
1981-82	348,173	3,128	3,128	920,863	4,476	4,476
1982-83	392,644	3,228	2,913	1,054,966	4,821	4,351
1983-84	431,109	3,393	2,895	1,139,688	5,001	4,267
1984-85	455,589	3,699	3,024	1,200,936	5,237	4,282
1985-86	487,800	3,896	3,062	n.a.	n.a.	n.a.

[1]Total operating grant divided by numbers of full-time and part-time students (graduate and undergraduate in case of universities) as measured in FTEs (full-time equivalents).

[2]Grant per FTE divided by Consumer Price Index, using 1981$.

Sources: Ontario Universities Statistical Compendium 1970-71 to 1984-85, an annual report by the Council of Ontario Universities Total Revenue and Expenses for Provincially Assisted Universities of Ontario (for 1974-75 to 1984-85). An annual publication of the Committee of Finance Officers — Universities of Ontario. An affiliate of the Council of Ontario Universities. Published and unpublished data from Ontario Ministry of Colleges and Universities, College Affairs Branch. Statistics Canada Cat. 62-010 (quarterly) Consumer Prices and Indexes, April-June, 1986.

TABLE 3
Ontario University Enrolments, Participation Indexes and Degrees

Academic Year	1st Year[1] Enrolment	Age 18 Population	1st Year Enrolment as a % of Age 18	Under-graduate Enrolment	Age 20-24 Population	Undergrad. Enrolment as a % of Age 20-24	Bachelor[2] and 1st Professional Degrees Granted	Age 22 Population	Bachelor and 1st Professional Degree Granted, % of Age 22 Population
1920-21		50,986		9,050	239,931	3.77		47,986	
1925-26		—		8,785	265,599***	3.31		—	
1930-31		65,796		11,414*	291,268	3.92		58,253*	
1935-36		—		12,066	307,628***	3.92		—	
1940-41		67,823		11,693	323,987	3.61		64,797	
1945-46		—		20,278	338,174***	6.00		—	
1950-51		63,686		21,268	352,360	6.04		70,351	
1955-56		69,370		21,088	365,160	5.78	6,799*	77,393	8.79
1960-61		87,376		29,576	386,966	7.64	9,839	97,010	10.14
1965-66		119,839		51,611	485,053	10.67	20,946	132,045	15.86
1970-71		138,110		102,630	674,135	15.22	36,513	148,055	24.66
1975-76	35,057	157,665	22.24	139,422	744,365	18.73	36,233	156,520	23.15
1980-81	33,617	167,145	20.11	142,839	789,690	18.09	39,430**	166,700**	23.65
1985-86	37,051	140,500	26.37	162,366**	820,200**	19.80			

[1]This is total full-time enrolment from *all* sources, not just Grade 13 in Ontario. In every case in this table, enrolment is full-time enrolment only.

[2]First professional degrees includes professional degrees granted to graduates of professional schools, *including* faculties in which many or most students have already received a bachelor degree. A student who gets a B.A. and then a degree in law is counted twice.

*for 1962   **for 1983   ***Estimated

Note: The population figures are Census Years.

Source: Census Publications and Ministry of Colleges and Universities Reports.

TABLE 4
Ontario Grade 13 Enrolments, University Applications and Registrations, 1973-1985

Years	Grade 13 Enrolment (previous academic year) (1)	University Applications (2)	2 ÷ 1 as a % (3)	University Registrants (4)	4 ÷ 2 as a % (5)	4 ÷ 1 as a % (6)
1973-74	55,609	34,552	62.1	24,679	71.4	44.4
1974	55,173	36,426	66.0	25,821	70.9	46.8
1975	56,396	36,815	65.3	26,902	73.1	47.7
1976	59,997	39,241	65.4	27,195	69.3	45.3
1977	61,892	38,764	62.6	25,802	66.6	45.7
1978	60,733	36,529	60.2	25,069	68.6	41.3
1979	60,461	36,780	60.8	25,458	69.2	42.1
1980	60,212	38,523	64.0	26,747	69.4	44.4
1981	53,408	42,532	67.1	28,396	66.8	44.8
1982	66,669	45,214	68.0	29,919	66.1	44.9
1983	71,567	47,902	66.9	30,808	64.3	43.1
1984	72,216	47,840	66.3	30,260	63.3	41.9
1985	69,932	47,737	68.3	30,298	63.5	43.3

(1) Public and private school enrolments.
(2) University applicants from Grade 13 in Ontario *only,* e.g., 34,552 applicants from 1972-73 Grade 13 students for University places in 1973-74.
(4) University registrants in September from Grade 13 in Ontario previous academic year, e.g., 24,679 registrants in 1973-74 from 55,609 Grade 13 students in 1972-73.

Source: Council of Ontario Universities (data from Universities Application Centre at Guelph University).

TABLE 5
Ontario Scholars and Grade 13 Mark-Averages for Registrants at Ontario Universities, 1983

University	% Scholars	Rank Order	Grade 13 marks	Rank Order	Registrants as a % of Applicants	Rank Order
(1)	(1)	(2)	(3)	(4)	(5)	(6)
Brock	15.4	11	72.7	10	69.5	8
Carleton	21.7	8	74.3	8	81.5	3
Guelph	20.9	9	74.0	9	73.0	6
Lakehead	15.2	12.5	70.3	13	57.4	12
Laurentian	15.8	10	71.6	11	93.5	2
McMaster	33.3	5	76.0	4.5	73.8	5
Ottawa	27.1	7	75.3	6.5	62.3	9
Queen's	63.1	1	82.0	1	42.3	15
Toronto	49.6	3	79.0	3	59.4	11
Trent	12.9	14	68.5	15	104.0	1
Waterloo	54.1	2	76.0	4.5	54.2	14
Western	41.1	4	79.3	2	60.7	10
W.L.U.	31.2	6	75.3	6.5	56.4	13
Windsor	15.2	12.5	70.0	14	79.8	4
York	11.0	15	71.5	12	72.8	7
Total	33.5					

$r = .954$ $r = -.617$

$r = -.618$

(1) % of registrants identified as Ontario Scholars, an accolade bestowed on about one Grade 13 graduate in four.
(3) Average of the Grade 13 mark of new registrants from Grade 13.
(5) *Number* of registrants expressed as percentage of the *number* of applicants who identified that university as their *first* choice (not exactly the same as saying *these* registrants identified the university they are attending as their first choice).

Source: Council of Ontario Universities (data from Ontario Universities Centre at Guelph University).

TABLE 6
Growth 1978-83 and Exclusion Rates in 1983
at Ontario Universities

University	Increase in Registrants 1978-83 as a %	Rank Order	Regis- trants as a % of appli- cants 1983	Rank Order	Applications for 1983 as a % of Registrants in 1982	Rank Order
	(1)	(2)	(3)	(4)	(5)	(6)
Brock	+ 115.9	2	69.5	8	163.1	7
Carleton	+ 72.0	4	81.5	13	138.3	11
Guelph	+ 26.1	9	73.0	10	137.6	13
Lakehead	+ 12.1	12	57.4	4	178.2	5
Laurentian	+ 35.0	8	93.5	14	124.4	14
McMaster	+ 22.6	10	73.8	11	139.7	10
Ottawa	+ 40.5	7	62.3	7	193.8	2
Queen's	(−)14.4	15	42.3	1	205.2	1
Toronto	(−) 5.6	14	59.4	5	185.6	4
Trent	+ 129.0	1	104.0	15	137.7	12
Waterloo	(−) 3.6	13	54.2	2	171.7	6
Western	+ 20.8	11	60.7	6	156.5	8
W.L.U.	+ 41.8	6	56.4	3	191.6	3
Windsor	+ 64.7	5	79.8	12	112.7	15
York	+ 81.4	3	72.8	9	140.9	9
Total	+ 22.9		64.3		160.0	

$r = -.664$ $r = +.857$

(1) Registrations from Grade 13 in Ontario previous academic year.
(3) Number of applicants who identified the university as their first choice.
(5) Number of applicants as % of number of registrants in that university previous academic year.

TABLE 7

**Registration Growth, 1978-83, and Percent Scholars in 1983
at Ontario Universities**

University	Increase in Registrations 1978-83 (1)	Rank Order (2)	% Scholars in 1983 (3)	Rank Order (4)
Brock	+115.9	2	15.4	11
Carleton	+ 72.0	4	21.7	8
Guelph	+ 26.1	9	20.9	9
Lakehead	+ 12.1	12	15.2	12.5
Laurentian	+ 35.0	8	15.8	10
McMaster	+ 22.6	10	33.3	5
Ottawa	+ 40.5	7	27.1	7
Queen's	(−)14.4	15	63.1	1
Toronto	(−) 5.6	14	49.6	3
Trent	+129.0	1	12.9	14
Waterloo	(−) 3.6	13	54.1	2
Western	+ 20.8	11	41.1	4
W.L.U.	+ 41.8	6	31.2	6
Windsor	+ 64.7	5	15.2	12.5
York	+ 81.4	3	11.0	15
Total	+ 29.9		33.5	

$r = -.756$

(1) Registrations from Grade 13 in Ontario previous academic year.
(3) Percent of Registrants identified as Ontario Scholars.

Colleges and Governments - An Evolving Relationship: Government Intervention into the Operations of Community Colleges in Canada, 1964-1986

by

John D. Dennison[1]

Introduction

An essay which attempts to address issues concerning the community colleges in Canada must begin with a number of *caveats*. The prime difficulty lies with the community college concept itself. There are such colleges in nine of Canada's provinces and both territories, with the arguable exception of Nova Scotia, but they defy generalization. Their many designs respond to their diverse environments - historical, socio-cultural, economic and educational. Canada's college systems were born and nurtured within that remarkable golden age of educational development which blossomed in the late fifties and withered in the middle seventies.[2] Few social organizations have bloomed so rapidly, been so fuelled by idealism, and grown so old so quickly. But, while they share a common period of development, each provincial college system crafted an organizational model which best met the expectations of government and society for a new and different type of postsecondary educational institution appropriate to their needs.

British Columbia and Alberta saw the new institutions as a response to the growing public demand for access to advanced education, as a means of overcoming traditional barriers to

---

[1] Professor of Higher Education, Department of Administrative, Adult and Higher Education, University of British Columbia, Vancouver, BC.

[2] John D. Dennison and Paul Gallagher, Canada's Community Colleges: A Critical Analysis (Vancouver: University of British Columbia Press, 1986).

participation, be they geographic, academic, financial or psychological, and as instruments in the process of "democratization" of higher education.[3] Saskatchewan's colleges were designed as primarily socio-cultural organizations which would contribute to the personal and collective advancement of their communities and as ingredients for enriching the quality of life in rural society.[4]

Ontario's colleges were much more clearly focused and carefully related to the long-term economic blueprint prepared for that province.[5] They were not intended to be "feeder" institutions providing the first year or two of undergraduate Arts and Science programs of the universities. The colleges of applied arts and technology (CAATs) were intended to provide occupational preparation at a technical and paraprofessional level to ensure a better flow of trained manpower for the Ontario labour market.

Quebec's Colleges d'Enseignement General et Professionel (CEGEP) were created as one of the components of a reform of the province's educational system which in turn was identified with the "Quiet Revolution", the socio-cultural change which revolutionized French Canadian society in ways as irreversible as they were dramatic.[6] The CEGEPs provided the link between the reformed secondary school system (which ended with Grade 11) and both the labour market and the university world. Their purpose was to increase access to higher education and also to produce new cadres of Quebec youth with improved technical, technological and business skills.

---

[3]D. Berghofer and A. Vladicka, Access to Opportunity, 1905-1980 (Edmonton, Alberta: Ministry of Advanced Education and Manpower, 1980).

[4]R. Faris, "Community College Development in Saskatchewan: A Unique Approach", Canadian Forum 51 (1972), pp. 60-61.

[5]Ontario Department of Education, Basic Documents: Colleges of Applied Arts and Technology (Toronto: Queen's Printer, 1965).

[6]A. Denis and J. Lipkin, "Quebec's CEGEPs: Promise and Reality", McGill Journal of Education 7, (1972), pp. 119-134.

The maritime provinces, particularly New Brunswick and Prince Edward Island, used the colleges to complement a university system which was traditional and academic, and therefore did little to prepare the kind of workforce needed for technical and industrial growth. Newfoundland, despite its great economic problems, responded similarly. The Territories, although their development educationally was delayed, eventually joined the provincial pattern of college establishment.[7]

In spite of their diversity in structure, organization and purpose, all of Canada's colleges share some common philosophic commitments. All have assumed some responsibility for widening access to higher education by diversifying admission requirements, charging modest tuition fees and decentralizing the delivery of programs. All have introduced changes (for Canada) in curriculum organization, primarily through the integration of academic or general studies with vocational and technical studies. Most provide employed and unemployed adults with the opportunity to upgrade or acquire the academic background needed to undertake postsecondary and university programs. More than any other educational institution in Canada the colleges place high priority upon student support services and provide effective counselling to accommodate the diverse needs and aspirations of their heterogeneous student body.

In fact, serving the needs of students in their community has become the central mission of these colleges, a commitment which is reflected in a variety of policy initiatives: through flexible scheduling, and evening and weekend programs designed for part-time students; through the deliberate recognition of teaching as the only responsibility of their faculty; and through the use of advisory committees to ensure relevance of occupational preparation for students intending to enter the workforce. No less important is the community college need to be responsive to expectations of their immediate communities, social, economic, cultural and other groups. This is demonstrated by their willingness to mount programs at the request of local employer groups, social agencies, associations

---

[7] Dennison and Gallagher, Canada's Community Colleges.

and even individuals. One would expect that the ability of a college to meet such challenges would rest upon the power and autonomy of its governing board to commit financial and other resources to program development. In other words it would seem reasonable that autonomy, with all of its implications, is essential to the attainment of a community college's mission. But the autonomy of a publicly funded organization rests upon the willingness of government to recognize the attributes of such status, and to refrain from intervention and intrusion in the institution's affairs.

This paper will review and comment upon the relationship between governments and public community colleges in Canada over the past quarter century.

An Historical Overview

Unlike universities, the community colleges in Canada from their establishment have been required to respond to the policy initiatives and directives of two levels of government - federal and provincial. On a less formal level, many have also had to relate to their local or municipal governments. The latter has been the case either because of the funding arrangements (British Columbia and Alberta) or because of the composition of their governing boards (Quebec and Ontario). From a constitutional perspective, it may be argued that in Canada the community colleges, as educational institutions, are totally within the jurisdiction of the provincial governments. The minister responsible determines overall policy for the college system. The provincial government allocates resources and demands accountability for the disbursement of public funds. In some provinces, authority over specific aspects of college life (e.g., programs and staffing) are delegated to an intermediary body. Authority for the management of individual institutions is delegated to governing boards.

However, colleges are also engaged in vocational training. Their programs prepare individuals for the labour market by providing them with specific job skills. Employment is a legitimate national concern of the federal government, consistent with its constitutional jurisdiction over national economic affairs. Therefore, federal governments, through legislated acts, have from time to time directly funded training programs for designated occupational groups. Following Canadian constitutional convention, however, these funds are usually channelled to institutions through the appropriate provincial ministry.

Such intervention into the funding of occupational training began early in this century, but it reached massive proportions in the 1960s with the Technical and Vocational Assistance Acts. Over the past twenty years federal government policy in this area has shifted several times, culminating in recent years with the National Training Acts of the last Liberal administration and the Canadian Job Strategies of the present Conservative administration. With each policy initiative the community colleges have been forced to adjust, adapting their programming to different levels of funding, in differing occupational training areas and under differing arrangements. This has created instability and a consequent inability to engage in long term planning with any confidence.

Nevertheless, it is the provincial governments which drive the direction and pace of college development with respect to programs, responsiveness, accessibility and educational function, and therefore it is the relationship between colleges and provincial governments which is the keystone to success. Since their original development in the mid-60s to the present day, the college systems in Canada have passed through three eras, in terms of their relationship to provincial governments.

Autonomy, Diversity and Expansion, 1960-1975

In the early days of the colleges, the grandest vision was one of a loose network of institutions throughout Canada, each shaping its own destiny within broad provincial guidelines, each capitalizing on its own strengths and individual personnel, each responding to its own community or locality or region in its self-determined, unique, and distinctive way. This prospect of heady institutional discretion was an immediate and effective stimulus to action and enthusiasm. Tremendous energy was expended by board members, employees, and students in making colleges "our own". College presidents and administrators were generally entrepreneurial and politely competitive with their neighbouring colleges. Instructors developed fresh programs, experimented with different teaching techniques, and threw themselves into developing "their own" colleges. Great institutional pride and loyalty were clearly evident.[8]

The literature concerning the establishment of the college systems in various provinces is laced with sentiment about the need for community control and institutional autonomy. Colleges were to focus their attention upon the varied program needs of their communities. Their boards had considerable delegated authority in the matter of personnel hiring, program planning, and the delivery of college services.

Even in provinces such as Quebec, Ontario and Alberta, where provincial interbodies were created to monitor and control college development, the intent was to preserve an arm's length relationship between government and the institutions. Institutional autonomy, in varying degrees, was seen as essential to success in providing broader learning opportunities for new segments of society.

The consequences of this essentially decentralized management policy was a rapid increase in enrolment and growth in the number and kind of programs, with little coordination and even less concern over standards and possible duplication. There was a touching belief that the new colleges could become "all things to all people". With reference to the Ontario system Pitman records:

> The creation of these colleges represented an opportunity to celebrate the entrepreneurial spirit at the local community level. Moreover, institutional expansion came at a point in time when the problem of fiscal restraint, with all its attendant implications,

---

[8]*Ibid.*, p. 185.

was not a threat.[9]

Consolidation and Constraint, 1975-1980

However, the euphoric experiment in local autonomy exacted a price. College budgets expanded at an alarming rate and it was soon apparent that the drain on provincial treasuries by the rapidly expanding college system was well beyond expectation and easy control. The 1960's commitment to accessibility had released a flood of prospective students, of varied ages and educational backgrounds, bringing with them a variety of aspirations and problems.

Recognizing that it was politically unwise to call explicitly and directly for restrictions on admissions, the provincial authorities chose instead to gradually increase their control over college expenditure. In doing so, they increased direct influence upon the college systems.

Other factors also played a role in contributing to the growing intervention of provincial governments. (1) Collective agreements between the rapidly unionizing instructor organizations and their employers (represented by college boards or provincial agencies) were producing generous salary increases and improved workload working conditions which had the effect of increasing staff complements. (2) Competing funding demands from health, social welfare, and energy took precedence over education. (3) Massive inflation affected the entire economy and anti-inflation measures directly affected the public sector. (4) Public deficits of both the federal and provincial governments caused cutbacks in all public services. (5) Debt at the federal level forced governments to impose ceilings on postsecondary education transfer payments.

The cumulative effects of these factors led to the determination by provincial governments to curb spending on all forms of higher education. They used the traditional powers of government - legislative amendments to control program

---

[9]W. Pitman, The Report of the Advisor to the Minister of Colleges and Universities on the Governance of the Colleges of Applied Arts and Technology (Toronto: Queens Printer, 1986), p. 3.

approval, limit collective bargaining, designate membership on policy making boards (or even abolish the boards entirely) - and through traditional regulatory powers - limits placed on funding formulae, expenditure ceilings imposed at the program level and control exercised over block grants.

The results of increased government intervention was a "consolidation psychology". There was a virtual moratorium on imaginative program development, a reduction in college services, and the imposition of controls and quotas on the admission of students. The college systems had adopted a maintenance mode!

Restraint, Retrenchment and Control, 1980-1986

Despite the limitations imposed upon college development and expenditure during the second half of the 1970s, in the early '80s provincial governments continued to be concerned about the colleges and the need to monitor their activities. Government deficits (at all levels) continued to rise - partly due to the accumulated consequences of rapid expansion of program services in the previous two decades, but also due to the severe economic recession which, though not peculiar to Canada, had a major impact in this country, largely because of the structure of its economy.[10] Provinces which depended heavily upon natural resource exploitation were particularly affected. Government expenditure was placed under more stringent review. Funds to community college systems were reduced. And, inevitably, ways had to be found to reduce the cost of programs with limited political support. Unfortunately, much community college activity falls into this category. Direct intervention by government into the college sector was the means to a desired end.

Intervention took several different approaches, varying according to province. The most common procedure was for the appropriate government department to define more clearly, in more restrictive fashion and with specific terminology, the role

---

[10]Donald Macdonald, (Chairman), Report of the Royal Commission on the Economic Union and Development Prospects for Canada (Ottawa: Queens Printer, 1985).

expected of the colleges. The role was usually reduced to one of contributing through training to the economic growth of the province. There was an obligation to provide occupational training in designated job categories to fill projected provincial needs, and such job preparation took precedence over all else - the traditional academic and social roles of the colleges and the non-vocational programs. Their funding was reduced, or even ignored. Instead, the colleges were encouraged to embark upon entrepreneurial activities which would generate income from the private and international sectors - a technique which had the added advantage of enhancing their role in economic development.

The means adopted by governments to ensure new college directions and program priorities were to introduce funding by formulae, targetting particular activities, and effectively transforming the program profile of the institutions. Designated funding ensured the demise of some activities, controlled the expansion of others and ensured the adoption of still others - all within an overall reduction of costs. A second procedure to ensure the same end was the reduction of general funding while concurrently allotting special funds designated for "programs of excellence". What qualified as excellence was established by the appropriate ministry through "guidelines" and similar compelling advice. Finally, the major component of college budgets and a significant factor in their growth, the salaries and fringe benefits of personnel, was controlled either through provincial level collective bargaining limitations or by legislation constraining local agreements.

The result of this government intervention has been community college systems tuned to provincial needs, with reduced accessibility to students seeking programs not perceived to be a priority, and increased productivity reflected in larger class sizes and heavier teaching loads.

Inevitably, the instructional staff has become increasingly demoralized about the quality of the teaching-learning environment[11] to the point where observers like Pitman have expressed concern that colleges have all but lost their educational role and the original basis for their establishment.

> In the last number of years, there has been a tendency to view these crown corporation, not as learning institutes, but as industrial organizations. The emphasis has been on the budget "bottom line", on entrepreneurism, on immediate response to market needs, and on bureaucratic models. Senior administrators have seen themselves as being observed and judged on their capacity to serve this industrial model - a model, ironically, that many progressive industries have eschewed in favour of more horizontal, operational styles. I think it is time the pendulum swung toward the college as an educational institution, with its strengths in its quality of teaching, decision-making and work relationships.[12]

What of the Future?

In a particular sense, Canada's colleges reached a watershed in the late nineteen eighties. Maturity has not come easily, as two decades of turbulent development have demonstrated. No doubt part of the problem stems from lack of agreement among government, college authorities, and the wider community as to whether these institutions are to be treated as tools for provincial and federal government planning, in educational and economic terms, or as postsecondary educational institutions which have the responsibility of responding to the diverse service needs of very different communities and are permitted autonomously to make the expert decisions which

---

[11]See Michael L. Skolnik, (Chairman), Surival or Excellence? Report of the Instructional Assignment Review Committee (Toronto: Ministry of Colleges and Universities, 1985) and John Dennison, "Some Aspects of Government Policy towards Community Colleges in British Columbia, 1982-1986" (University of British Columbia, unpublished paper, 1986).

[12]W. Pitman, Report on Governance, p. 5.

are necessary to play this role. Or perhaps the colleges are some kind of combination of both kinds of institution, in which an unlikely balance of provincial and regional priorities can be maintained.

Pitman, in assessing the Ontario scene, expressed the problem succinctly...

> If the colleges are to be seen solely as community colleges, then there seems to be little point to any provincial structure. On the other hand, if the colleges are really a provincial manpower supply system, then there seems to be little point to having local boards of governors in colleges, at all. Of course, neither of the above positions is tenable; governance must balance the implications of a number of competing expectations. That balance must be reflected in the governing structures, at every level.[13]

If the descriptive label "community", as applied to colleges, is to have any validity, they must have a measure of fiscal and planning independence which will permit them, under the management of quasi-autonomous boards, to respond to the needs of a designated regional community. Whether such needs be for social and personnel development, intellectual enrichment, services to native people, senior citizens and women preparing to enter the workforce, human resource and environmental programs, or a wide diversity of career and personal interests, they can only be assessed flexibly if the local interests are paramount. To many observers the foregoing has been the real strength of the college sector, and the strongest justification for its development. The colleges have been able to respond effectively to segments of Canadian society whose educational interests have long been ignored.[14]

---

[13]*Ibid.*, p. 7.

[14]F. Beinder, The Community College in British Columbia: The Emphasis is on Community (Nanaimo, B.C.: Quadra Graphics, 1983).

If this role is to be protected, however, ways must be found to fund the colleges in a manner which allows for considerable local discretion in deciding upon and spending their operating budgets. While the board must be held accountable for its decisions, it must be recognized that there will be great diversity of standards and emphases. It is inevitable that colleges will develop quite different program profiles in response to the character of their communities.

At the same time, it is also reasonable to expect that the colleges be responsive to the training needs of the province in designated occupational groups. Not all their students will remain in their own community. Many graduates will travel elsewhere in the province and in Canada to seek a job. To this end a limited amount of the funding should be specifically targetted for programs of high provincial and national priority.

Under such a system the legitimate responsibility of governments to control the financial growth of public institutions and special mission of colleges to be responsive to their communities can both be met. When funding must be reduced, it would be for a college to determine which programs must be protected and which can be curtailed.

A note of caution is necessary with respect to the role of the federal government. Based upon dubious assumptions about unemployment and the relevancy of certain occupational skills which the college can develop, the present federal government has redirected training funds from the public to the private sector under the Canadian Job Strategies Program. The potential unfortunate consequences of this policy are many. They cannot be discussed in this paper, but it would be irresponsible not to at least sound a warning. The institutions which are close to their communities and are in constant touch with the local employers concerning their labour needs have a much better chance of designing relevant training activities than does a federal bureaucrat in an office many kilometres distant. Moreover, in addition to designing training programs in cooperation with employers, the educators in the colleges can integrate general program components which will provide students with a greater capacity to adapt to technological changes in the workplace. Therefore, even in the use of specified federal training funds, the individual colleges should be granted greater freedom to direct the programming to regional priorities.

A Final Comment

Despite the concept of "community" as applied to Canadian colleges, provincial governments have long exercised a considerable centralized control over their development. While there is considerable variation, it is evident that the colleges were established by governments to meet economic, socio-cultural or education objectives during a period when postsecondary education was accorded a very high priority. In the establishment period, the institutions were granted a reasonable degree of autonomy in matters of governance, program development, staffing and admissions. But, following that, there emerged a clear trend towards increased government intervention. In recent years, government influence upon college operations has reached such a stage that several observers have called for a review and reassessment of college roles.[15]   The original mission of the community colleges, as comprehensive educational institutions, seems to have been superceded by their increasing responsibility as extensions of government departments, primarily in the area of occupational training. The consequence has been a lowering of faculty morale and a perceived erosion of quality in the education being provided by the college sector.[16]

If Canada's colleges are to achieve the high expectations of their early years, in particular with respect to their responsiveness to community needs, it is vital that they retain autonomy and flexibility in matters of curriculum, budgeting priorities and allocation of personnel. The initiative lies with provincial governments. The latter must review their

---

[15]For example, see Skolnik, Survival or Excellence; Pitman, Report on Governance; Dennison, "Some Aspects of Government Policy"; R. Isabelle, Quebec Colleges: Provincial Colleges or Autonomous Institutions? (Montreal: Conseil des Colleges, 1982 [unpublished]); A. LeBlanc, "A Brief to the Council of Colleges on the CEGEP of Tomorrow" (St. Laurent, Quebec, 1984 [unpublished]).

[16]See Skolnik, Survival or Excellence and LeBlanc, A Brief.

perception of, and their relationship with, their college systems. There is every hope that governments will recognize that the real value of a community college lies in its role as community leader, contributing to community development by undertaking flexible and adaptable educational enterprises. Policies necessary to realize such ends should be introduced without delay. Only then will Canada's community colleges successfully meet the optimistic challenges set for them in their early years.

The Political-Economic Record

by

Kenneth Rea[1]

What stands out in any examination of social policy in the post-World War II period is the abrupt change which occurred in the mid-1970s, here in Ontario and apparently almost everywhere else in the Western World. What I wish to explore is the juxtaposition of developments in economics, politics and the real-world environment which appear to underlie this pervasive shift in attitudes, and to make some reference to what may or may not prove to be uniquely local considerations. First, let me review the particular experience in Ontario so as to establish how it conforms to the more general pattern.

The Period of Expansion: The Origins of a Social Policy Consensus

In Ontario in the early 1940s the context in which government involved itself in such things as education and social matters generally was remarkably similar to what it had been decades earlier. Provincial government spending was actually declining at the beginning of the period. The total outlays of the province and its municipalities (including school boards) fell by about thirty percent between during the years of World War II. The government's total spending amounted to less than seven percent of the estimated value of provincial production.

After the war, the economy of Ontario was almost completely transformed. Remarkable as the unexpected postwar boom was, what stands out in this period with respect to economic policy is the change in the way the public and their elected representatives perceived the functioning of the economic system and their relationship to it.

As elsewhere, in Ontario there was a marked decline in confidence in the market system. There was a corresponding burgeoning of interest in the possibilities of deliberate

---

[1] Professor of Economics, University of Toronto, Toronto, ON.

management of the economy to achieve certain widely accepted social objectives. While there remained some enthusiasm for the cooperative and other forms of voluntary collective activity, most of the responsibility for such efforts had come to be lodged with the government. At the federal level interests focused on the possibility of stabilizing the economy at high levels of income and employment by using the instruments of fiscal and monetary policy - although this possibility was only partially realized.

The appropriate role of the provincial governments was not so clear, partly because of the constitutional uncertainties inherent in the country's federal system, but also, I would guess, because the theory of economic management was not articulated for sub-national units in the way that the Keynesian doctrine was for a nation as a whole. Nevertheless, the provincial government did come to be held responsible for, and did come to accept responsibility for, intervening in the economic life of the province, including its educational system, in a deliberate and at times aggressive manner.

While an active economic role for government at any level was far from being a new concept in Canada, the scale and openness of the intervention demanded in the 1939-75 period was unprecedented.

Surprisingly little attention was given to the rationale for this. Although no one in a position of responsibility spoke openly about dismantling the market system the way Pierre Trudeau did many years later, it is difficult to find any area of economic activity which was not subjected to some form of deliberate intervention during this thirty-five year period.

The overall effects of this intervention are even now not easily identified. Despite the advances in economic knowledge over the period, policymakers and their advisors lacked a sufficient understanding of the forces bringing about economic change to affect them in predictable ways. This was as true of interventions in the field of education as in the more traditional areas such as promoting investment in physical forms of overhead capital. But even if they had possessed better information and all the technical ability needed to act upon it, the record shows clearly that the real problem lay not

146

in implementing policy but in determining the goals to which it should be directed.

Oddly, however, the period began with just such an exercise, an undertaking to formulate a general plan for reform of the political-economic system. Shortly after World War II began, the Conservative Party in Ontario formulated a remarkably broad and aggressive economic plan for the province, a plan which formed most of its platform for the 1943 provincial election. Thirty years later, the Conservative government, after an uninterrupted succession of election victories, renounced such interventions in the economy and dedicated itself to bringing under control, not the economy, but its own involvement in it.

The Toronto Globe and Mail in 1943 hailed the "22 Points" declaration of the Conservatives as a "Great Social Document", something more than just another collection of campaign promises. It could properly be regarded, the paper asserted, as a "whole plan" for the future of the province, a plan through which the people of Ontario could begin "intensively to plan the use and development" of the province's resources.[2]

In many ways the 22 points declaration was an accurate indicator of the attitudes and expectations which underlay much of the economic and social policy activity of the next quarter of a century. Ideologically, it carried forward something of the tradition of the old Canadian conservatism of John A. Macdonald, a tradition which incorporated the view that active government participation in the economic development of the country was appropriate so long as it was consistent with the fostering of business enterprise and general expansion. It also owed something to the ideology, or at least to the rhetoric, of the Canadian left. By 1943 it was no longer difficult even for non-socialists to talk freely about the idea of "planning" for a better world, all the time rejecting fervently the idea of complete collectivization of economic life.

Following the War the provincial government's attempts to shape and control the economic boom called for vigorous, if not

---

[2]Toronto Globe and Mail, 10 July 1943, editorial.

often effective, public policy measures. Of course the usual Canadian problem of federal-provincial relations enormously complicated the situation. But there was a will to intervene and an unclear but perceptible public expectation that such intervention was desirable, even after the spectre of a return to chronic depression began to wane. The stimulus of the Cold War, and particularly the challenge of Soviet technology filtered from the U.S. into Ontario and was vigorously taken up. Although shortages of skilled workers were largely met by heavy immigration, as in other periods of rapid Canadian economic expansion, the perception of the need for more education and training of all kinds in the environment of the 1950s and early 1960s made concern over the means and the finer points of educational policy of minor importance.

At the end of World War II Ontario had three publicly supported universities, and by the mid 1970s fifteen. The number of non-university postsecondary institutions increased from a few trade and vocational schools to a system of some twenty-two colleges covering the entire province. Full-time university enrolments increased from 12,410 in 1940 to 159,701 in 1975; full-time postsecondary non-university enrolment increased from less than 11,000 in 1955 to almost 60,000 in 1975. There were 1,179 university teachers in Ontario in 1940; by 1975 there were 12,290. Total expenditures on education in the province exceeded ten billion dollars annually by the mid-1970s about 60 percent of which was disbursed by the provincial government, 20 percent by the municipalities, and 10 percent by the federal government. Fees and other sources covered the remaining ten percent.

The role of the provincial government in the administration and financial support of the educational system changed considerably over the period, reflecting a tendency toward centralization and - possibly - an increasing reliance on expert knowledge and opinion. Yet there is little evidence that the provincial government was able to formulate any very clear set of objectives with respect to the province's educational system. Perhaps the most remarkable thing about this is that many people apparently expected it to.

While there were frequent studies of the system, including several which were supposed to answer the question of what its goals and objectives should be, and despite the aggressive action taken on occasion to meet perceived "shortages" of particular kinds of labour, no general pattern of purpose emerges with respect to what was becoming one of the province's most important industries.

Whether this was a fault or a virtue depended (and continues to depend) on the view held as to the appropriate role of public policy with respect to higher education. What I have found remarkable in studying the 1940s and the postwar decades in Ontario is the extent to which people accepted the general idea of economic planning as an appropriate context for social policy formation. This is hardly surprising in the case of the communists, socialists and others on the political left. The two communists in the provincial legislature in the early postwar period were articulate advocates of serious planning and the more numerous members of the CCF-NDP (Cooperative Commonwealth Federation-New Democratic Party) were often easily drawn out on the subject. But even Conservatives spoke well of planning - although they often meant something more limited than the defining of economic objectives and the development of instruments by which to attain them - community planning, manpower planning and other unsystematic and implausible attempts to impose a degree of central control over a more-or-less market-based economy.

The popularity of "planning" was on the wane, of course, by the 1960s, and survived only in the vague commitments of practical socialists to government intervention and the criticisms levelled by neo-Marxists at the government's ("the state's") complicity with private business.

What had happened, as we can now see, was that Keynesianism carried the day and provided governments with the means of participating actively in many areas of economic life without having to accept the rigours of detailed planning.

"...Keynesianism... provided the ideological and political foundations for the compromise of capitalist democracy. Keynesianism held out the prospect that the state could reconcile the private ownership of the means of production with democratic management of the economy... Democratic control over the level of unemployment and the distribution of income became the terms of the compromise which made democratic capitalism possible."[3] In the field of education, it was possible for the government of Ontario to undertake a massive expansion of the system in response to the demographic and social forces which were operating and to centralize certain aspects of the administrative and financing system without having to intervene directly in what was becoming the province's largest "industry".

Postsecondary education was in the hands of universities, whose autonomy was seldom challenged. Many were substantially self-supporting, although the University of Toronto and the other non-sectarian institutions did receive substantial grants from the province.

Vocational education was provided by the provincial Department of Labour which operated an apprenticeship training program and by a number of private secretarial and trade schools. Most nurses were trained by hospital schools of nursing. Elementary teachers received their special training in provincial government operated teachers' colleges and high school teachers at the Ontario College of Education. Adult education was offered by the universities through "extension" programs and by such voluntary organizations as the YMCA and the Workmens' Educational League. Specialized organizations, such as Frontier College, provided education to particular groups of workers.

One of the first areas of a perceived shortage of skilled workers was in the educational system itself. The demand for trained teachers greatly exceeded the available supply. But the need for vocational training was also recognized in other occupations. The province established a number of special schools after the war to teach particular manual and technical skills.

---

[3] Adam Przeworski and Michael Wallerstein, "Democratic Capitalism at the Crossroads", Democracy, Vol. 2, No. 54 (July, 1982) as cited in D.A. Wolfe, "The Rise and Decline of the Keynesian Era in Canada: Economic Policy, 1930-1982", in M.S. Cross and G.S. Keley, Modern Canada, Readings in Canadian Social History, Vol. 5, p. 48.

After World War II the returning veterans flooded the province's degree-granting institutions. University undergraduate enrolment in 1945 was about the same as in 1940. By 1947 it had doubled.

In the field of adult education, a "Community Programmes Branch" was established within the Department of Education to provide services to communities which took the initiative in organizing recreational and adult education activities.

The policy of providing support, while leaving responsibility for initiating and operating programs to local bodies, was in keeping with the provincial government's apparent objective of centralizing financial and administrative functions in education while decentralizing curriculum development. Such practices were reinforced by the findings of the first major inquiry in the postwar period into the workings of the educational system in the province. The Hope Commission, appointed in 1945 and reporting five years later, broke little new ground. It failed to find an acceptable solution to the government's main problem at the time - the highly sensitive issue of public financial support for Roman Catholic separate schools.

The general policy position of the provincial government remained conservative in the 1950s, with much attention still being given to problems of financing education. As to the purposes of the system, government's view appeared to be that the main task of the elementary and secondary schools was to provide good basic education and socialize students, into good citizens. The question of the economic returns to education received little attention. Human capital theory had yet to be invented. Thus, the Minister of Education in 1952 could report:

> The objective of our work in this Department is to produce loyal, intelligent, right-thinking, religious and freedom-loving citizens to take their places in developing, by all legitimate means at their disposal, this rapidly-expanding Province and Dominion. In the schools of Ontario the young people and the boys and girls are being trained to realize what true democracy really means and it is hoped that their loyalty to Queen and country will be such that they

will be ready when their turn comes, to render their
share of public service in the communities in which
they make their homes.[4]

Within only a few year both thought and practice changed
radically. Enrolment increases in the elementary schools as
the baby boom children flooded in, combined with a sharp rise
in the secondary schools' retention rates, shocked the system.
Total spending on current account by elementary and
secondary school boards increased from over 54 million dollars
in 1945 to more than 99 million in 1950. By 1955 the annual
current outlay had more than doubled again. Capital spending
increased even more rapidly, rising from 7.7 million dollars in
1945 to 35.5 million a decade later.[5]

Demographic forces, rising per capita incomes, and a growing
belief in the economic benefits of education were supplemented
during the 1950s by federal government policy, especially as it
related to vocational and technical education, as major causes
of expansion in the educational system. To maximize Ontario's
benefits under the terms of the new federal programs, the
provincial government restructured the educational system in
the province. In the 1960s the Ontario government assumed
direct responsibility for a large part of secondary school
spending, thereby increasing the base on which federal grants
would be calculated. Because of time limits imposed on the
capital grants part of the agreement, Ontario initiated a crash
program of school construction. It also changed the
curriculum, implementing a streaming system in which there
would be three "distinct but equal" branches: arts and science;
business and commerce; and technology and trade. While
pedagogic reasons were cited for this change, it also had the
effect of greatly increasing the number of high-school courses
eligible for federal financial support. By 1965 approximately
half the secondary schools in Ontario were offering technical
and vocational programs.

----

[4]Ontario Department of Education, Annual Report (Toronto: Queen's
Printer, 1952), p. 2.

[5]K.J. Rea, The Prosperous Years, (Toronto: University of Toronto Press,
1985), p. 108.

The physical expansion of the primary and secondary school system proceeded at a remarkable pace in the 1960s. Between 1945 and 1969 the province had spent more than 2.3 billion dollars on more than 9700 building projects to provide spaces for 1,820,000 elementary and secondary school students.

The cost of operating this expanding system remained a concern, as did uncertainty about what the system was supposed to be producing. Both matters were aggressively addressed during the decade: the first through an elaborate financing arrangement known as the "foundation tax scheme" and the second by a highly controversial inquiry carried out by the "Provincial Committee on Aims and Objectives of Education in the Schools of Ontario", better known as the Hall-Dennis Committee.

While it was concerned with the primary and secondary levels of schooling, the Hall-Dennis inquiry is important because of how clearly it demonstrates the difficulty of finding meaningful definitions of the purposes of education in general. Although the Hall-Dennis Committee was specifically instructed to "identify the needs of the child as a person and as a member of society, to set forth the aims of education for the educational system of the province, and to propose means by which these aims and objectives may be achieved", its 1968 report, <u>Living and Learning</u>, sidestepped the problem of defining the purposes of education by declaring that "The aims and objectives of education are an intrinsic part of the proposed educational process, and are inherent in the very spirit of the report".

Despite a great deal of attention paid to the influence of changing technology on educational needs and methods, the report had nothing substantial to say about the connection between education and the fostering of technical change.

The Committee accepted the prevailing view that "money spent on education is a sound investment" citing the Economic Council of Canada to support this view and suggested that new ways of financing education should be sought.

One of the great practical problems of this period was the inability of labour markets to absorb the large numbers of young adults who were entering the market with specialized but low-level training in various skills and trades. One plausible remedy for this was to provide such labour force entrants with further training. But while some of them could be accommodated in the existing technical institutes and a few by the universities, additional facilities would be required.

The government responded to recommendations from a number of bodies by creating in 1965 the Colleges of Applied Arts and Technology. The existing technical and trades institutes were incorporated in some of the new institutions and new colleges were built throughout the province. By the end of the decade twenty-two CAAT's were in operation. The capital outlay was substantial, rising from annual expenditures of about 2.5 million in 1966 to more than 63 million in 1971. The annual operating costs rose from about five million in 1966 to over 100 million in the early 1970s. A substantial part of these costs was met by government grants to the province, but the burden on the province was considerable at a time when the cost of other forms of education was becoming a matter of increasing concern. The government's reasons for developing a whole new tier of educational facilities under these circumstances have given rise to considerable speculation. The availability of federal funds was undoubtedly a consideration. It has also been suggested that the legacy of the Robarts "streaming" plan was a flood of unemployable young people who either had to be absorbed by some new kind of institution for upgrading or allowed to drift into chronic unemployment.

Although the creation of the CAAT system removed much of the pressure on the existing universities to expand their diploma and other programs of low academic content, it caused concern lest the new institutions siphon off much of the public funding upon which the universities were becoming increasingly dependent.

The financial problems of the universities were addressed as early as 1951 when the Royal Commission on National Development in the Arts, Letters and Sciences recommended that the federal government provide universities in Canada with per capita grants in recognition of their "national importance".

Universities in Ontario, like those in other provinces, subsequently obtained financial support from the federal government to help cover both operating and capital costs. After 1967 the federal government provided fifty percent of the operating costs of postsecondary institutions under the terms of the Federal-Provincial Fiscal Arrangements Act. Federal funds to support research in the universities were also provided through the Canada Council and the National Research Council.

The provincial government's funding of university education in the early part of the period was carried out on an *ad hoc* basis, with governments responding to individual universities' requests for money. As the requests grew after the war, the Ontario government had instituted a system of making grants to universities based rather loosely on the available "surplus" in the provincial budget. As the number of universities eligible for support increased, the government found it necessary to develop more formal mechanisms for allotting funds among them. The bureaucracy directly involved in the process grew from a part-time consultant hired in the early 1950s to a large committee which by the mid-1960s included several businessmen as well as the Chief Justice of Ontario, the Deputy Minister of Education and other senior officials of the government. When representatives of the universities were eventually added, the committee became the "Committee on University Affairs". In 1967 it was given a full-time chairman, Dr. D.T. Wright, a former dean of engineering of the University of Waterloo.

Many of the functions of the Committee on University Affairs paralleled those of the Department of University Affairs which had been created in 1964. Both were involved in the task of allocating government funds to the universities. By the mid-1960s the latter had become almost entirely dependent upon government grants both for operating and capital needs.

Although the government continued to maintain a general policy of *laissez-faire* with respect to actual university operations, it was clear that the latter would be increasingly influenced by public policy considerations. Indeed, the provincial government made clear its intention to require universities to meet the demands placed upon them with respect to turning out trained manpower in an efficient manner. It they would not do so voluntarily, the government would be forced to "move in and take over".[6] "Formula financing", which was implemented in 1967, deflected these threats, providing a complex but acceptable system for allocating funds among the universities of the province. The institutions remained free to apportion resources among their various divisions and faculties as they saw fit.

While it was possible for universities to seek funds from private sources, even the new institutions which received considerable community and local business support, derived only a small percentage of their total operating expenses in this way.[7]

By the late 1960s the government's commitment to provide higher education opportunities for all qualified applicants had resulted in a system so large that, as with the primary and secondary sector, it seemed obvious that the rate of growth in spending on postsecondary education in Ontario had to be curtailed. But there was no easy way to do this. To explore the possibilities, in 1969 the government appointed a large committee of inquiry to investigate the whole matter of postsecondary education in the province.

The Commission on Post-Secondary Education in Ontario (COPSEO) was an odd collection of academics, "educators, youthful activists, businessmen, and representatives of various cultural constituencies in the province". Full of dissension within, the Commission was faced with barely concealed hostility by many members of the university community who feared that its purpose was to undermine the traditional values of higher education in the province. Its first report, a deliberately sensational newsprint flyer, did nothing to allay such suspicions. Its tone suggested that the Commission

---

[6] See Rea, The Prosperous Years, p. 114.

[7] For a discussion of this see Paul Axelrod, Scholars and Dollars: Politics, Economics and the Universities of Ontario, 1945-1980, (Toronto: University of Toronto Press, 1982).

156

intended to launch an all-out attack on the existing system. A subsequent interim report published in 1971 suggested that the government should support "socially useful alternatives to postsecondary education", should channel all funding for postsecondary education through a single department, and should broaden the definition of postsecondary education to include museums, theatres, schools of nursing and similar institutions.[8] But the Commission's final report in 1972 was more moderate than expected. The 126 recommendations included proposals to broaden the system, to increase accessibility, to promote life-long learning, to expand French language facilities. It also proposed that a number of advisory bodies be established and that formula financing be retained but improved by basing grants on projected enrolment data to facilitate planning. Increased student aid was also called for.[9] Most of these proposals were promptly lost, however, in the context of the provincial government's restraint program.

The Period of Contraction: Collapse of the Social Consensus

The subsequent measures adopted by the provincial government to control growth in the postsecondary system in Ontario followed similar trends elsewhere. Total (real) spending on education in the province continued to increase, but when related to the level and pattern of enrolment, the effects on the postsecondary sector were particularly drastic.

While the enrolment share of elementary and secondary schools in the province fell in the 1970s, the share of total educational expenditure going to the elementary and secondary sector was rising. Within the postsecondary system the most rapid growth of enrolment was in the Colleges of Applied Arts and Technology, although the actual shift in the 1970s saw the Colleges' share of total postsecondary enrolment

---

[8] Ontario, Commission on Post-Secondary Education in Ontario, Draft Report, (Toronto, 1971).

[9] Ontario, Commission on Post-Secondary Education, The Learning Society, (Toronto, 1972).

rise only from 31 to 32 percent; but the Colleges' share of total postsecondary expenditures rose from 15 to 26 percent. For the universities of Ontario, using full-time equivalent data, real per capita spending fell 21.5 percent from 1970 to 1980. Real per capita spending peaked in 1970 for the universities, and in 1975 for the colleges.

The Ontario experience has been particularly extreme. Operating expenditures per student in Canada as a whole actually increased slightly during the 1970s (from $4068 to $4146, compared to the reduction in Ontario from $4490 to $3592).[10] The reasons for this severity are not clear, although a possible explanation may lie in the fact that Ontario's expansion in the 1960s was particularly rapid. The cessation of growth in the mid-1970s may have led the Ontario government to react with something approaching panic to the prospect of being seen to have been responsible for greatly overexpanding the system in the 1960s. The political implications of such a perception would be greatly heightened, of course, by the change in public attitudes toward education in particular and government intervention in general.

The real-world events to which government policy in Ontario was responding were reasonably clear by the early 1980s. The rate at which demand for places in postsecondary institutions was growing had fallen sharply since the late 1960s. This was obviously in part due to a slower growth rate for the postsecondary age cohort: from over 5 percent per year in the 1960s to 2.2 percent in the 1970s. Even more important was a decline in the rate of participation in higher education: postsecondary participation in Ontario had more than doubled during the 1960s, whereas in the years from 1970 to 1982 the rate increased only from 19 to 21.5 percent.[11] In part this may simply mirror the effect of the rapid expansion in the supply of postsecondary places in the period of rapid growth of the

---

[10]Data from J.B. Davies and G.M. Macdonald, Information in the Labour Market, Ontario Economic Council, (Toronto: University of Toronto Press, 1984), pp. 107-9.

[11]Ibid., p. 115.

system - Ontario created so many new institutions throughout the province that the cost to students of going on to postsecondary schooling must have dropped significantly. By the 1970s this effect would have disappeared. There were also significant changes in the volume and form of federal government subsidies to postsecondary education: from a system of population based subsidies paid to each province which were then allocated among particular universities on the basis of enrolment, to an open-ended system of financing half the operating costs of all postsecondary institutions in the period 1968-77 and after 1977, a system of grants to provinces for health and education expenditures lumped together (Established Programs Financing or EPF).

The latter represented, in effect, a marked reduction in federal support committed to subsidizing higher education in most provinces. Whether it played a part in explaining Ontario's particularly drastic curtailment of higher education funding is not clear.

There was also an unmistakable disillusionment with the benefits of investing in higher education, both from the standpoint of the individual and the society. At the individual level, the least documented but most widely reported evidence was of Ph.D.s driving taxicabs. But such exaggerations contained more than a kernel of reality: with the recurrence of mass general unemployment, much of it induced as governments reduced aggregate demand in an attempt to control inflation, many job-market entrants were disappointed in the immediate returns to their personal investments (however highly subsidized they might have been).

Such experiences were the subject of extensive investigation at the federal level. As noted in a 1981 paper: "Concerted and sustained efforts are required to avoid university and college graduates finding themselves unemployed because of an oversupply of their particular skills, while industrial expansion is hampered by shortages of other skills."[12]

---

[12]*Ibid.*, p. 95.

In a similar vein, the flawed but widely cited report by Statistics Canada, Job Market Reality for Postsecondary Graduates (March 1981), reported employment experiences of university and college graduates surveyed in 1978 and interpreted them in highly pessimistic fashion.

A peculiarly Canadian aspect of this otherwise general deterioration in the outlook for what was increasingly being thought of once again as "highly trained manpower" was the extent to which the demand for it was a function of public policy itself. The public service sector throughout the postwar period was a particularly important source of employment for Canadian graduates. Policies of restraint in the public sector consequently impinge strongly on these markets, a phenomenon attributed by some analysts to the "truncated" nature of Canadian industrial development. In 1978 the commercial service industries employed less than half the proportion of bachelors graduates employed by the public sector.[13]

As Joel Novek observed in a recent article, "... it was the expansion of the social services in the postwar period which underpinned the development of the Canadian university system far beyond the level which Canadian industry, with its dependent structure and limited demand for highly-qualified manpower, could conceivably need or support. The private sector presently funds approximately 1 percent of all university research in the natural sciences, an even smaller proportion in the humanities and social sciences, and employs 40 percent of all bachelors, 30 percent of all masters and 20 percent of all doctoral graduates."[14]

As for the social returns to education, the reaction to the euphoria induced by the exercises in human capital theory contributed to the revolution in the economics of education

---

[13]See W.G. Picot, University Graduates and Jobs: Changes During the 1970's (Ottawa: Statistics Canada, 1983), (Cat. No. 80-501E).

[14]Joel Novek, "University Graduates, Jobs and University-Industry Linkages", Canadian Public Policy, Vol. II, No. 2, p. 193.

which occurred in the 1970s. How much impact this had directly on decision-makers here or elsewhere is impossible to measure, but if the convictions of experts have any bearing on policy, some account must be taken of these developments in the world of ideas.

Crudely put, the development of the economics of labour following the lead of Gary Becker's major book, Human Capital, in 1964, led to apparently objective demonstrations of the returns to education of a kind which could legitimize much of the broad subsidization and expansion of educational system which was undertaken by governments here and elsewhere. With the subsequent work of Edward Dennison and Robert Solow it became part of conventional wisdom that the skill, dexterity and knowledge of the population was an important determinant of an economy's rate of growth and, ultimately, of the population's level of living.

This concept of "human capital" arising from the "investments" in education was quickly picked up by the media, politicians and other opinion-makers.[15] While the view survived that educational standards and health levels were high in Canada, and particularly in Ontario, where there had long been a certain smugness about the quality of the province's educational system in comparison with the American, it was soon noted that one reason why productivity and incomes were lower in Canada than in the U.S. might be that the Canadian labour force was demonstrably less well educated.

The efforts of economists to measure the returns to education in the early 1960s were somewhat crude, but they were important because they appeared to support the traditional assumption about the "value" of a good education. Early studies suggested that the private returns to higher education (that is, the additional income individuals could expect to receive over their lifetime after deducting the direct expenses such as tuition fees and the indirect cost of foregone income

---

[15] As used by economists, the concept was usually defined as the knowledge, skills, energy and motivation acquired by people which contributed to their ability to produce goods and services.

during the years spent obtaining additional schooling) were well worth the costs. Some indicated that these returns were substantially above the returns which could be expected from investments in physical capital.

Canadian studies found that the returns to investments in higher education in this country were probably even greater than in the U.S. Thus, the Economic Council of Canada suggested in its annual report of 1965 that the overall rate of return to investment in education, taking into account not only the private but the public costs involved, would range from ten to fifteen percent, levels which compared favourably with even the pre-tax returns available from investments in physical and financial assets. The policy implication was clear: greater emphasis should be placed on expanding investment in education relative to investment in other assets.

The importance of the new "scientific" knowledge, especially the concept of human capital, lay in the effect it had in transforming governments, certainly in the case of Ontario, from agencies forced to accommodate such an expansion into agencies enthusiastically promoting it. Unfortunately, this enthusiasm proved to be ill-founded. By the 1970s the work being done on the economics of education was showing that the earlier estimates undoubtedly had exaggerated the returns to investment in further schooling, partly because they failed to take into account factors such as differences in individual ability, family background, the "screening function" performed by the educational system, post-graduation experience and other considerations which might have been responsible for the higher incomes earned by the more highly educated.

Combined with a tendency for estimates of lifetime earnings of university graduates to fall, the re-estimation of the rate of return to investments in higher education taking account of such considerations was yielding figures, by the mid-1970s, more in the range of four to five percent rather than ten to fifteen. At the same time, however, new approaches to the whole question of identifying returns, both private and public, were being developed which raised the possibility that the earlier estimates, while based on biased data and inadequate techniques, may have been close to the "true" rates of return after all.

But by then there was another reason for skepticism about rates of return analysis applied to education. Quite apart from whether the rates were right or not, a "new" theoretical argument gained prominence that in its extreme form suggested that the entire relationship between education and economic growth was specious.

A new generation of radical economists in the U.S. began to attract attention. The movement was exemplified by Samuel Bowles and Herbert Gintis whose book, Schooling in Capitalist America (1976), argued strongly that formal schooling systematically encourages the development of non-cognitive personality traits and that these, not cognitive knowledge, determine the effectiveness of the individual in the work place. At the lower level, the schools develop punctuality, persistence, concentration, docility, compliance and ability to work with others while higher education produces the qualities of self-esteem, self-reliance, versatility and leadership ability.

This and related arguments along the lines of the "signalling hypothesis" have had a significant impact on economic theories of education. Professor Mark Blaug in a recent article [16] accepts the rejection of cognitive development, claiming that "... most employers, whether public or private, care less about what potential workers know than about how they will behave" and that "The vast bulk of jobs in an industrial economy involve competencies that are acquired on the job in a few weeks and require, not a given stock of knowledge of facts and concepts, but the capacity to learn by doing."[17]

This not only wrecks the earlier assumption implicit in much educational theory that formal schooling is needed as preparation for specific jobs, but it also appears to destroy the connection between the supply of education and the rate of economic growth. Thus Blaug concludes that under the revised assumptions, "... there is no real sense in which a given level of

---

[16]Mark Blaug, "Where Are We Now in the Economics of Education?", Economics of Education Review, Vol. 4, No. 1, (1985), pp. 17-28.

[17]Ibid., p. 20.

education in the economically active population of a country can be said to be technically 'required' to permit the achieved level of economic growth of that country." While education may make a contribution to economic growth it may do this simply by providing a framework which accommodates the growth.[18]

Whether induced by the screening hypothesis or by doubts about rate of return estimation, the economics profession appears to have backed away from many of the orthodoxies of human capital theory as developed in the 1960s. Thus, Canada's elaborate inquiry into the future of the Canadian economy, the MacDonald Commission, observed in its final report that while estimates of the rate of return on education had "a considerable impact in the 1960s", their influence declined in the 1970s.[19]

Closely related to these lines of revision in the economics of education was the task of explaining why the great expansion in educational opportunity in the postwar period had so little apparent effect on the distribution of income. Again the implications of the screening hypothesis suggest that "the expansion of post-compulsory education is simply passed down the line and ends up in a chronic core of unemployed school leavers without ... much visible effect on the distribution of earned income from employment".[20]

These developments in the economics of education may now be considered within the context of the Ontario government's general change of direction with respect to social policy. The breakdown of crudely Keynesian-based interventionism locally is associated with the adoption of an alternative philosophy which appeared to be rooted in some notion of returning to the market system; perhaps it was "neo-conservatism".

---

[18]*Ibid.*, p. 28.

[19]Canada, Report of the Royal Commission on the Economic Union and Development Prospects for Canada, (Ottawa: 1985), note 1, chapter 18.

[20]Blaug, "Where Are We Now", p. 21.

During their declining years in office the Ontario Conservatives explicitly accepted much of the rhetoric of the neo-conservatives in the U.S. and Britain to legitimize their retreat into the restraint programs of the mid 1970s - a return to the market decision-making system; downsizing government; deregulation; privatization.

In Ontario, as elsewhere, there were expressions of disillusionment with government management of the economy, a growing sense that government spending was "out of control", and that government intervention, instead of improving the performance of the system, was at least partly responsible for its perceived "failures" to maintain full employment, stable price levels, a high rate of economic growth and a "fair" distribution of the fruits of economic effort. The Ontario government picked up on this loss of confidence in the positive economic role of government with remarkable agility. It may, in fact, have seen the opportunity it was presented with to deal with what was otherwise an increasingly untenable position. By 1969 it seemed that the province had failed in its long struggle to wrest enough discretionary budgetary power from the federal government to permit it to continue with further expansion of major programs.

While the government continued in the early 1970s to justify its own budget deficits on the grounds they were needed to alleviate unemployment which was being generated by Ottawa's spending restraints, by 1973 the provincial treasurer was taking the position that Ontario was no longer able to afford such large deficits and that it had no choice but to leave full responsibility for the poor performance of the economy to Ottawa. He could also suggest, however, that reduction in the rate of growth of provincial spending in the major social policy fields was warranted on grounds of controlling inflation.

What was particularly novel by the end of the period, however, was the frequent reference government spokesmen made to the desirability of restricting the growth of government activities and the need to promote the growth of the private sector.

In the first budget speech under the leadership of Mr. Davis, the government proclaimed as its first priority the restoration of "full employment growth" in the province, but went on to indicate that this would be achieved by measures to encourage the expansion of the private sector. The government would attempt to "maintain firm control over public spending in order to contain tax levels and the generation of inflationary pressures".[21]

By the mid-1970s the government was going further, asserting that it would seek not only to control the growth of the public sector, but actually to shrink it.

Certainly the government was disposed to begin dismantling, if it could, the more esoteric of its commitments to intervention. It began a general retreat from local government rationalization and from the process of implementing province-wide economic planning in general. While it would continue to embrace the principles of "planning", it could also advocate a belief in the free market system as the best means of achieving its planning objectives. It appeared that special interest groups, agencies and local authorities would be given scope to exercise their ingenuity in reducing their claims on the province for financial support. The government for its own part undertook to cut back on its services and on construction activities, not to solve its taxation dilemma, but to set free capital and labour for use in what it claimed would be an expanding private sector. The best way to preserve the social and material environment which had been built up in the province in the future would be by "maintaining a healthy climate for free enterprise". As for social security, the position now was that "Employment security is the only real income security a free society can afford for the vast majority of its citizens".[22]

This approach was refined in a number of government studies and policy papers in the late 1970s and early 1980s, some of which set it within a framework of reforming the administrative and policy process in general. In major fields such as education, health and welfare, specific policy revisions

---

[21] Ontario, Debates, 26 April 1971, p. 863.

[22] Ontario, Debates, 6 April 1976, p. 1131.

were considered and widely debated both within and outside the government apparatus. In the field of higher education perhaps the most bluntly indicative manifestation of the change in attitude with respect to government was provided by the report of a rather obscure task group established by the Ontario Ministries of Education and Colleges and Universities.[23] Its report contained a number of radical-sounding observations about changes in public attitudes with respect to education and government involvement in the economy, noting that "the general climate of opinion has become in itself an issue of major importance" and suggesting that a frustrated public has developed a distrust of institutions in general and the usefulness of educational institutions in particular.[24]

The report mentioned three options with respect to the future role of government: (1) reduce scope and scale of present education system; (2) continue to try to meet needs of various interests despite declining resources; (3) find new ways to mediate the complex needs that will arise. The report generally supported the third option, placing emphasis on the mediating role of government, improving adaptive learning, reducing government's involvement in service delivery, and improving communication between government and various groups in society. In keeping with the privatization theme, Towards the Year 2000 suggested that independent agencies have the potential for providing the increased diversity of services required. Since they are more highly customized to individual and group needs, they are likely to be seen as more responsive and less alienating, and they might provide some services at lower costs.[25]

---

[23]Ontario, Ministry of Education, Towards the Year 2000: Future Conditions and Strategic Options for the Support of Learning in Ontario, Review and Evaluation Bulletins, Vol. 5, No. 1, (Toronto: 1984).

[24]Ibid., p. 38.

[25]Ibid., p. 68.

The provincial government's own interpretation of the social and other trends operating in the early 1980s was understandably less than consistent. The main message was clearly that there were grounds for cutting back on the growth of the system and, indeed, in the Ontario case, for contracting it. There was, however, a regression to vocationalism which, as in the case of federal policies, made little sense in the light of what was known about the changes taking place both in the economy and in expert confidence in our ability to reconcile trends in the supply of and demand for skilled labour.

The general orientation of policy-makers in Ontario may be inferred from the utterances of the Minister of Education and Minister of Colleges and Universities in a legislative statement in 1983. Dr. Stephenson observed that it now appeared likely that there would be a reduction in the demand for undergraduate postsecondary education in its traditional forms as the economy changed from an "industrial" to an "information" base and that, while Ontario universities had been meeting this shift, the time had come for government to exercise leadership through a "short-term intervention in the planning process".[26]

The alarm induced in the university community by such comments was aggravated by the appointment of yet another Commission on postsecondary education. As with the COPSEO exercise of a decade earlier, the Bovey Commission was seen as a thinly disguised agency to legitimize drastic government intervention in the system of higher education in Ontario. Again, however, its final report proved less drastic in its recommendations than had been feared.[27] The report confirmed what was well known, that the quality of the Ontario university system was in jeopardy. It made no fewer than fifty-one recommendations for improvements. They included: higher student fees, entrance exams, reduced enrolments,

---

[26] Ontario, Debates, 15 December, 1981.

[27] Ontario, Commission on the Future Development of the Universities of Ontario (The Bovey Commission), Ontario Universities: Options and Futures, (Toronto: 1984).

retirement of older professors, and the establishment of a stronger Provincial Intermediary Body (to replace the Ontario Council on University Affairs). It was suggested that these changes be made in stages, with enrolment cuts and increased tuition fees followed in a later stage by efforts of the government to increase funding to restore accessibility and, if necessary, further fee increases combined with an income-based contingent repayment loan plan.

The end of the Conservative party's more than four decades of rule in Ontario brought little perceptible change in the new direction of social policy or apparent principles of government intervention in the economy or the system of higher education. Particularly in view of the renewed influence of the NDP in the policymaking process, this suggests that some new social consensus may be emerging.

Section II

The British Experience

by

Maurice Kogan[1]

The British case is so extreme an example of policy reversal
and of break up of established relationships between the state
and higher education that it will test well the principles being
canvassed in this conference.

Government in Britain is more unrestrained in its power than
in virtually any other democratic country. The executive is so
well integrated with the legislature that the very act of election
and the parliamentary majority confer entrenched legitimacy
on it. We have no effective balance of powers. Only recently
has forensic challenge, through judicial review, become a direct
way of tackling administrative actions. The politics of higher
education are well contained within the small groups with a
direct concern in them. No one suffers any political penalties
for doing down higher education.[2]

Relationships Before the Cuts

The British case is most easily evaluated if restricted to the
supposedly autonomous university sector, although the
government's legitimacy in so strongly controlling the local
authority maintained polytechnics and other colleges would
make a good discussion in its own right. Here there are
certainly issues of the legitimacy of central government in
controlling locally run higher education.

Although the universities have always assumed that their
autonomy was endorsed and accepted by the state, they have
never been entirely free. Royal Commissions have been
brought in to remedy their working, and not only in the period

---

[1]Professor and Head, Department of Government, Brunel University,
Uxbridge, Middlesex, UK.

[2]M. Kogan with D. Kogan, The Attack on Higher Education (London: Kogan
Page, 1983).

of virtually complete public subsidy either. There were Royal Commissions on the Scottish universities (1826), Oxford and Cambridge (1850), London (1909), Wales (1916) and a Privy Council "trial" in 1902 over the division of the Victoria University. A Royal Commission settled the controversies over the relationship between St. Andrews University and Dundee University College in 1951. Universities may license knowledge but the state has had the last say on the licensing of their products, such as doctors, lawyers and teachers, if only to hand back the job to the professional bodies mainly consisting of academics themselves. The universities of 50 years ago were closely integrated with the state as it then was, and they formed just as indispensable a part of the framework of national institutions as they do now. "The links, however, were personal and social, not bureaucratic or formal."[3] Throughout, the universities have hardly ever played an oppositional or critical role and have figured within a consensual elite system.

In the post-war period of expansion, the new universities, founded on Royal Charters, were created on the advice of Ministers, themselves depending on University Grants Committee (UGC) advice, and were thus ultimately the product of government decisions. Only the University of Buckingham did it alone, and were fortunate to have a radical Conservative government to make an honest woman of them. Since 1945 when expansion began, the issue has not been whether higher education is self generating but whether once created God has given it free will.

In any event, autonomy is by no means derived from a state of nature. Many highly esteemed European universities are under legal and administrative controls quite alien to those known in the Anglo-Saxon systems. In Sweden and elsewhere, new professorships require Acts of Parliament and new courses are approved by the centre after consultation with the professoriate at large.

In post-war Britain, three phases can be identified. From 1945 until 1967, the legitimacy of the state in expanding higher

---

[3] J. Carswell, Government and the Universities in Britain. Programme and Performance, 1960-1980 (Cambridge: Cambridge University Press, 1985).

education, in itself, of course, an intervention, arose from strong public demand. This was based on rising expectations generated by the phenomenal expansion of schooling as well as general support for an increase in the trained manpower base. The Robbins Committee Report[4] did not so much create expansion as strongly legitimate it, this being the way that government tended to seek support for its actions.[5] The appointment of the Robbins Committee itself entailed a decision to regularize established policy. Government assessors made sure that the Committee's recommendations were well assimilated into the policy bloodstream before the day of publication when the Report's recommendations were instantly accepted by the Conservative Prime Minister, Lord Home. The growth of the university system had already been put on its way. The binary system, dividing the universities from the newly designated polytechnics came later, in 1966.

During this period, although initially some institutional leaders expressed misgivings, nobody contested the need for expansion. Student demand was the undisputed imperative. The misnamed "social demand" principle of Robbins, that all who were qualified should gain entry to higher education somewhere, was assumed to be serendipitously compatible with the economy's needs. In fact, although this seemed to work for the burgeoning public sector and other service occupations, the system has failed to fill its places in the hard sciences and technologies from 1945 until the present day, in spite of constant inducements and pressure.

Expansion involved two interlocking sets of decisions. The government would determine the extent of student demand and meet the costs. The decisions about what to expand, and where, would be taken by the academics themselves through a process

---

[4]Report of the Committee on Higher Education (Robbins Report), Higher Education (Her Majesty's Stationery Office, 1963).

[5]See M. Kogan and T. Packwood, Advisory Councils and Committees in Education (London: Routledge and Kegan Paul, 1974); and M. Kogan and M. Atkin, Legitimating Education Policy: The Use of Special Committees in Formulating Policies in the USA and UK (Stanford, CA: Stanford University Press, 1982).

of interplay between the institutions and their colleagues on the UGC. Academics were thus co-opted into the allocation process. This happens, of course, in most systems, but the UGC had remarkable freedom to award grants for five years in advance and to hold the universities on a very loose rein on what they did with the money.

Only from 1967 did the UGC provide a General Memorandum to Guidance which still "reflected the UGC's unwillingness to encroach on university autonomy" as did successive Memoranda until 1977.[6] Universities still remained remarkably free to take the money and follow but also ignore parts of the advice. All the same, the 1967 Memorandum provided the first strong guidance about the balance between graduate and undergraduate students and the different subject areas. The UGC had long taken the largest decisions on where, for example, to put a new medical school or law faculty.

This happy state, so greatly admired by people working in other systems, with its ability to move forward without much strain, to maintain high standards of scholarship, research and teaching, and to meet new social demand, was legitimized by a *beau* ideal of higher education. It allowed for the acceptance of multiple objectives which seemed to be reached without undue conflict. The hidden hand was at work. Student demand was not in conflict with employment. Arts students and social scientists could find work in the burgeoning areas of marketing, in the public sector, which was undergoing a whopping expansion in the 1950s, 1960s and early 1970s, and in teaching, which doubled its numbers in the post-war period.

A subtle dual system provided for the financing of research. UGC grants assumed that a good proportion - later calculated at one third - would be devoted to non-teaching academic activity. Money also came from research councils, and from public and private customers. The unspoken assumption was

----

[6]M. Shattock and R. Berdahl, "The British University Grants Committee 1919-1983 - Changing Relationships with Government and the Universities", Higher Education, Vol. 13, No. 5 (1984), reproduced in I. MacNay and J. Ozga, Policy Making in Education: The Breakdown of Consensus, Open University Set Book, (Elmsford, NY: Pergamon Press, 1985).

that that which was deemed good by the academy would also be good for society. Academics could incorporate the public good in their choice of subjects for study. At minimum, scholarship was cultural embellishment for which society would willingly pay.

There were, too, educational ideals which underpinned the fairly luxurious funding for teaching. Hardly a new university failed to follow the Oxbridge model of personal and academic tutoring of students. By contrast with both the European and American practices the expanded system was familial and thus costly.

With this background in mind, of a government which felt legitimate in supporting an increasingly expanding higher education system and of universities which felt secure in the state's support, and bear in mind that the decision makers were all university alumni, I now turn to more recent events.

From 1970 the prescriptions tightened and, by the time of the first OPEC oil crisis, it was becoming clear that money would be cut and that the famous quinquennial system was under threat. Throughout the rest of the 1970s the cries of pain at the government's failure to meet inflation costs were loud. The first intimations of the end of the love affair between universities and the public began to be felt. It was suggested that they should widen access and their range of courses, and government was affronted by the Vice-Chancellors' refusal to consider what now seems moderate change. One former Vice-Chancellor thought them "pampered darlings". A Labour Secretary of State anticipated his apostasy to the Conservatives by suggesting that the universities sell a few oil paintings. Student recruitment began to falter. At the end of the decade government was making serious efforts to reconcile the prospective decline in age groups with existing capacities and with potential sources of new student demand.[7]

Throughout the 1970s, grants had been cut by about 10 percent, generally by failure to meet the full cost of inflation. But in

_____

[7]Oakes Report (The Brown Paper), Higher Education into the 1970's (Her Majesty's Stationery Office, 1978).

1979 the Thatcher government arrived with a clear mandate, refreshed in 1983, to roll back the boundaries of the state, to enhance spending on defence and public order, and to find the money to do so from such areas as higher education. Nothing had been specified but the tenor of the party's manifesto and other public declarations was clear enough. There was a clear change in the political and social atmosphere. It had both the power and the moral legitimacy. It could claim to have read public disenchantment with publicly paid for services about which it now determined to take firm action. That disenchantment had already been perceived by its Labour predecessors.[8]

In 1979 and then most sharply in 1981, the British government cut the amount of money channelled to universities through the University Grants Committee. It then turned round to deal with the parallel public sector, led by the polytechnics. In this process we can observe increased convergence between the status of universities in their relationship with the state and that of the public sector institutions.

Government took away large sums of money, and over such a short time that the universities had no alternative but to buy out staff at quite high prices. But it was quite unconcerned about the effect on student places and left the UGC to decide whether to cut numbers or cut the unit of resource. It then supported the UGC's decision to cut numbers. It was certainly not concerned about the system's ability to increase the numbers of students from "new" and under-recruited groups.

In the event, the government was extraordinarily lucky. It allowed the UGC to knock out 20,000 places in a period of two years, at the peak of the age group bulge. But in spite of the cuts the numbers of people entering the higher education system as a whole have gone up. No doubt juvenile unemployment has strengthened their decisions. The public sector institutions took in much larger numbers, at the cost of reasonable staffing ratios. The net result for the government could hardly be more fortunate. On severely reduced funding the age participation rate (APR) has gone up from 12.7 percent

---

[8]Carswell, Government and the Universities.

to 14.1 percent in seven years. Only recently did we reach a point where it is clear that if government did not put back more money soon, perhaps five universities would be bankrupt by 1990. And now the government has said, a year before a general election, that it will not let universities go bankrupt. And it has given more money to the polytechnics.

The reductions, according to Ministers, were forced by the need to save money.[9] But once the government found it could break the social demand principle of the Robbins Report and suffer no political penalties, it also discovered that it could impose its own preferences on the other, more detailed, objectives of higher education.

There was a change of Ministers, and under the remarkable Sir Keith Joseph the government caught its ideological wind. Applicants still strongly favoured the traditional arts subjects but their preferences would now take second place to a planning imperative. Ministers' readings of the needs of the labour market, readings that employers did not wholly share, would now frame the access policies. So we had yet another determined attempt to produce more engineers, and to breed a race of business managers and information technologists.

The government had thus within a few years demolished the Robbins principle of social demand, although by a sheer fluke it was able to preserve and slightly increase the established recruitment ratios. It has, through the UGC, taken away the last shred of pretense that universities determine their own subject profiles. And it has taken away the autonomy implicit in a five year planning lead which universities so happily enjoyed. Henceforth all would dance to some very short tunes. A promise to allow level funding, once the traumas of 1981 were over, has been blatantly broken.

The next step towards higher education's subordination came in 1985. Ministers had long implied, without stating their evidence, that higher education, and particularly the universities, needed to put their houses in order. One theme was that they needed to improve their management. The

---

[9] Kogan and Kogan, The Attack on Higher Education.

Committee of Vice-Chancellors and Principals responded loyally to this and the Jarratt Report on University Management finally demolished the assumption that universities were guilds of masters.[10] Although all the Jarratt proposals are stated with qualifications the message is clear: universities are management systems and Vice-Chancellors are chief executives. The Committee of Vice-Chancellors and Principals (CVCP), with ardent UGC support, has now produced performance indicators, and there is some evidence that they are already being put to work by the UGC.

These changes are consistent with the growth of managerialism in higher education. They weaken the assumption of the self regulating community of scholars and make more explicit the assumption that universities are cost creating institutions whose functioning will be subordinate to *a priori* objectives. These will be achieved through management hierarchy, and rewards and sanctions, as much as through the self motivation of individual academics on tenured freeholds.

The most recent episode concerns the UGC's evaluation of research. It demonstrates how the state has managed to advance its encroachment with the cooperation of the academics themselves.

The UGC has had a hard time in trying to keep faith with its own colleagues while fending off the encroachment of the state. In 1981 it wrongly decided to preserve the unit of resource. The choice between sustaining research quality and student places is one which they should have thrown straight back to Ministers. They also responded reluctantly but too efficiently to government's demands that they judge the competence of the 1,500 departments which constitute our universities. These evaluations determined the distribution of the cuts, some of which were all but lethal. Its then Chairman has since said that the UGC usually gets its judgments 80 percent right. That means they got their judgments of 300 departments wrong.

---

[10]Jarratt Report, Report of the Steering Committee for Efficiency Studies in Universities, Committee of Vice-Chancellors and Principals (1985).

My critique of this process at the time remains unchallenged.[11]
The UGC works through quite small committees whose
members have to pass judgment on the quality of as many as 45
departments, or many more, because each represents a broad
range of subjects and each discipline has, of course, its own
sub-disciplines. The UGC also claims to have consulted the
learned societies and the research councils. In the case of the
social sciences, they are said to have sat for one day with the
Chairman and Deputy Secretary of the ESRC who simply
passed off-the-cuff judgments.

In 1986, the UGC went a step further, grading all subject areas
on their research competence. In doing so they met demands
from two groups. Some of the elite have never believed that
expansion of the universities was a good policy although they
accepted the desirability of expansion of the public sector.
Particularly in the hard sciences and technologies, some of the
leading academics are prepared to be assertive about standards
with a certainty not found in the arts or social sciences. The
great majority of our Vice-Chancellors are now recruited from
the non-arts areas, this being a significant change of recent
years, and many of them would go along, in principle, with the
notion of research selectivity.

In doing so, I believe that they followed an inappropriate
analogy with the US concept of the research university. Our
universities take about six to seven percent of the age group,
and it can be assumed that the tenured teachers are
correspondingly selectively recruited. The majority are likely
to be well within the range normally denoted by research
universities. Putting this small group within four evaluative
grades is surely just crazy.

The second impulse came from a highly opinionated Secretary
of State who was both fastidious and narrow in his belief in
higher academic standards. One of his young advisors is
reputed to have said that Britain needs only three universities.
So convinced was he that mediocrity needed to be driven out
that he made it a condition of his support for the continued
level of funding for higher education.

---

[11] Kogan and Kogan, The Attack on Higher Education.

Two issues arise from this UGC activity. Was it fairly administered? The press is full of well documented cases of wrong assessments. Two have been retracted because of clerical errors; the Oxford Law Faculty was reported to have threatened legal action. The findings in one area, politics, are seriously challenged by a separate academic exercise.[12] This analysis claimed a 75 and a 66 percent lack of correspondence between the UGC and Crewe's more quantitative assessment. The UGC process was secret, anonymous and based on no stated criteria. It seems to have been innocent of the key rules of peer review.

But, secondly, should it have happened? Certainly there is a strong case for higher education in Britain making a far more serious job of its peer review systems. Such improvements should be directed towards helping departments and academics improve themselves. They should be undertaken primarily in a consultative rather than in a prescriptive or allocative mode. Instead of evaluating in order to improve, however, the UGC evaluated in order to reveal publicly the alleged weaknesses of the universities. And the exercise was undertaken by co-opted academics, at the behest of the State and not by the Republic of Letters regulating its own for its own purposes. The UGC academics and their advisors thus prepared some university departments for public humiliation - the lists were published in the press - as well as for reduced or enhanced grants. It was on these terms that the state was prepared to continue support and to sustain the legitimacy of higher education.

Moreover, it is possible that the co-opted academics have delivered some departments, and perhaps faculties and universities, to the government for closure. The worst graded will get less funds over the next four years. They will recruit less good students and presumably obtain fewer external grants and endowments. The UGC's prophesies will thus become self-fulfilling.

---

[12]See Felicity Jones, "Internal Politics Out in the Open", The TImes Higher Education Supplement, 3 October 1986, p. 11; and Professor Ivor Crewe, Essex University (unpublished).

Legitimacy is a moral entity dependent on its acceptance by others. By allowing peer review, albeit shakily administered, to be used as a tool of the state, the academy itself legitimated the state's intrusion into the most intimate areas of higher education's private life.

Higher Education and Responsiveness

Moving away from these particular exercises we can begin to figure out how institutions are responding to more general pressures from the environment. A research project which I am leading is concerned with the responsiveness of higher education to external influences.

Let me mention some of the emerging findings. First, institutions have met requirements, as far as they can recruit students, to change the balance between arts and science. Many institutions, including those least favourably treated by the UGC, have increased their externally funded research, although the research councils now say that they are less able to fund basic research and are turning away alpha applications.

There is evidence from our limited number of cases that employment consciousness is growing among both students and teachers. Thus one prestigious history faculty now mounts a course which asks why the British elite do not favour work in productive industry. The course is the best subscribed. Another strong history department puts more emphasis on group discussion and presentation, these being skills expected by employers. Many are building in computing courses. Modern language and English language courses may take up applied linguistics because it is seen as marketable.

These moves must not be exaggerated but they certainly represent a move away from the traditional researcher-teacher norm of the curriculum.

Do the pressures of the state and of employment cut even

deeper? Is there what Elzinga has called "epistemic drift"?[13] Are the academy's knowledge rules, its respect for evidence and the like, affected by external pressure? It seems likely that they are not. Research and scholarship may be triggered by external pressures or wishes. There has long been the distinction between work based on disciplines and that based on domains. Domains (the term is taken from Eric Trist[14]) start with a problem, such as drug dependency or planning in the inner city, and then use constructs and knowledge from the disciplines to help solve them. The setting of the question and the answers given to it are not solely in the hands of the academics but also in the hands of the policymaker or practitioner who cannot veto the science but may affect the agenda. It may well be that there will be a shift between the disciplines and domains as a result of recent funding pressures. But government should not confuse the outside world's view of this. Employers and others seem to want academic standards to remain high and pure. Those who commission research may often be as critical of its scientific quality as of its relevance.

An obtrusive government might wish to see much more of the traditional heartlands of higher education transformed into domain based work. That does not seem to be happening in Britain, except at the important margin. Our government is schizoid in wanting both a move towards instrumentally useful courses and the retention of elite traditional education, but for a smaller number. The traditional elite, reading any of the traditional subjects, are still snapped up by employers and government where they preside over a robust economy. In this sense higher education continues to be legitimized by employers who want good generalists, able to think flexibly, to communicate well and to engender good human relations.

---

[13] A. Elzinga, "Research, Bureaucracy and the Drift of Epistemic Criteria", in Bjorn Wittrock and Aant Elzinga (eds.), The University Research System: The Public Policies of the Home of Scientists (Stockholm: Almqvist and Wiksell International, 1985).

[14] E. Trist, "Types of Output Mix of Research Organization and Their Complementarity", in A.B. Cherns et. al. (eds.), Social Science and Government: Policies and Problems, (London: Tavistock Publications, 1972).

So the knowledge rules will not change but the balance between different styles and objectives of teaching and research might do so. The attack has not been on the power of the academy to determine what it will regard as good academic work. It has been on the subject balances, the resource used, and on the uses to which academic evaluation are put. The behavioural model that government wants imposed is that of rewards and punishments related to visible products. It is now in a position to do what it wants because the academics themselves have legitimized the process. And, as a result, the normative concomity of higher education has been broken.

Some Possible Explanations

The general questions which arise from the British case are, first, how can we typify and explain the recent encroachments of the state and, secondly, what are the moral bases of government's legitimacy to act in this way. The answers to the questions are linked.

We have been watching two potentially conflicting legitimacies at work. The freedom of the basic unit has always been a dominant norm in the universities, associated with beliefs that the growth and transmission of knowledge are legitimate in themselves, not depending on stated public demands for their right to flourish; and that it is a proper function of academic institutions to act as centres of alternative opinions within the political system. At the same time, central authorities influence the higher education system so as to make its norms compatible with the needs of the society which nourishes and sanctions it.[15] Stated in maximum terms, the academy's desired state was one in which "academic autonomy, whether defined and guaranteed by law, by financial independence, or by customary tolerance, is thus the necessary safeguard for the free and unfettered discharge of every university's primary duty, which is to permit intellectual nonconformity as the

---

[15]T. Becher and M. Kogan, Process and Structure in Higher Education, (London: Heinemann Educational Books, 1980).

means of advancing knowledge".[16]

Yet there has never been a time when higher education has had the moral right to be wholly free of society's demands, as mediated by government. Kant attempted to state the boundary, in terms of knowledge that might be conditioned by government's wishes and knowledge that should be free.[17] The frontier limiting the power of the state has often moved in either direction.

Neave typifies the intention of European governments generally as being "to alter the public life or the external environment of higher education..." and "to bring about deep and abiding modifications to certain aspects of that institution's private life or inner environment".[18] Writing of recent West German, Swedish and Greek legislation, he cites the legislative changes creating various models of "participation" which extended "very considerably the boundary within which state intervention was seen as legitimate and necessary". And, quoting Trow, these changes reinforced the planner's view of higher education, which saw it more as the object than the subject, and tended to define its role in terms of service to society - its public mission - rather than emphasizing its autonomous functions.[19]

The assertion of such public functions led to an increase of government control over the external frame of higher education and also in its inner workings. There was a

---

[16]G. Templeman, "Britain: A Model at Risk", Cre-Information, (2nd Quarter, 1982).

[17]G. Neave, "La Notion de Limite, Modele des Liens Existant entre l'Universite et l'Etat", Cre-Information, (2nd Quarter, 1982).

[18]G. Neave, "Higher Education in a Period of Consolidation: 1975-1985", European Journal of Education, Vol. 20, Nos. 2-3 (1985).

[19]M. Trow, "Dilemmas of Higher Education in the 1980's and 1990's", Paper presented at the Conference of Learned Societies, Montreal, June, 1980, quoted in Neave, "Higher Education in a Period of Consolidation".

"thickening administrative overlay in the form of agencies intermediary to government and institutions".

And what underlies current radical changes in relationships? Several explanations are possible. If the earlier expectations of universities were that they would enhance the culture, the current demands are for a contribution towards technology and productiveness, both expensive to fund, and not the first preference of the academy as areas for development. A second contribution to government's determination to plan decisively is the perceived need to consolidate the enlarged system.[20] Thirdly, the academics are seen as resistant to change.

A further set of reasons are psychological and political. The turning point was in the late 1960s and occurred independently of economic or demographic crisis. It was then that the academy made its first fundamental concessions to the laity, which were only later to be converted into cash deductions. The professoriate's monopoly of power was broken through student and junior staff participation in decision making. Although those movements have in time been largely assimilated, there were attacks on the credibility of academic knowledge, the rise of critical theory through which the academy's own children called their parents' credibility into question. At the same time, with the move from an APR of three to fourteen percent, the far greater numbers of both faculty and students made what had been precious, in both its positive and negative senses, more demotic, less esoteric, less "expert" in the eyes of the public, the press and the bureaucratic and political groups whose confidence in dealing with and taming academics thus grew in reciprocal fashion.

The government's right to alter the boundary may have been strengthened by the behaviour of the UGC which has been described as indecisive in its leadership of the university system,[21] until the 1979 cuts gave it "vigour and snap" which restored its position in Whitehall. The government was then

---

[20] Neave, "Higher Education in a Period of Consolidation".

[21] Shattock and Berdahl, "The British University Grants Committee".

legitimated in its turn by the willingness of the co-opted academics to act on its behalf, very likely in the belief that that would bring more money back to the universities. In one, highly contestable, view they saved the university system by doing so.[22]

Theoretical Aspects

The theoretical aspects of this case study require us to consider what constitutes legitimacy on both sides of the boundary. Citizens' obligations to each other bestow legitimacy on a government which is made definite by the fact of public election, than which there is no higher truth in a democracy. But Pitkin argues that government is legitimated by reason of its just and benevolent procedures and policies.[23]

If we take Pitkin as our starting point, three theoretical frames might help us modify the crude democratic assumption that once a government is elected it is legitimated to follow its own value preferences without reservations, this being the style adopted towards the universities in Britain since 1979.

The first derives from exchange theory and its subsidiary, resource dependency theory.[24] This argues that in an exchange relationship too much dependency on one side generates an unhealthy imbalance of power. The contribution of the academy to science, technology, social control, culture and the licensing of individuals for employment will deteriorate if the state presses the academy into a dysfunctional dependency. But that is a functional argument, and not a moral one disputing the state's legitimacy. The state can spoil things if it wants to.

---

[22]*Ibid.*

[23]Quoted in B. Goodwin, Using Political Ideas (New York: John Wiley & Sons, 1982).

[24]See P. Blau, Exchange and Power in Social Life (New York: John Wiley & Sons, 1964).

There is also the growing body of normative thought about the nature of successful policy implementation. This concerns the need of government to refresh its mandate by consultation and by empathy with those affected by its decisions.[25] Policies are meaningful only if their impacts are considered. Government cannot hope for good results if it fails to exploit the knowledge of those whom it governs. Consultation and participation by those affected by decision making are both morally right and functionally necessary if policies are to achieve their desired effects. Here the beleaguered universities would argue that if the government has any belief in higher education at all, it would have done well to have worked more closely with its practitioners in discovering the likely impact of its policies. The new policies would then have been better tested and justice to those affected would have been more secure. This argument is both normative, in that it argues a reformulation of proper democratic behaviour, and instrumental in arguing how government must act if it is to be effective. The normative argument takes us back into the sources and justifications of legitimacy.

A longer-standing theme concerns the legitimacy of public institutions. The conservative tradition in Britain has been anything but anarchic or anti-institutionalist. It has invested faith in parliamentary procedure, the courts, and the permanent civil service. These ideals were converted to more collectivist purposes in Richard Titmuss' defence of institutionalism that the public good must be incorporated into public institutions and not rely simply on residual devices.[26] The notion of the beneficent public institution with a long term mandate is thus present in many otherwise conflicting strands of political and social thought.

Until recently, the universities figured in this scheme of things as the acknowledged certifiers of both knowledge and the

---

[25]J.J. Richardson and A.G. Jordan, Governing Under Pressure: The Policy Process in a Post-Parliamentary Democracy, (Oxford: Martin Robertson, 1979).

[26]See R. Pinker, Social Theory and Social Policy, (London: Heinemann Educational Books, 1971).

knowledgeable. It will not do without several reservations, some of which are being forced upon us. Publicly funded institutions must not become safe havens for the idle who exploit the protection thus given them. The second is that though university operations may be free from prescriptions of the state, their objectives and scale are now out of their own hands in Britain, and the remaining question is whether their academic working is being affected by the closer prescriptions of the state, as aided by the co-opted academics.

To conclude, in higher education in Britain the legitimacy of the state is formally unimpaired. After all, it saved public money and lost no student places in the recent cuts, although big science complains that real damage is being done. Higher education has no irreducibly defensible boundaries. It is an optional extra. The notion that the public purse will support free and entrenched institutions demands an extraordinary degree of civilized tolerance of dissent and a belief that society needs many points of value setting which must be allowed long periods of security and self-confidence. The case for higher education is thus dependent on basic values which are highly contestable.

The state's assault has done damage; it might lead to good if higher education in Britain establishes more firmly, professionally and openly its own evaluative systems with a mandate to secure improvement and development rather than reduction and humiliation.

Ministers are elected to be prophetic and they have the right, though they would be unwise, to adopt the heroic rather than the negotiative style if they wish. They may well find, however, that exchange theory rules, and that if they insist on taking too much power in their relationship with the academy the results will not be worth having.

The Australian Experience

Governments and Tertiary Education: Increased Centralization at Four Levels

by

Grant Harman[1]

Introduction

What is in question in Australia today is not the legitimacy of governments sharing in policymaking and control for tertiary education. The fundamental legitimacy issue was settled with respect to state governments late last century and early this century, and with respect to the national government during and immediately following the second world war. Shared control between the Commonwealth or Federal Government, state governments, the governing bodies of individual institutions and their component parts is an accepted part of Australian education life. What is at issue, however, are questions about how far government controls and power should go, which level of government should do what, what areas of university and college life should be affected by government regulation, and how government control and regulation should be exercised.

In many respects the most important questions about the relationship of governments and tertiary education centre on issues of institutional independence and government interference. The strong belief of the tertiary education community, and especially of the university sector, is that governments interfere far too much and that the degree, the scope and the frequency of such interference is rapidly increasing. This view is expressed forcefully by university spokespersons. For example, at a conference of Australian university governing bodies held in 1982, Professor David Caro, Vice-Chancellor of the University of Melbourne,

---

[1]Professor and Head, Centre for Administrative and Higher Education Studies, The University of New England, Armidale, NSW, Australia.

Australia's second oldest university, warned that "the autonomy of universities is now less respected than it used to be" and asserted "there is little doubt that there have been substantial inroads into autonomy in the last few years".[2] Government officials and Ministers view the situation differently. They argue that universities are privileged in the large measure of independence they enjoy and bemoan the fact that universities are often so unresponsive, so unheeding, to society's needs as interpreted by officials of the government of the day. Significantly, at the 1982 conference of Australian university governing bodies, the Commonwealth Minister of Education publicly disagreed with Professor Caro's statements and dismissed his complaints about the serious loss of autonomy by universities. He told delegates that the Federal Government did "not seek to interfere unnecessarily in your day to day affairs". But, he went on,

> We do not expect you then to try to escape from accepting responsibility for your management decisions by blaming them on us. While you are funded as you are, you can demand no blank official cheque which ignores other priorities and needs... You cannot dismiss the changing needs of a society which you serve and which, in its turn, sustains and accepts you.[3]

Thus, in Australia today, there is considerable tension at the interface between tertiary education, especially universities, and government.

In this paper, I propose to explore aspects of this tension, but to do so within the broader context of shifts in effective power in the whole system of tertiary education governance. My argument is that over the past decade and a half there have been at least four major shifts in effective power:

---

[2] David Caro, "The Institutional Experience" (1982), in J.E. Anywl (ed.), University Government Relations. Proceedings of the Conference of University Governing Bodies, August 1982, (Canberra: Australian Vice-Chancellors' Committee, 1983), p. 19.

[3] Peter Baume, "Opening Address" (1982), in J.E. Anywl (ed.), University Governments Relations, p. 8.

1. at the institutional level, from departments and faculties to central administrations, central committees, and senior administrative officers;

2. from individual institutions to governments;

3. within government, from state governments to the Federal Government; and

4. at both federal and state levels of government from special coordinating agencies to Ministers, Cabinet and central departments.

By power is meant simply the capacity for independent discretionary decision-making and the ability to take and enforce decisions which are or might be opposed by other actors in the system of governance. I should make it clear that my argument about the shift in power at four levels is not that all effective power has moved from one set of points to others, but rather that the balance of power has changed.

Before proceeding two qualifications need to be made. First, more attention will be devoted to universities than to other tertiary education institutions. There are considerable differences between the three sectors of tertiary education with respect to governance and institutional government relations and there is not space here to try to map even some major differences between the sectors on various key dimensions. Further, issues of governance and relations to government also are more interesting and controversial with respect to universities. But it is worth pointing out that, among the three sectors of tertiary education, not only arrangements concerning governance, but norms about governance vary in curious ways. The notions of academic freedom and institutional autonomy essentially relate to universities, and are shared to a lesser extent by the colleges of advanced education (CAEs) and even less by technical and further education institutions (TAFE). Thus, while university people may be outraged at a proposal to bring some university practice into line with that of other sectors, university spokespersons are strangely silent when governments interfere in new ways in non-university institutions.

A second qualification is that, while the analysis presented here could reasonably be accused of taking more of a tertiary education institution view than a government perspective, the paper is based on the belief that both tertiary education institutions and governments need to be involved to a major degree in governance and control. Universities in particular need a large measure of independence if they are to perform their specialized and unique work well. But, on the other hand, governments need to have a substantial role in the interests of effective coordination and use of scarce resources, and to ensure that tertiary education is, in a broad sense, working to achieve broad agreed-upon objectives.

The Australian Tertiary Education System

For readers unfamiliar with the system of tertiary education in Australia a brief sketch of current arrangements and key characteristics is necessary. For the past decade, Australia has used the term "tertiary education" in basically the same way that many other countries use the term "higher education". The Australian tertiary education system is made up of three distinct sectors or groups of institutions - universities, CAEs, and technical and further education colleges.[4]

The nineteen universities constitute the strongest and best developed sector, although they enrol only about 13 percent (or 175,000) of total student numbers. They were all established under state legislation, except for the Australian National University in the national capital of Canberra, but are wholly funded by the Federal Government, except for relatively minor levels of endowments, and research grants and contracts from state governments and industry. They tend to be mainly coordinated at the Federal Government level and view themselves essentially as part of a national system. Most students enrolled in universities are studying at the undergraduate level, but in relation to other tertiary education institutions universities have a special role in post-graduate education and research.

---

[4]See B.R. Williams, Systems of Higher Education: Australia (New York: International Council for Educational Development, 1978); and G.S. Harman, "The Universities of Australia" in Commonwealth Universities Yearbook 1986 (London: The Association of Commonwealth Universities, 1986).

The CAE sector which has 196,000 students, was created in the second half of the 1960s largely by bringing together a range of different non-university institutions, operated mainly by state government departments - senior technical colleges, agricultural colleges, paramedical institutions and teachers colleges. At the beginning of 1981, there were seventy-three CAEs but, as a result of mergers, their number has been reduced now to forty-seven. While CAEs continue to place considerable emphasis on undergraduate diploma and associate diploma courses, almost 70 percent of their students are enrolled in bachelors degree and post-graduate courses. As a group of institutions, they are less homogeneous in character than the universities and range from large, multi-faculty institutes of technology to small "single purpose" agricultural or paramedical colleges. Like universities they are now funded wholly by the Federal Government, but are coordinated mainly at the state level and enjoy less autonomy than universities.

The TAFE sector is by far the largest but was the most recent to have developed nationally as a separate and recognized component of tertiary education. It has over one million students located in 300 colleges plus numerous annexes and branch campuses. The main emphasis is on training for skilled trades, apprenticeship programs, and remedial and preparatory work, but there are also substantial efforts in non-credit adult education. TAFE colleges are controlled directly by government departments or agencies and the main funding comes from state sources. For more than a decade, however, the Federal Government has provided substantial funds, especially for capital projects and special projects.

By far the most curious feature of this tertiary education system relates to governance and funding. Within each of the six states, almost all tertiary education institutions are public creations, legally responsible to a state Minister and government. Yet, for the university and CAE sectors, since 1974 the Federal Government has accepted full responsibility for providing all regular recurrent and capital funding. Further, since 1974 no tuition fees have been charged in the three sectors. The result is that universities and CAEs are wholly dependent on the generosity of the Federal Government and often there is considerable ambiguity and tension about the location of the real power of control when Federal and state priorities do not coincide. For the past two decades the Federal Government has taken the major role in policy initiation for universities and CAEs, and works mainly through its specialist coordinating agency, the Commonwealth Tertiary Education Commission (CTEC). Constitutionally, the Federal Government has no direct legal power control over universities and colleges, but instead exerts its influence mainly via conditional (section 96) grants of funds to the six states for specified purposes in particular universities or colleges. Although funding responsibilities for universities and CAEs lie with the Federal government, state governments have made it clear that they have not abdicated their traditional responsibilities for tertiary education and all states have established special tertiary education coordinating agencies - sometimes just for CAEs, but in other cases for universities and CAEs or for all tertiary education institutions.

Over the past decade student load in universities and CAEs has increased by over 25 percent and in TAFEs by over 30 percent. Funding levels, however, for universities and CAEs have not kept pace with this growth and a recent government report[5] indicates that, for universities, while student load increased by 14.4 percent in the past decade, operating grants rose only by 11.9 percent, academic staff numbers by 6.4 percent and general staff numbers by 2.9 percent. For CAEs the trend has been more adverse.

From Departments and Faculties to the Centre of Institutions

The centralization of power at the institutional level has been much more pronounced in universities and CAEs. It has sprung from a number of sources. In part, it has been an almost inevitable response to a greater measure of government control and regulation, and to increased demands for information and more effective and explicit accountability. These trends have worked to increase the size and importance of central administrations and central committees; since the central bodies are increasingly being held responsible for the activities

---

[5] Review of Efficiency and Effectiveness in Higher Education, (Canberra: Australian Government Publishing Service, 1986), p. 37.

196

of components units they respond by claiming and exercising greater control over them. But centralization at institutional level has also been a response to tight budgetary conditions. Whenever possible, spare resources must be reclaimed from departments in order to support new or growing activities. There is also a need to review activities, and to make selective cuts. Apart from these two factors, the trend to increased centralization at the institutional level has been aided by increased democratization at faculty and departmental levels, and often a resulting failure or unwillingness by deans and heads to take tough decisions. Significantly, a recent report of a committee chaired by the Chairman of CTEC calls for stronger academic leadership in universities and CAEs and recommends that deans and heads of schools should be appointed rather than elected positions.[6]

This centralization at the institutional level gives reason for concern. Universities and CAEs clearly need strong leadership at the senior levels, especially if they are to engage in effective strategic planning and develop clear policies with regard to strong teaching programs and targeting of research funds to higher producers and to priority areas. The dilemma is to ensure that effective independence is maintained at faculty and department levels since the key arguments in favour of a larger measure of institutional independence relate to the special characteristics of academic work. As Martin Trow has argued, there is a danger that decisions taken at central levels of universities may be at odds "with the very values they are intended to defend".[7]

From Tertiary Education Institutions to Government

For convenience the analysis of this shift will focus first on universities, but some brief comments will be made on the other two sectors. The year 1969 provides a good point to establish some benchmarks by which to identify and evaluate

---

[6]*Ibid.*, p. 255.

[7]Martin Trow, "Dilemmas of Higher Education in the 1980's and 1990's", paper presented at the Conference of Learned Societies, (Montreal, June 1980).

recent changes. At that time, there were only fourteen universities compared to nineteen today, and the student population was continuing to expand rapidly as it had for more than a decade. The Australian Universities Commission, modelled on the British University Grants Committee, had been operating for ten years and the universities were financed on a matching system of state and federal grants for both capital and recurrent expenditure. New South Wales was the only state that had established a tertiary education coordinating authority whose responsibilities included universities.

Universities at that time enjoyed a large measure of effective independence. This independence can be conveniently categorized under the headings of legal status, educational policies and programs, staff and students, and administration and financial control. Each deserves separate discussion.

- *Legal status* Each university was an independent public corporation able to own property, to sue and be sued, and to regulate its own affairs within wide powers delegated to it by its instrument of incorporation. Each was free from direct day to day control by a government department. Each had a governing body charged with management responsibility and responsible to a minister and parliament. The chief formal constraints were the obligation to keep within the powers granted by legislation and the need to secure parliamentary authority to alter the instrument of incorporation. This, of course, was apart from being subject to the ordinary laws of the land and any specific conditions imposed by governments with regard to financial grants.

- *Educational policies and programs* Universities enjoyed a large measure of independence with regard to the educational programs they offered, the subjects or disciplines they taught, the content of units, the structure of programs, the nature of examinations and other assessment procedures used, and the standards required for admission to the university and for the award of particular degrees or diplomas. At the same time, freedom with regard to programs was limited by the amount of finance available and major new academic developments, such as a new faculty or an expensive department, required formal approval by the Australian Universities Commission.

- *Research* Each university had the right to make its own decisions concerning the encouragement and conduct of research. However, acceptance of research grants, such as through the Australian Research Grants Committee, provided limits to this freedom.

- *Staff and students* Apart from the fact that by their acts of incorporation a number of universities were specifically forbidden from applying any religious test in the selection of staff and students, universities were essentially free to recruit their own staff and students. With regard to staff they had considerable freedom to set terms and conditions of employment, although from the early 1960s unified salary scales for academic staff had become common. The few attempts at government interference in academic staff appointments had been strongly resisted and condemned.

- *Administration and financial control* Universities had considerable independence in establishing their own administrative procedures, forms of academic government and administrative control over staff, and discipline over students. They also had considerable freedom to make their own decisions about how they allocated funds to different purposes. But there were well-entrenched limitations, such as on the ability to switch funds at their own discretion between capital and recurrent expenditures and controls over the planning and construction of buildings. Further, there were some controls over recurrent expenditure. In making its requests for funds each university had to make a case for resources to undertake new major developments.

The year 1969 also saw a conference of university governing bodies at the Australian National University in Canberra, held to consider the role and responsibilities of governing bodies. The conference discussed changes in relations between governments and universities and some concern was expressed about the effects on autonomy of procedures introduced by the Australian Universities Commission and by the Australian Research Grants Committee. Some concerns were also expressed about possible future developments. But, overall, the conference proceedings do not indicate any high level of concern about university independence and the Commonwealth Minister for Education assured delegates that "the Commonwealth Government has neither the intention nor the wish to dictate to Universities".[8]

Since 1969 a substantial centralization of power to governments has taken place with a corresponding reduction in university independence. Table 1 (Appendix) attempts to summarize some of the main changes under the same headings used above when discussing university independence in 1969. It will be noted that the changes are extensive and include numerous cases of both state government and Federal Government action. In some cases changes resulted from pressure exerted by university interests (such as with the establishment of the Academic Salaries Tribunal in 1974 by the Whitlam Government) or at least with the support of the interests involved (for example, the 1981 amalgamation of the University of Wollongong and the Wollongong Institute of Education), but in most cases the initiative came from the Commonwealth Government or a state government alone. Frequently changes were announced as policy by governments without prior consultation with the institutions affected. Some changes, such as those which were part of the "Razor Gang" cuts of 1981 by the Federal Government led by Malcolm

---

[8]Malcolm Fraser, "Governments, Universities and the Community", in A Report on the Conference on the Role and Responsibilities of Governing Bodies held at the Australian National University, 22-23 May 1969, (Canberra, 1969), p. 103.

Fraser,[9] were strenuously opposed by individual universities and the Australian Vice-Chancellors' Committee, but in other cases the university community accepted particular reductions in independence with little or no protest. To outsiders this lack of protest may well appear curious, but the explanation lies essentially in elements of Australia's political culture. In particular, there is the Australian tendency to look to governments to solve all kinds of economic and social problems; consequently, government involvement in a new sphere is not automatically viewed as being undesirable.

Space does not allow a detailed explanation of the various encroachments on university independence since the late 1960s, but three forms of intervention deserve comment. First, the CTEC inquiry of the late 1970s into study leave was largely driven by an anti-education and anti-university public mood at the time. The end result was not as bad as universities feared. Application and reporting procedures were made more formal and restrictions were placed on the number of staff which could be away at any one time and the proportion of budgets which could be spent on study leave travel. In fact, however, these so-called restrictions were close to the operating norms for many institutions. But the instructions to universities which followed the inquiry represented another case of government interference in a matter which previously had been left to universities to decide. It also was a damaging period in university-government relations in that this inquiry and other government actions conveyed to university personnel an attitude of distrust of universities on the part of government.

Second, Federal Government intervention in 1981-82, as part of the so-called "Razor Gang" cuts, marked the first time that governments in Australia had announced without consultation with the affected university that a major program and school would be closed and the first time that a number of universities were virtually ordered to amalgamate with nearby colleges of

[9]See Grant Harman, "The 'Razor Gang' Moves, the 1981 Guidelines and the Uncertain Future" in Grant Harman and Don Smart (eds.), Federal Intervention in Australian Education: Past, Present, Future (Melbourne: Georgian House, 1982).

advanced education.[10] But the political events which led to the "Razor Gang" cuts were somewhat unusual and colleges of advanced education were much more affected than universities. In fact, 30 out of the 78 CAEs operating at the time were told that, unless they combined with larger institutions before the end of 1981, they would lose all Federal funding. Significantly, few university voices were raised against these drastic moves against CAEs.

Third, particularly important but not well documented to date has been the influence of both state and federal legislation on matters such as equal opportunity and employment, anti-discrimination, freedom of information and appeals on government decisions.[11] In New South Wales, for example, all universities and CAEs are required to prepare, implement and report on their equal opportunity management plans. The Director of Equal Opportunity in Public Employment has the power to approve or reject plans. In Victoria and the Australian Capital Territory, universities and CAEs are subject to freedom of information legislation and have had to produce all kinds of documents and so bring internal decision-making processes under public scrutiny.

The reduction in university independence since 1969 can be attributed to the operation of a combination of factors. In the first place, it is one consequence of tighter government budgets and of quite substantial demographic changes. The attempts of the early 1980s at forced amalgamations affecting four universities, for example, stemmed largely from problems encountered by the CTEC in securing substantial reductions in teacher education enrolments, especially in CAEs, in order to free scarce resources for expanding areas.

---

[10]*Ibid.*

[11]Helen Sungaila, "The Growing Influence of Legal Considerations on Education Decisions", paper presented at October 1986 Jubilee Conference, (Centre for Administrative and Higher Education Studies, University of New England, Armidale, 1986).

Second, to a substantial extent the changes in university independence can be seen as a fairly natural outcome of the transition from an elite tertiary education system, where only a very small proportion of young people had an opportunity to enrol, to a mass system. Tertiary education in Australia now takes a significant proportion of the resources of society and large numbers of individuals and families have a direct interest in what universities and colleges do. In turn, this has created pressures for governments to regulate and monitor more closely their activities.

Third, the drive for greater accountability and greater interference has been related to changing community attitudes to tertiary education. Partly because of changing employment prospects for graduates, in the second half of the 1970s and early 1980s universities and CAEs lost in public esteem and support, and many prominent business leaders as well as politicians urged governments to bring institutions back into line. But in recent months this mood of public criticism has subsided and there are clear signs of a more supportive public attitude emerging.

Fourth, the reduction of university and CAE independence is, to some extent, an outcome of the acceptance by the Commonwealth government in 1973 of full responsibility for the normal recurrent and capital funding for all universities and CAEs and the abolition of tuition fees. At the time universities generally favoured the end of shared federal-state funding; they hoped this would provide more liberal financial support and confirm the fact that universities had primarily a national rather than a local or state orientation. But the longer term effect has been that, apart from gifts and income from investments, research grants and contracts, the universities have become totally dependent on the Commonwealth Government. Not only have recurrent grants failed to keep pace fully with inflation, but the Commonwealth has used the power of the purse, mainly through section 96 grants, to insist on particular policies being followed. Prior to 1974, state governments often acted as buffers to Federal Government initiatives and pressures.

A fifth factor has been the growth of the college of advanced education sector to be a direct competitor of universities for both funding and students, and the move to see universities as constituting merely one sector of a three sector system of tertiary education. In 1969, only a very general way could CAEs have been considered as being in direct competition for students with universities. Now there is considerable overlap between CAE and university courses in terms of course levels. Distinctions between the two sectors are becoming increasingly similar policies for them. The fact that CAEs still enjoy somewhat less independence than universities poses a threat to universities. Colleges argue for equal treatment with universities, but it seems likely that on balance the outcome will be a gradual reduction of university independence towards CAE conditions, rather than to allow CAEs to enjoy current university privileges.

A further contributing factor has been the inability of the universities to effectively counter various encroachments by government, and the tendency of the university community itself to use the arm of government in order to secure desired goals. To a substantial extent, Australian universities have shown a surprising lack of interest in issues relating to university independence. They have been reticent in trying to explain to a community used to the wide use of government to achieve objectives why universities need a substantial degree of freedom in order to do their work well. Some encroachments have been resisted but, on many occasions, few voices of opposition have been raised. But perhaps more serious has been the fact that, while academic staff and university leaders say they are opposed to the notion of increased government intervention in university affairs, at the same time they often see no inconsistency in seeking government intervention to right a particular wrong or to overcome a perceived disability.

For the other two sectors of tertiary education, the experience of the last two decades has had a number of parallels. Both CAEs and TAFE colleges have experienced new forms of government intervention; CAEs, in particular, were particularly affected by the "Razor Gang" cuts of the early 1980s. On the other hand, as they have become increasingly like universities, CAEs have gained some new freedoms; for example, CAEs generally have more administrative independence today, and in some states the larger CAEs have been given effective control over the accreditation of their own courses. TAFE colleges too have gained in independence, and especially in those states where the larger colleges have been legally constituted in a similar way to CAEs under their own governing bodies.

How serious are all these changes that have been outlined? Do they constitute a substantial reduction of independence in the case of universities? The answers you would receive to these questions in Australia would vary, depending largely on where the person providing the reply sits. Many of my academic colleagues, for example, see the changes as resulting in serious infringement of university institutional autonomy. Ministers, or senior officials, on the other hand, treat university complaints as special pleading and as academic efforts to return to some ideal relationship between government and universities that never existed. As someone convinced of the desirability of universities having a large degree of independence, I am concerned about any real reduction in freedom of independent action, and consider that, with the marked increased degree of different kinds of regulatory legislation, universities are becoming increasingly difficult to manage. On the other hand, I must admit that Australian universities still have a great deal of discretionary power and, in particular, they have a large measure of control in areas which are central to the academic enterprise - the selection of students; the selection of staff; control over what is taught and how it is taught.

From State Government to Federal Government

Commonwealth Government influence in policymaking for tertiary education began in a small way prior to the second world war and, for universities, grew substantially during the war and in the post-war era. Establishment of the Australian Universities Commission in the late 1950s led to the Commonwealth Government taking on a major role in planning and financing university expansion and from 1965 the Commonwealth Government undertook a similar role for CAEs. Then in 1974, following agreement by the states to the Commonwealth taking over full responsibility for the regular recurrent and capital funding of universities and CAEs, the previous powerful role of state governments was significantly reduced and the Commonwealth Government achieved the advantages that the power of the purse can bring. Since 1974 the Commonwealth Government has been the dominant partner in policy determination for universities and CAEs but, as already noted, state governments have made it clear that they have not foregone and have no intention of foregoing their constitutional and legal responsibilities for their universities and CAEs. This situation leads to tension and ambiguity where the real power lies.

Generally a high level of state and federal cooperation exists, with federal authorities tending to take the major initiating role in planning and policy formulation. But from time to time issues emerge where there are sharp differences in federal and state priorities and policies. This happened, for example, in the early 1980s when, as part of the "Razor Gang" cuts, the Fraser Government insisted that thirty CAEs amalgamate with other CAEs or with universities. In some states, CAE personnel looked to their state governments to resist Commonwealth dictation, but in the end practically all amalgamations went ahead as state governments were unwilling to risk loss of federal funding or closure because of institutional insolvency.[12] At the present time two major battles are being fought - one relating to a New South Wales government plan to create a new university in the western suburbs of Sydney[13] and the other a proposal of the Western Australian Government to upgrade its largest CAE to university status. But unless the respective state governments are prepared to provide financial resources to fund their proposals, it is unlikely that state government wishes will succeed, provided the will of the Federal Government does not weaken.

The future of Commonwealth-state relations with regard to universities and CAEs is somewhat unclear. It seems unlikely that any Commonwealth administration would wish to retreat from having a substantial involvement in the university and

---

[12]G.S. Harman, "Restructuring Higher Education Systems Through Institutional Mergers", Higher Education, (forthcoming).

[13]Higher Education Development in Western and South-Western Sydney, (Canberra: Commonwealth Tertiary Education Commission, 1986).

CAE sectors, and there is much to support such a stance. From a longer term perspective, Commonwealth involvement had decidedly worked to the financial advantage of universities and CAEs. It has also tended to promote a national rather than a parochial outlook - a characteristic that members of the academic community generally value. In terms of professional training and research, Commonwealth ministers and authorities point to the desirability of national approaches and priorities. At the same time, state governments have made it clear they do not wish to continue to exercise their responsibilities and, significantly, in the period since the Commonwealth took over full financial responsibility most states have developed or strengthened their tertiary education coordinating machinery, while a number have sponsored major inquiries into tertiary education. State governments quite rightly point to the desirability of policies that will taken into account local and regional needs and that in some senses universities and CAEs should be seen as contributing to a state system of educational provision. They also point to the need for effective coordination between universities and CAEs on the one hand, and technical and further education on the other. Various proposals for change have been made over the past decade, but state governments have shown little enthusiasm for varying existing arrangements, except that in recent months two state governments have provided some financial resources for particular CAE developments (one government financed a major new campus and another provided funding for 1500 additional students) while the Northern Territory to date is financing the initial development of a University College in Darwin. One major problem of the present system is the long delays that result when federal and state governments disagree, and the tendency for some planning decisions to be compromises between state and federal governments that are not necessarily in the best issues of universities and CAEs.

From Coordinating Agencies to Ministers and Central Departments

This trend has operated at both state and Commonwealth levels, but it has been most marked over the last few years at the Commonwealth level. There the Minister for Education and the Federal Cabinet, together with the Department of Education and central departments, have acquired a more dominant role at the expense of the CTEC.

This centralization of power is the result of a number of influences. One is the general trend in modern government for cabinet ministers to develop a more activist style and for central departments to become decidedly more influential. In the case of the Commonwealth level, this tendency appears to have accelerated under recent Prime Ministers. Another factor was the acceptance by the Commonwealth Government of responsibility for the total funding for higher education. Under the previous system of shared funding, the effective limits on expenditure generally were set by state governments since, with its superior financial resources, the Commonwealth Government in most cases was willing to be more generous to universities and CAEs than were state administrations. But with the system of total Commonwealth funding, the Commonwealth alone had to determine expenditure limits and, in practice, these soon came to be set on the advice of central departments, particularly the Department of Finance and the Department of Prime Minister and Cabinet. Another influence still has been the financial constraints which began with the Hayden budget of August 1975 and which led in turn first to the temporary abandonment of the triennial system and then to the system of the rolling triennium. This meant for a period of some years operation of a practice of virtually annual budgeting for universities and CAEs, with the expenditure limits being set more in terms of what the government was prepared to spend rather than what institutions believed they needed to pursue their work. A further influence has been a tendency by recent Federal governments to distrust advice from statutory bodies and to rely more on departmental advice. Finally, universities, CAEs and the academic community in some respects have perhaps unknowingly encouraged these developments to which they are opposed, since a natural reaction to what is seen as unfavourable decisions by either a Minister or the Cabinet is to lobby both directly. This in turn possibly has encouraged Ministers and the Cabinet to intervene more directly in university affairs.

This form of increased centralization also gives reason for concern. While Ministers and government clearly have the right to decide where to look for expert advice, the worry is that central departments are often not well informed on details with regard to universities and CAEs. Specialist coordinating agencies have a difficult job, and their efforts frequently are not fully appreciated by universities and CAEs. But generally they are better informed than other government agencies about the needs and specialist interests of tertiary education. On balance, the idea of a specialist coordinating agency to provide independent advice to Ministers and to act as a buffer between institutions on the one hand and governments on the other has much to commend it. Recent changes in the structure of the CTEC can be interpreted as an attempt initiated by the CTEC Chairman to increase the effectiveness and influence of CTEC in relation to other Commonwealth Government agencies.[14]

Conclusions

The argument of the paper has been that the changing relationships between governments and tertiary education can best be understood in the broader context of quite important centralizing shifts of power taking place in the governance of the Australian tertiary education system. The various shifts provide some reason for concern, but perhaps more serious is the worry about how effectively Australian universities and CAEs may respond to future changes in governance and to threats to their essential academic functions. To date, in my view, the essential functions of universities and CAEs have not been unduly restricted, although a network of federal and state regulatory provisions makes the tasks of institutional management increasingly difficult. But more serious are the further threats on the horizon and the question of whether universities and CAEs will be able to develop viable political strategies to resist interference and to develop the will to do so strenuously and effectively.

---

[14]Review of the Structure of the Commonwealth Tertiary Education Commission and Arrangements for Coordination and Consultation with States and Institutions, (Canberra: Australian Government Publishing Service, 1985).

Appendix

Table 1

Reductions in University Independence Since 1969

Legal Status and Powers

- In 1981-82 four regional universities pressed by the Commonwealth Government to amalgamate with a nearby CAE. (In the end two universities escaped amalgamation through a change of government.)

- A 1981 amendment to the James Cook University Act gave Queensland Minister of Education power to adjudicate in disagreements between the University and the Queensland Advanced Education Board over the conduct and content of advanced education courses offered by the University.

- Legislation passed by various state parliaments limiting compulsory membership of student associations.

- In New South Wales composition of university governing bodies changed against the wish of universities.

- Inquiries by Ombudsmen into university decisions.

- Universities brought under powers of various federal and state "social" legislation (e.g., anti-discrimination, freedom of information).

- In a number of states universities must give notice of making submissions to CTEC.

- From 1987 all universities will be required to charge a student administration fee of $250.

Education Policies and Programs

- CTEC approval now required for the introduction of all new courses.

- In some states universities must secure approval to introduce new courses or to significantly amend existing courses.

- In 1981 Deakin University forced by the Federal Government to close its school of engineering.

- Through the recommendations of the Inquiry into Management Education, CTEC achieved some rationalization of management programs - closure of some MBA programs threatened.

Research

- New "research centres of excellence" allocation on the recommendations of a essentially "lay" committee.

- Tighter controls instituted over government research contracts.

- Further restrictions on use and management of special research funds.

Staff and Students

- All universities forced to revise study leave rules, and to provide more information on operation of study leave programs.

- Universities instructed on minimum and maximum student enrolment numbers.

- In 1979 universities instructed to reduce numbers in teacher education programs and not to replace staff for those programs.

- Universities pressed to modify composition of student intakes and student selection procedures.

- Universities instructed by Fraser Government to reduce proportion of academic staff at rank of lecturer and above to 50 percent of total academic staff.

Administration and Financial Control

- In 1974 establishment of Academic Salaries Tribunal with power to determine salary levels for each rank for the Australian National University and to make recommendations for other universities.

- 1980 Commonwealth legislation limited university salary levels to those set by Academic Salaries Tribunal.

- 1981 Commonwealth legislation required universities to supply audit certificates showing actual salaries paid.

- More use of "ear-marked" grants by the CTEC for recurrent expenditure.

- Abolition of Academic Salaries Tribunal in 1985 and provision for university salaries to be fixed nationally by the Arbitration and Conciliation Commission.

Bi-Lateral and Multi-Lateral Aid and the University: A Chinese Case Study

by

Ruth Hayhoe[1]

Introduction

Most of the papers in this volume look at issues of national or provincial government intervention in facets of university life in North America or other OECD countries. These countries share two characteristics which make the experience of their universities somewhat different from that of most universities in the rest of the globe. First, they share a tradition rooted in the history of the medieval university of Europe, which provides a common point of reference in debates over the appropriate nature and level of university autonomy in the changing political-economic circumstances of advanced capitalist societies.[2] While this tradition of university autonomy was exported to many former colonies in the period of Empire,[3] in no other societies has it been so culturally at one with overall social and political tradition as in Europe and, to a lesser extent, North America.[4] Secondly, OECD countries

---

[1] Assistant Professor, Higher Education Group, OISE, Toronto, ON.

[2] Robert Nisbet, The Degradation of the Academic Dogma: The University in America 1945-1970 (London: Heinneman, 1971) is perhaps one of the best examples of the application of traditional values to a critique of the "modern" university.

[3] Eric Ashby, Universities: British, Indian, African (London: Weidenfield and Nicolson, 1966).

[4] Richard Hofstadger and Walter Metzger, The Development of Academic Freedom in the United States (New York and London: Columbia University Press, 1955). This book identifies the roots of the American university in the colonial college which derived from the British college, yet Protestant lay government had made very different from the European university. Autonomy and academic freedom were won with considerably greater struggle in democratic America than in autocratic Germany, for example.

enjoy a position of political-economic supremacy in the global community which may be challenged through United Nations organizations, but has a remarkable solidity and strength due to their control of such institutions as the International Monetary Fund and the World Bank.[5] Universities within the OECD are not only unlikely to be threatened with intervention from international government organizations, but they enjoy a special status in the world community as the likely source of expertise for the ministrations of these organizations in the developing world.[6]

In making these two points, I don't in any way intend to minimize the important debates and struggles over university-government relations going on in North America in conditions of economic recession and a general mood of social conservatism. These raise serious questions relating to how the university's characteristic value of scholarly autonomy is to be re-interpreted for our age. But I do want to emphasize the even greater difficulties facing scholars of the developing world who have to contend not only with the intervention in university affairs of national governments but also of powerful bi-lateral and multi-lateral aid agencies, and for whom university autonomy may not be a part of a longstanding cultural tradition.

A further distinction should be made between the conditions of bi-lateral and multi-lateral aid. The extent and scope of bi-lateral aid projects is usually modest and their direction is likely to be shaped by the particular character of university culture in the donor nation. The degree to which it constitutes

---

[5]For a radical critique of this situation, see Teresa Hayter and Catherine Watson, Aid: Rhetoric or Reality? (London: Pluto Press, 1985); and Cheryl Payer, The World Bank: A Critical Analysis (New York and London: Monthly Review Press, 1982), The Debt Trap, the IMF and the Third World (London: Penguin, 1974).

[6]The efforts made by the AUCC to assist Canadian university scholars in getting World Bank contracts doubtless are not merely a matter of the economic advantage involved, but the prestige value of such contracts for Canadian institutions. See Monica Gruder, A Guide to the World Bank for Canadian Universities (Ottawa: AUCC, February, 1985).

government interference in a cross-national setting is linked to two issues, the nature of university autonomy in both societies and the particular political-economic relations linking the two nations. In the case of British relations with former colonies and American relations with such Latin American nations as Columbia[7] bi-lateral aid is likely to consolidate dominance and coopt the university to the service of certain political interests. In such a situation as Chinese aid to African universities or Eastern European aid to Chinese universities, this is less likely to be the case. With multi-lateral aid, such as that of the World Bank, cultural influences are likely to be more eclectic, while issues of the international political economy tend to dominate. External aid may constitute a channel for ensuring that the receiving university conforms to national development plans which in turn favour the preservation of an international *status quo* dominated by the economies and political interests of OECD countries.[8] Cultural dynamics are nevertheless operative in this situation, and they may be used to promote a diversity of influences that strengthens the autonomy of the knowledge base in a "developing" university.[9]

The question of the legitimacy of the intervention of government into the affairs of universities in developing countries thus can be explored on two levels. First, it should be considered in relation to a scholarly culture to which the western values of university autonomy and academic freedom may be foreign. What is accepted as "legitimate" intervention

---

[7]See, for example, Gilbert G. Gonzalez, "Educational Reform and the University of Columbia", Comparative Education, Vol. 17, No. 2 (June, 1981).

[8]The special issue of Comparative Education devoted to the World Bank educational policy paper of 1980, Vol. 17, No. 2 (June, 1981) contains several articles that show how World Bank educational aid is linked to overall national development strategies worked out between economists within the receiving country and World Bank advisors.

[9]Ali Mazrui, "The African University as a Multi-National Corporation", in Political Values and the Educational Class in Africa (London: Heinneman, 1978). Two of Mazrui's suggested strategies for strengthening the autonomy of the African university in a highly unequal global environment are the domestication and diversification of the higher curriculum.

by scholars in a "developing" university may therefore be different from what would be acceptable in a western situation. Their government-university relations have to be understood in terms of local scholarly and cultural tradition. This is not to suggest an acceptance of total cultural relativism, but that behind the terms "university autonomy" and "academic freedom" used in developing countries may be a different set of connotations than those we assume from the western perspective.

The second level to be explored relates to the legitimacy of the intervention of foreign or international government agencies in a "developing" university. Here it may be a question both of national government strength in the particular relationship that occasions intervention and in the university's ability to shape and control the knowledge introduced through "aid" towards ends its scholars define as appropriate.[10] I have suggested elsewhere standards drawn from World Order Models Scholarship for judging whether or not international intervention is "legitimate" in particular situations. Equity draws attention to the agreements on which it is based, autonomy alludes to the degree to which it strengthens the independence of local scholarship,[11] solidarity to the measure in which it encourages local networks of scholarly cooperation and participation to the extent to which it draw "developing" scholars into mutual theoretical interaction with the global scholarly community.[12] Forms of intervention intended to promote conformity to the international *status quo* and a dependent knowledge relationship which serves to make economic or political dependency appear as "normal" or

---

[10]Arturo Escobar, "Discourse and Power in Development: Michel Foucault and the Relevance of His Work to the Third World", Alternatives, X (Winter, 1984-5), pp. 377-400, suggests that the discourse of development, largely produced by universities in Europe and North America, may contribute to the maintenance of domination and economic exploitation.

[11]In Escobar's terms, this would be the ability to produce and use counter discourses.

[12]R. Hayhoe, "Penetration of Mutuality? China's Educational Cooperation with Europe, Japan and North America", Comparative Education Review, Vol. 30, No. 4, (November, 1986). These four counter values to cultural imperialism are drawn from J. Galtung, The True Worlds: A Transnational Perspective (New York: The Free Press, 1980).

"inevitable" might be judged as illegitimate within this framework.[13]

In this paper, I am going to focus on the Chinese university and sketch out a background for considering the bi-lateral and multi-lateral aid projects now affecting it. From an economic perspective China is a poor developing country, whose universities have come later to the game of international aid than those of India, Africa and Latin America. It is also a nation with a tremendously rich cultural heritage and universities whose modern shape continues to be informed by values of a scholarly culture which ruled the Chinese Empire for two millennia. Western-derived values of university autonomy and academic freedom have often been invoked in the history of the modern Chinese university, yet the real question of its relation to government can be more effectively understood in terms of values of intellectual authority and scholarly monopoly, derived from the dominant Confucian scholarly tradition.[14]

In this paper I seek to outline the conceptual background from which an analysis of contemporary bi-lateral and multi-lateral aid to the Chinese university could be developed on a deeper level than the technocratic one of efficiency, effectiveness and impact in the transfer of knowledge and technology. These are important issues of accountability for such agencies as the Canadian International Development Agency (CIDA),[15] yet they do not touch upon the deeper-level questions which will determine the long-term future of aid to Chinese universities. Does aid strengthen them so that they are able to make an independent contribution to Chinese development and ultimately to global transformation, or does it coopt them into temporary service to foreign interests?

---

[13] R. Arnove (ed.), Philanthropy: Cultural Imperialism (Boston: C.K. Hall, 1979) shows how the great American foundations have used assistance to the social sciences in this way.

[14] R. Hayhoe, "Chinese, European and American Scholarly Values in Interaction", LACE Occasional Paper No. 13, (July, 1984).

[15] For an example of this kind of evaluation see Doris Ryan and Thomas Fleming, Evaluation Report of the Canada-China Management Education Program (Toronto: OISE, March, 1986).

This conceptual background has two parts. The first essential point is an understanding of China's scholarly tradition and thus the meaning that lay behind the values of autonomy and academic freedom which were adopted in China's early modern universities, giving them a superficial similarity to European and American institutions. Only from an understanding of the meaning of university autonomy within Chinese culture, can we go on to consider the issue of the legitimacy of national or foreign/international government intervention in the contemporary period.

Secondly, the place of China's universities in the international political economy is a question of great importance. China's extensive experience of bi-lateral aid with Soviet bloc countries in the fifties has parallels with both the bi-lateral and multi-lateral aid of the present period, and a careful analysis of what went wrong in Soviet aid to China's universities may shed light on the second question of interest to this paper - government intervention in the university in a situation of global dominance and dependency, whether within the capitalist or the socialist imperialist bloc.[16] Intervention might be seen as legitimate if it contributes to a strong and independent university able to serve the nation and offer something fresh to the international scholarly community. It might be seen as illegitimate, if it serves the political or economic interests of the donor country/bloc and prevents the university from developing a fresh and critical knowledge base from which to contribute both to national development and to the international academic community.

In the following two sections, the historical experience of China's modern universities in relation to Republican and Communist governments is reviewed. Under the Republican government, the dominant theme of interest is the emergence of a Chinese view of university autonomy, expressed in terms very similar to those of the European patterns being emulated, yet having a different substance due to the traditions of Chinese scholarly culture. Under the Communist government, the theme of interest is the role of the Chinese university in a situation of external domination and forms of aid that served to

---

[16]What the Chinese have dubbed "Soviet Social imperialism", I am simply calling socialist imperialism, in contrast to capitalist imperialism.

shape China's development towards Soviet global interests. The outcome of this situation, which appeared highly successful between 1952 and 1957, is of the greatest relevance to present multi-lateral and bi-lateral aid projects involving China's universities.

The University and Government in Republican China

The relationship between university and government in modern China is an extremely complex one, yet it has one clear point in common with other developing societies: the fact that the values of university autonomy and academic freedom were not central to its own scholarly tradition, as they had been to the modern European and North American university. Furthermore, the contours of this relationship were worked out after the revolution of 1911 in world conditions under which the dominance of the great western imperialist nations had serious consequences for Chinese development, as was later to be the case again under the hegemony of socialist imperialism in the sixties. Thus, Chinese scholars over the whole modern period have had to face the question of university-government relations and the legitimacy of government intervention under conditions fundamentally different from those of universities in North America and Europe, and also in the Soviet Union.

In this essay I wish to focus on two institutions which have probably done most to shape the ethos of the modern university in China: Beijing University which dominated the Republican period and has continued to be China's most illustrious university in the post-1949 period, and People's University, which was consciously established by Communist leaders in the early fifties as a prototype of a truly modern Chinese university, whose role was to set a model of reform for the universities that had grown up under capitalism.[17] I will draw upon previous research in creating profiles of these two institutions and their relation to the Chinese government, which should lay a foundation for reflecting on both the

---

[17]Interestingly the history of these two institutions, first Beijing University, then People's University, are placed first in the recently published Zhongguo gaodeng jiaoyu jianjie (A Brief Introduction to Higher Education in the P.R.C.), (Beijing: Educational Science Press, 1982).

possibilities and the difficulties associated with contemporary projects of bi-lateral and multi-lateral aid for the Chinese university.

Without question, Cai Yuanpei was the scholar who did most to define the role of the modern Chinese university in relation to the Republican government.[18] As a scholar who had received the highest accolades within the Chinese traditional system, being made a Hanlin academician in 1895,[19] he had a thorough understanding of the traditional role of China's higher institutions in a society which he characterized as "several thousand years of scholarly despotism".[20] The traditional Chinese scholarly community had never experienced or aspired to university autonomy or academic freedom, rather it had held an intellectual authority and scholarly monopoly that was inextricably meshed with the imperial system. In such a community, questions of the legitimacy of government intervention were irrelevant, since the scholarly community was, more or less, the government.[21] The exception to this picture were the fragmented groups of scholars who withdrew or abstained from bureaucratic participation for a period and created enclaves of intellectual freedom within the private *shuyuan* (colleges) or scholarly societies. For them government intervention consisted in either cooption to

---

[18]W. Duiker, Ts'ai Yüan-p'ei: Educator of Modern China (University Park and London: The Penn State University Press, 1977).

[19]Cai Yuanpei Nianpu (A Biography of Cai Yuanpei) ed. Gao Pingshu (Beijing: Zhonghua shuju, 1980).

[20]Cai Yuanpei Quanji (Cai Yuanpei's Complete Writings) ed. Gao Pingshu (Beijing: Zhonghua shuju, 1984), Vol. III, p. 21.

[21]Adam Liu Yuen-ching, The Hanlin Academy: Training Ground for the Ambitious (Connecticut: Archon Books, 1981). A British observer in the 19th century commented "The whole of China may be said to resemble one vast university, which is governed by the scholars who have been educated within its walls", quoted in Teng Ssu-yu, "Chinese Influence on the Western Examination System", Harvard Journal of Asiatic Studies, Vol. 7, No. 4 (1942), p. 290.

serving the imperial examination system or a suppression which they could not easily counter.[22]

After the revolution of 1911 and the overthrow of the imperial system, the task of creating a new role for the university in modern China fell to Cai Yuanpei, first in his brief tenure as Minister of Education, when he drafted the first republican higher education legislation, later more substantively in his leadership of Beijing University as Chancellor from 1917 to 1923, and finally in his attempts to establish the framework for an 'apolitical' university which should protect the whole national education system from political manipulation under the Nationalist government (1927-1949). Cai had spent a total of 8 years in Europe, partly in France but mainly in Germany, where he studied at the universities of Berlin and Leipzig. Clearly the spirit of the university of Berlin, created by Wilhelm von Humboldt a century earlier, left a deep impression on him and inspired him with the vision of a modern Chinese university that would play a totally different role *vis-a-vis* China's modern government than the traditional relationship between Chinese intellectual institutions and the imperial government.

The legislation drafted by Cai in 1912 defined the aim of the modern university as teaching and research in advanced scholarship and forming persons with broad learning for the needs of the country. On the European model, Cai identified a collection of modern knowledge disciplines, then classified them as pertaining to scholarship (*xue*), including the pure arts and sciences, or as pertaining to professional development (*shu*), covering the professions of medicine, engineering, agriculture, law and commerce. To be called a university (*daxue*), the legislation stipulated that a higher institution had to have a curriculum made up of 1) pure disciplines of the arts and sciences or 2) arts plus law, or commerce or 3) sciences plus medicine, agriculture or engineering.[23]

---

[22]John Meskill, Academies in Ming China (Arizona: University of Arizona Press, 1982).

[23]Cai Yuanpei Quanji, Vol. II, p. 283.

When Cai became Chancellor of Beijing University in 1917, he had the opportunity of putting into practice the principles drawn from his European experience which had informed the legislation of 1912 but had had little effect on the actual conditions of Chinese higher education in the intervening years. Looking back on the period in 1917, he noted how most higher institutions were dedicated to professional training in law, commerce and other practical fields and the students were not interested in scholarship but in a certificate that would enable them to find positions within the corrupt warlord bureaucracy.[24] It may have been this observation which strengthened his determination to turn Beijing university into a truly scholarly institution, removing commerce and engineering and having them combined with other professional higher institutions, in order to focus on the pure arts and sciences, which he saw as integrated under the fundamental unity of philosophy.

Beijing University became a self-governing institution, the first to have its own senate, and Cai's great hopes for its national and even global role can be seen in the article he wrote for the inaugural issue of its scholarly journal in 1917. The role of a research university, he wrote, was not simply to introduce European research achievements, but to build upon these achievements progressive new discoveries of its own. It was not simply to preserve the essence of Chinese national culture, but to use scientific methods in exploring and exposing this essence. He encouraged Beida's research scholars and students to make use of what simple facilities the university was able to provide in order to produce something new which would contribute both to national scholarship and to the world scholarly community.[25]

The heady atmosphere created by China's first real university, shaped according to the western values of autonomy and academic freedom, soon overflowed into national and international political activities with the May 4th Movement of 1919. Chinese students and scholars under Beida's leadership

---

[24] Cai Yuanpei Quanji, Vol. III, p. 110.

[25] Cai Yuanpei Quanji, Vol. III, p. 210.

succeeded in preventing China's signature to the Treaty of Versailles with its humiliating implications for Chinese sovereignty.[26] In this movement, Cai was caught between a national government determined to suppress student activism and an intellectual community of his own creation which could not limit their scholarly research interests to pure fields of knowledge in face of national and international conditions threatening China's very existence in the modern world of nations. His resignation and return some months later at the insistence of both the university community and the government did not solve the question of the legitimacy of government intervention on the one hand (in suppressing the student movement) or of direct student/faculty political involvement on the other.[27]

This was clearly an issue which he thought about very deeply in the ensuing years, and with the long awaited establishment of a genuine republican government under the Nationalist Party in 1927 he attempted to settle it for once and for all. As a trusted member of the Party and probably China's most widely respected scholar, he tried to establish, in place of a ministry of education, a national scholarly academy which would be headed by an academician and composed of the presidents of all of China's universities. They, in turn would control all educational institutions within the university district which they headed.

Clearly inspired by the French exemplar, Cai tried to legislate for an absolute separation between education and politics by ensuring the legal independence of this academy and safeguarding the university community's role in conserving, advancing and disseminating knowledge.[28] While this plan failed, Cai did succeed in keeping some distance between politics and the university by preventing the Nationalist Party

---

[26]Chow Tse-tsung, The May 4th Movement (Stanford: Stanford University Press, 1960).

[27]See Cai Yuanpei Quanji, Vol. III, pp. 312, 341 for Cai's letter of resignation and speech on return to the university.

[28]A. Linden, "Politics and Education in Nationalist China: The Case of the University Council 1927-1928", Journal of Asian Studies, Vol. 27, No. 4 (August, 1966), pp. 763-776.

from turning the well organised national student movement into the political arm of the Party among China's youth. Instead the movement was disbanded and student activism was to be contained within individual university campuses and directed towards local concerns rather than national or international issues.[29]

The values of university autonomy and academic freedom, which Cai strove to promote, were not easily adopted by Chinese institutions whose cultural and political conditions were so different from those of Europe and North America. Nevertheless, with Beida in the lead, some universities did become institutions of considerable scholarly reputation. When, in 1931, the League of Nations Institute of Intellectual Cooperation was invited by the Nationalist government to send four experts to study the Chinese education system and make recommendations for reform, they commented on the achievements made in creating a modern higher education system, probably the most successful aspect of Nationalist educational efforts. They suggested the further enhancement of the system through measures which drew on European scholarly values, the strengthening of academic disciplines, the establishment of chairs in the basic disciplines to stimulate the advancement of knowledge, standardized examinations to be used both at the end of upper secondary for unified recruitment purposes and at the end of university to ensure high standards of knowledge acquisition, the strict monitoring of academic appointments on a national basis to ensure high standards and the subjection of the whole system to financial and geographical rationalization.[30]

Some of these reform measures were adopted, as can be seen in Nationalist legislation for the years from 1933 to 1937.[31] While they may have contributed to the remarkable vigour of the Chinese university community in these years, a vigour which helped sustain its activities under war-time conditions of

---

[29] John Israel, Student Nationalism in China 1927-1937 (Stanford: Hoover Institution Press, 1966).

[30] C.H. Becker et. al., The Reorganization of Education in China (Paris: Institute of Intellectual Cooperation, 1932).

[31] Jiaoyu faling (Shanghai: Zhonghua shuju, 1947), pp. 144-7, 182.

retreat to the interior from 1937 to 1945,[32] they also proved useful to the Nationalist government as tools of political repression. Activist scholars and students could be subjected to harassment through the rigid application of the monitoring process for academic appointments and renewals of contract, and through academic entrance and graduation examinations. University presidents differed in the degree to which they allowed pressure from Nationalist Party cells within the university to affect academic decision-making, but there were enormous pressures for academic freedom to be transmuted into a new intellectual authority which legitimated Nationalist government policy and increased the differences between progressive scholars critical of the regime and the government.

Although the League's intervention did not involve financial aid, it served to confer prestige and international respectability on a set of policies which strengthened the hand of a government becoming more and more repressive in its style of operation. Policies justified in terms of "academic standards" proved in reality to be useful tools for political control. This aspect of China's historical experience has much in common with that of many developing countries where the political allegiance of university students and scholars is crucial to the survival of national governments, and where a position of economic weakness in the international community makes for a deep concern within the scholarly community over issues of national foreign policy. This concern cannot rest content with academic analysis; it is likely to find expression in activist measures which threaten government itself. Bi-lateral and multi-lateral aid from powerful institutions that represent the political and economic interests of Europe and North America may thus create tensions in university-government relations which are likely to be far more severe than those experienced in the first and second worlds.[33] The absence of a cultural tradition in which university autonomy and academic freedom are well understood further exacerbates the situation. In many

---

[32]Cha Liangzheng (ed.), Kangzhan yilai zhi gaodeng jiaoyu (Higher Education in the war-time period), special issue of Jiaoyu zazhi, Vol. 31, No. 1, (1941), (republished in Hong Kong: Zhonghua Chuju, 1966).

[33]P. Altbach (ed.), The Student Revolution: A Global Analysis (Bombay: Lalvani Press, 1970); Donald Emmerson (ed.) Students and Politics in the Developing World (New York: Praeger, 1968).

developing countries this tension is resolved by the extreme measure of closing down the university or creating an alternative set of higher institutions.

The case of Cai Yuanpei is an instructive one. He tried to develop in China modern institutions embodying the values of university autonomy and academic freedom. Yet in a Chinese cultural environment suffused with traditions of intellectual authority and a scholarly dictatorship, these western values were easily coopted to the service of political repression.

What might have protected China's universities from a level of intervention that was finally to destroy them was the revitalization of progressive values of intellectual freedom which had been nurtured by Daoist thought and found institutional expression in the *shuyuan* of traditional China. These might have laid a foundation for a modern Chinese university less vulnerable to political manipulation and more able to generate the kinds of knowledge which could contribute to healthy economic and political development. Cai was not unaware of this. He shared with Mao Zedong a great admiration for the *shuyuan* tradition and for such institutions as the Hunan Self-Study University which both saw as embodying some of its values in a modern form.[34] However, when it came to establishing a formal higher education system, his recourse to western values of autonomy and academic freedom made the system vulnerable to underlying values of intellectual authority and scholarly domination issuing from the Confucian tradition. Conflicts between progressives and a Nationalist government which had gained international legitimacy for its repressive measures through the use of western academic terminology erupted in open violence by the forties and finally culminated in the success of the Communist revolution in 1949.

The University and Government in Communist China

Mao and other Communist leaders had both an understanding of progressive aspects of the Chinese scholarly tradition and

---

[34] For Cai's admiration of the Hunan Self-Study University, see the article he wrote about it in Xin jiaoyu Vol. 5, No. 1-2 (August, 1922), pp. 81-89. For the links Mao drew between the *shuyuan* tradition and the Hunan Self-Study University, see Zhang Liuquan, Zhongguo shuyuan shihua (Beijing: Jiaoyu kexue chubanshe, 1981), p. 135.

experience, in Yan'an and other border regions, in creating higher institutions which expressed an approach to scholarship both modern and Chinese. Yet when they came to power in 1949, they followed a similar short-cut to that taken by Cai Yuanpei - modelling their "modern" university on a foreign source, this time the Soviet Union rather than Germany. Soviet success with socialist modernization was seen as the model for China. The Soviet Union was prepared to give substantial aid for industrialization and for the creation of a higher education system suited to the new period. What resulted was not really a university system but an alternative that appeared more suitable to China's needs.

The first key point of departure from Cai's views was the separation of teaching and research. A national Academy of Sciences was made responsible for major scientific research projects, and the higher education system was given a mandate solely for advanced teaching, not for research. In 1952 the disciplines of knowledge, and the way in which they were organized in higher institutions, were reformed - a task similar in scope and dimension to that carried out by Cai Yuanpei in 1912. The concern was to ensure that the knowledge being transmitted had maximum relevance to socialist modernization needs. The pure disciplines of the arts and sciences were preserved in 14 "comprehensive universities" which were to nurture theoreticians and researchers, similar to Cai's aims in 1912. A parallel group of polytechnical universities, also directly administered by the Ministry of Higher Education, would transmit the range of applied scientific disciplines. With the exception of six normal universities and a few language institutes, all other higher institutions were administered by specialist ministries, agriculture, public health, metallurgy, machine building, railways etc., which shaped the knowledge content to fit the precise manpower needs of the economic sector for which they were responsible. Provincially administered higher institutions likewise were closely coordinated to meet provincial manpower needs. With the possible exception of the 14 comprehensive universities, these institutes were not universities in the western sense of the term. They were manpower training institutions.

However, this new system seemed well suited to China's needs. It served to overcome what had appeared to be the frivolity of broad commitment to academic knowledge which had characterized the Nationalist regime and the bourgeois scholars it had produced. Communist leadership recognized the need for the new higher education system to have a guiding intellectual rationale, but it would no longer be drawn from the European university tradition with its values of autonomy and academic freedom. At the core of the system, in place of philosophy, which Cai had seen as the unifying discipline of the university, they placed Marxist-Leninist teachings in political economy, giving to them the responsibility of bringing together all forms of knowledge in some comprehensive, intelligible way that would make sense of China's new road to development.

As Cai had striven to create one university, Beida, which would be an examplar of the truly modern Chinese university, the Communist leadership singled out People's University as the institution to lead the way in transforming China's universities for their role in socialist China. Its curriculum encompassed all the 'modern' social sciences, law, political economy, economic planning and cooperatives, as well as diplomacy and Russian. It was to provide both accelerated academic programs for the new cadres of the Communist regime and political science teachers who would be given positions throughout the higher education system and use the 'modern' social theory that they had acquired to transform the consciousness of students and academics. From 1957, the People's University also embraced the more traditional social science disciplines, such as philosophy, history and economics, and accepted some students through regular academic channels, as well as those being groomed for particular positions of power.[35]

Stalin himself was said to have been involved in the planning of People's University and right across the street from its campus in the North West suburbs of Beijing was the large complex which housed all of the Soviet experts sent to assist China's modernization efforts. A large number of these Russian specialists worked within departments of People's University, and the university was responsible for translating quantities of Russian social science texts into Chinese and disseminating

---

[35]C.T. Hu, "The Chinese People's University: Bastion of Marxism-Leninism" in Universities Facing the Future ed. W.R. Niblett and R.F. Butts (London: Evans Brothers, 1972).

them throughout the Chinese higher education system.

People's University thus stood at the peak of a sustained effort to transform the consciousness of China's intellectual community and enlist its whole-hearted support for, and commitment to, socialist modernization tasks. The Communist government was able to consolidate and transform the traditional Chinese values of intellectual authority and scholarly monopoly of power with much greater success than the Nationalist government. The scholarly community was to elaborate and disseminate the Marxist-Leninist texts which constituted the basis of socialist government. People's University had the role of arbiter of correct knowledge within the university system, a role similar to that of the Hanlin Academy in traditional China.

The challenge to this development lay in the issue of bi-lateral aid. The new higher education edifice was modelled exactly after Soviet patterns and held in place by an institution which not only expressed authoritatively the economic and social theories vital to socialist modernization but constituted a direct channel for the penetration of Soviet personnel, texts and materials. The way in which knowledge was regimented throughout the system made this penetration very successful.

My own sense of the situation is that the re-instatement of harmony between government and university, and of intellectual authority in a revived Confucianism turned to modern ends, might have been successful if it had not come to be seen as a mechanism for subordinating China to the political and economic interests of the Soviet Union. The Confucian role which China's Communist leaders gave to the scholarly community, particularly to People' University, could easily be accepted and effectively carried out. However, when these scholars came to be seen as the agents of foreign penetration in a world situation in which the Soviet Union assigned China to a position suited to its own political interests, they came under strong criticism. It seems clear that the Soviet "aid" of the fifties had real economic benefits for China's industrialization,[36] but, on a political level, the Chinese found Soviet domination unacceptable. Relations between the two

---

[36] A. Eckstein, China's Economic Revolution (Cambridge: Cambridge University Press, 1977).

nations became strained and resulted in an open split in 1960, with the sudden withdrawal of all Soviet aid.[37]

China's strident criticism of Soviet socialist imperialism in the early sixties, after the Soviet withdrawal, was parallelled by a strong anti-authoritarian movement within the universities, which finally culminated in chaos during the Cultural Revolution. For a time all universities were closed. When they were re-opened in 1971, massive efforts were made to transform the content of curricula away from the Soviet-defined specializations, teaching plans, course outlines and texts of the fifties towards practical areas of knowledge linked to local economic and political needs. The institution which was to have led the way to socialist modernity, People's University, remained closed for the full decade from 1967 to 1978, as did the four regional institutes of political science and law, which had extended its role of educating leading cadres and teachers for the socialist system.

I'd like to suggest that the dominance exercised by People's University over Chinese society became unacceptable because of the close linkage of bi-lateral aid to Soviet political and economic interests. Chinese government interference in the higher education system was not really the issue. China's modern universities naturally adopted the role of being the intellectual arm of government, responsible for a scholarly legitimation of government policy. It was within their traditions - they did not strive for the university autonomy and academic freedom which in the West is seen as synonymous with the idea of the university. However, when this harmony of interest between scholarly community and government was set against national interests, when it was seen in the context of world power relations, within which Soviet bi-lateral aid began to be perceived as a measure for maintaining China in a subordinate position to Soviet interests, it was no longer acceptable. In my opinion, the extremism of the Cultural Revolution and the passion with which universities were attacked for their role in legitimating an oppressive government was linked to this international situation.

---

[37] John Gittings, Survey of the Sino-Soviet Dispute (London: Oxford University Press, 1968).

230

China's two historical experiences of multi-lateral and bi-lateral aid thus have interesting implications for the present, when her universities are experiencing unprecedented access to all forms of interaction with the world academic community, particularly that part which is dominated by the OECD countries. In the case of the multi-lateral League of Nations' intervention, serious efforts were made to shape institutional patterns which would give fuller expression to the European vision of autonomy and academic freedom, seen as vital to genuine scholarship. The actual result, however, in China's internal political conditions of the time, was to strengthen the hand of an authoritarian government, exacerbating the contradictions which led many university scholars to ally themselves with the Communist cause.

In the case of the fifties and sixties, a reformed set of institutions of higher education, headed by People's University, was intended to serve socialist modernization, making possible a whole new beginning for China within the modern world. However, bi-lateral aid, expressed through knowledge patterns which came to be seen as tools of political control, strengthened the forces which finally erupted in the Cultural Revolution of 1966. External aid to the university again contributed to revolutionary ferment. The intellectuals were torn between the attractiveness of the revolutionary educational aspirations put forward by Mao and a commitment to forms of knowledge tested by time and the development experience of Europe and the Soviet Union.

China's recent history thus demonstrates the tremendous sensitivity and delicacy of the issue of foreign aid to the Chinese university. Western assumptions about autonomy and academic freedom simply do not hold in China's very different scholarly climate. Any form of aid which comes to be perceived as an instrument of intellectual imperialism is likely to prove abortive in the long term. China's historical experience is unique, yet political and cultural sensitivity of a parallel nature are clearly present in most universities of the developing world which are being subjected to intervention through international aid projects.

Implications for Current Bi-Lateral and Multi-Lateral Aid to Chinese Universities

The historical discussion which has formed the main body of this paper draws attention to issues which are crucial to the long-term success of present bi-lateral and multi-lateral aid programs. China's pre-Liberation experience showed how foreign aid conferred international scholarly prestige on forms of knowledge organization that served Nationalist government manipulation, thus stimulating among progressive scholars more and more sympathy for the Communist revolutionary cause. European academicism in the Chinese context actually contributed to Liberation and thereby to its own demise as a meaningful discourse in Chinese universities.

Soviet academicism appeared to promise the Chinese Communist leaders a higher education system that could serve socialist modernization. Ironically, however, it too served a government which came to be perceived as foreign dominated and oppressive, and so it contributed to its own demise in the Cultural Revolution of 1966. Soviet aid was not perceived as engaging Chinese scholars in a creative participatory way, but as imposing a structure and organization of knowledge that ultimately served Soviet interests. The fact that research was removed as a primary function of the university exacerbated this situation, leaving no forum for the re-interpretation and adaptation of the foreign knowledge being introduced. While Chinese intellectuals now condemn the Cultural Revolution, the truth is that many of them were deeply ambivalent at its outbreak in 1966, identifying with the need to transform the structure and organization of knowledge, if not with its more radical aspects.

After the Cultural Revolution patterns were rejected in 1978, the Soviet-derived patterns of the fifties were re-instated, in the absence of any acceptable alternative. However, this did not signify a return to centre stage of Soviet academic discourse and Soviet educational assistance. Rather it opened up a period in which Chinese scholars have had the space and time to digest and gradually revise the Soviet legacy, discarding certain aspects of it in their subsequent reforms. Probably the most significant of these is the restoration of the research function to universities. There have also been changes in the structure and organization of higher education towards greater curricular flexibility and adaptability.[38]

In this new situation, a whole set of bi-lateral and multi-lateral aid projects have been initiated with major nations of the OECD and with the World Bank. These represent a new form of international intervention in China's universities and the historical sketch above leads us to ask whether the knowledge flowing into Chinese institutions, and the ways in which that knowledge is constituted, will support good relations between the Chinese university and government or whether, once again, the academicians will be led into roles that come to be seen as serving foreign rather than national interests. This conviction accompanied revolution in both the Nationalist and the Communist periods. Will China's university scholars be indicted for acting as the intellectual arm of policies that favour the world interests of OECD countries? Or will they not only be able to interpret, adapt and domesticate the foreign knowledge but do so in such a way as to be seen to make an independent, balanced and critical contribution to China's development within the world community?

Elsewhere, I have analyzed in detail both the policy and practice of the educational aid of major OECD nations to China.[39] Here I will consider briefly only the cases of USA and France, since they have adopted rather different approaches, each of which has serious implications for the Chinese scholarly community. I will also consider issues raised by the extensive involvement of the World Bank in China's higher education reform.[40]

American intellectual involvement in China has two different sides. While official governmental support is given to forms of intellectual cooperation that make possible joint research, a

---

[38] R. Hayhoe, "China's Higher Curricular Reform in Historical Perspective", China Quarterly, No. 110 (June, 1987).

[39] R. Hayhoe, China's Universities and the Open Door (in press), chapters five and six.

[40] Ibid. chapter seven.

strengthening of American intelligence about China and the introduction of American approaches to the social sciences, another whole range and level of cooperation takes place through university-level linkages which receive little American government support and have created a spontaneous set of contacts and relations. Governmental aid is channelled through the Fullbright program, which supports centres for teaching American literature, history and culture within Chinese universities, as well as the presence of Chinese scholars and university teachers in American universities. These provide important conditions for mutual intellectual understanding and there is little evidence of their being used as channels for control or dominance in an overt way. However, the other major official support program, the National Centre for the Management of Industrial Science and Technology which is located at the Dalian Institute of Technology (DIT), a major Chinese polytechnical university, may have more serious implications for the Chinese university and its relation to government.

The Dalian Centre was created in 1980 as a result of a protocol between the U.S. Department of Commerce and the Chinese State Economic Commission. Its aim was to offer training in American management theory and technology to Chinese managers at senior and mid-levels. This was recently extended to include an MBA program in cooperation with the State University of New York at Buffalo, for the formation of young talent in the field of management. American government support contributes to the salaries of the American academics and law and business magnates who lecture in the program. In addition, the American corporate world has contributed considerable financial support, mainly through donations of equipment. A large number of Chinese managers have been trained in this program, and many of them have moved up within the Chinese bureaucracy as a consequence.[41] Political penetration in terms of an American concern for China's re-integration into the world capitalist order through the adoption

---

[41] One graduate of the program, for example, became chairman of the Communist Youth League and subsequently head of the Communist Party's central office.

of "rationalized" forms of administration is clear. One American professor even went so far as to claim 10 percent credit for the Dalian centre in the success of Deng Xiaoping's pragmatic policies! Whatever one thinks about such claims, the economic advantages to the United States of knowledge of the state of the Chinese economy and a network of linkages through the growing group of Dalian graduates are unmistakable. This alumni network seems to have broken through the traditional vertical integration patterns of the Chinese economic structure and created new horizontal links across sectors and echelons.[42]

But what has been the consequence for the Chinese university? How is this intervention likely to affect its relation to the Chinese government? No parallel network of influence has been created in the university community, although a consortium of 8 universities were originally linked with the Dalian Institute in the project. They have now withdrawn, and DIT itself is extremely frustrated. Rather than becoming a school of management for the university and contributing to a national university network of management schools, the Centre has been kept closely affiliated with the State Economic Commission (SEC). This was the preference of both the U.S. Department of Commerce and the SEC, which has created its own system of management institutes, including parallel institutes organized in cooperation with Japan, West Germany, Canada and the European Economic Community. These are entirely outside the higher education system, they have no links with Chinese universities.[43]

On the Chinese side there is deep concern with the need to foster research into management theory and practice, as well as to form a strong body of teachers for the Centre. On the American side there is much interest in strengthening the network of management talent within the Chinese economic system itself. The adaptation of American management theory

---

[42]R. Hayhoe, "Penetration or Mutuality?" documents reports on this development which constituted American embassy attempts at evaluating the project.

[43]*Ibid.*

and technique to the Chinese context is thus taking place in a situation where practice within the system is the major mechanism for the interpretation of foreign theory. The university community, with its interest in, and talent for, reflective theoretical scholarship is excluded. A whole new set of intellectual institutions are being created which have no connection with the university system but are intended to serve economic development needs directly under the State Economic Commission. There is the danger that a split may emerge between the supposedly neutral managerial techniques fostered through the SEC centres and likely to have wide coinage in the economic system, and the approaches to management developed in the Chinese universities which are likely to be more consciously theoretical and to take seriously the task of adapting western theory to Chinese socialist thought.

The problem with American bi-lateral aid is that it has three sources, not necessarily in unanimity, not predictable and not controllable: governmental aid, indirect government aid by means of American official support to U.S. academics and students (many of whom will be opposed to their government) and corporate aid in search of influence and ultimately of markets. The former seeks to subordinate China to its world influence and alignments. The Chinese government recognizes that fact and will accommodate it as far as it is in their interests but they cannot become vulnerable to the charge of being "lackeys of American imperialism". If governmental bi-lateral aid is far-sighted rather than short-sighted it will not rest with the Dalian type of assistance but see a strength in Chinese scholarly adaptation of western management to socialist goals and Chinese traditions of public administration.

However, the great promise of bi-lateral American aid is that it also involves experts and academics - essentially uncontrollable people. If American and Chinese academics can interact long enough to "learn each other's language", there will be a fruitful adaptation, a sharing of wisdom and knowledge from both sides because both sets of scholars are fuelled by curiosity and both regard "learning" as a challenge.

In this regard, unofficial forms of cooperation between American and Chinese universities seem to offer promise for an approach to bi-lateral aid that will strengthen Chinese intellectuals' ability to articulate, interpret and legitimate the modernization being tried out by current Chinese leaders. One example that shows possibilities of mutuality is the Hopkins-Nanda Center, jointly established by Johns Hopkins and Nanjing universities on Nanjing's campus. There collaborative teaching and research in a broad range of the social sciences began this year. While the American side expects that participating American students will be persons likely to take up careers in business, journalism and diplomacy, the Chinese hope that some of the young participants will become scholars for the burgeoning social science departments of Chinese universities. The opportunity they have to gain an understanding of such practical fields as management and foreign policy against the background of a wide-ranging program in political science, economics, history and sociology offers some promise for conditions in which a foundation can be laid for a solid Chinese intellectual adaptation process.

In reflecting on the American approach to bi-lateral aid, I wish to return to the four values suggested as a framework for judging the legitimacy of such projects. While the Dalian approach to American government intervention has legitimacy on the level of equity - in the sense that it is based upon the mutual agreement of both governments and can't be held to be an American imposition, the Hopkins-Nanda project seems to approach a deeper legitimacy at the level of autonomy, a potential for strengthening the independence of China's intellectual community. This could be the key to avoiding the kinds of contradictions which were exacerbated by western and Soviet interventions in China's historical experience and erupted into open revolution in both cases.

In the French approach the issue of cultural autonomy has even greater centrality within the educational aid and cooperation that is underway. The French have not so far jumped on the bandwagon of the cooperative management institutes, with their promise of short-term economic benefits. They have focused their aid on a major comprehensive university in central China - Wuhan University. Through an unusual agreement between the French Ministry of Foreign Affairs and Wuhan University, first signed in 1980, Wuhan was earmarked as the national centre of intellectual cooperation with France. The French send 12-15 French professors each year in fields such as mathematics, sciences and French language and literature. The Chinese have made special arrangements for cooperative teaching within the departments of mathematics and French. They have also established a multi-disciplinary social science research centre on French problems. Each year up to ten Wuhan faculty spend a year in research or study in France, and gradually a community of Chinese scholars with a shared exposure to French culture is taking shape.

The knowledge emphasis of this project is of special significance. Theoretical disciplines (mathematics, sciences and literature) provided the initial focus. Gradually, however, cooperation in applied fields, such as engineering and management, has come under discussion. This means there are conditions for cultural autonomy and for the creative re-interpretation and adaptation of the knowledge and technology being introduced from France.

If the standards of equity and autonomy are met in the French case, and in some aspects of the American case, standards of solidarity and participation are much more difficult to achieve within the context of bi-lateral aid projects. Solidarity refers to the creation of local networks of cooperation involving a large number of persons in the task of critically and collectively re-interpreting foreign-derived knowledge. Participation as the creative theoretical involvement of peripheral scholars cannot easily be extended to include a large proportion of the Chinese scholarly community since the projects of bi-lateral cooperation have limited scope and resources.

In conclusion, I'd like to turn to the activity of the World Bank in Chinese higher education, since it is precisely in relation to solidarity and participation that it shows promise. Between 1980 and 1986 eight higher education projects have been organized with World Bank assistance, and a total of nearly one billion U.S. dollars (mostly in soft loans) has been borrowed, with an even greater financial commitment from the Chinese side. There can be little doubt on the issue of equity in this relationship. The Chinese have shaped the projects to suit their own views of the needs of the four modernizations. As for autonomy, the only question at issue might be the overwhelming emphasis on the applied physical sciences, on the purchase of sophisticated equipment rather than of books -

a situation not conducive to the strengthening of theoretical reflection and cultural vitality. However, the eclectic nature of the external cultural influences being introduced through these projects does not make foreign domination as serious a threat as it might otherwise be.

Where World Bank projects hold promise is in the areas of solidarity and participation. Altogether 186 Chinese higher institutions are taking part in the eight projects now underway, a scope of involvement that would be impossible under conditions of bi-lateral aid. These 186 institutions are geographically located in all of China's provinces except Tibet and over the four echelons of the higher education system - local institutions under city governments, provincial institutions, national institutions under specialist ministries and national universities under the State Education Commission. In the past only higher institutions at the national level had the opportunity for serious cooperation and exchange with foreign universities, so a whole new group of actors have been brought into the international arena through World Bank projects.

Of the eight projects, four are administered through the ministries of agriculture and public health, all involving agricultural and medical universities. In these projects the ministries exercise strong Chinese supervision, inviting foreign consultants of their own choice, mainly overseas Chinese, as needed. The other four projects are administered through the State Education Commission and involve local, provincial and national higher institutions. In order to ensure academic quality in the implementation of these projects, it was agreed between both sides for two parallel bodies to advise on implementation, the Chinese Review Commission and the International Advisory Panel, composed of distinguished scholars from China and from the OECD countries respectively. The role of these two bodies may be of special importance as a kind of buffer ensuring the application of scholarly criteria to the four university development projects and assuring the integration of the Chinese intellectual community with that of the OECD nations.

Both by its scope and a cultural eclecticism involving Japanese, South Asian, European and North American scholars, World Bank assistance seems to provide conditions for a critical and participatory contribution of the Chinese scholarly community to Chinese national development and to the world academic community. However, the other side of the picture, one that should not be overlooked, is the fact that the World Bank represents the political and economic interests of the OECD nations and China's long-term allegiance to these interests cannot be counted upon. If China's scholars are able to digest in a critical and discriminatory way knowledge drawn from World Bank networks and assist their nation to chart an independent yet integrative course within the world community, current aid projects may have long-term benefits for all. If, however, foreign knowledge is transferred mechanistically and can be held to be assuring the global dominance of these countries at China's expense, the present rapprochement with the advanced capitalist world is not likely to last. That, at least, seems to be the lesson of the Soviet aid in the fifties.

Government Intervention and University Autonomy in Guyana and Tanzania - A Third World Perspective

by

Vivian D.O. Patterson[1]

Introduction

That we question the legitimacy of government intervention in higher education is a symptom. All over the Western World universities are becoming concerned about government intervention in university affairs. Historically the presumption of non-government intervention in the university has its genesis in the concepts of university autonomy and academic freedom, and is also related to the "idea" or the "ideal" of the university.

University autonomy has been defined as "essentially the freedom to use resources and to define and execute programs consonant with institutional (university) purposes".[2] Among others, such purposes involve decisions on students, programs, faculty, instructional practices and research. In fact, it is these very areas that Governments today seek to influence, even control. Often, the rationale advanced for such intervention is the concern over university accountability for the increasingly large amounts of public funds spent on universities.

---

[1] Ph.D. Student, Higher Education Group, OISE, Toronto, ON.

[2] For more extensive treatment of the concept of university autonomy see: Paul L. Dressel and W.H. Faricy, Return to Responsibility, Chapters 1-3, (San Francisco: Jossey-Bass Inc., 1972), pp. 1-47. The concept of academic freedom has been defined by, among others, Sir Robert Birley KCMG, The Real Meaning of Academic Freedom, (UK: World University Service, 1972); and Edmund L. Princoffes, The Concept of Academic Freedom, (University of Texas Press, 1972).

In view of the political weight and the financial burden of universities, Governments show an increasing tendency to make them accountable to the public and to strengthen central control of finances, teaching and research, personnel appointments and curricula.[3]

But this is not the only reason why governments seek to influence and control universities. I shall return to this point later.

Meanwhile, it is instructive to note that a fundamental component of university autonomy is that "it recognizes professional competency and its role in fulfilling the purposes of the university. Without any autonomy, the university probably could not exist as we understand the term today".[4] Polin was more emphatic than Dressell and Faricy in his convictions about the autonomy of the university. He is convinced that:

> Any individual worthy of the academic vocation, considers the autonomy of the university an essential condition of its existence. For the university is par excellence, the place where people gather who are devoted to the life and freedom of the mind. The activities of the mind, from whence spring every culture, are imagination, invention, creation and synthesis. These require the absence of any external authority or constraint. In a word ... mind is freedom. Universities are associations created to cultivate the activities of the mind, that is to say, the activities of freedom. Their mission is the pursuit of truth through freedom, the free work of the mind ... Autonomy of the university is intrinsic to our understanding of education. It is necessary for fertile

---

[3]Dietrich Goldschmidt, "The University as an Institution Present Problems and Future Trends", Higher Education in Europe, Vol. IX, No. 4, (October-December, 1984), pp. 66.

[4]Dressell and Faricy, Return to Responsibility, p. 14.

teaching, effective research and creative invention.[5]

Writing in a similar vein, Moos and Rourke observed:

> The case for the freedom of the university ... rests upon a characteristic of Higher Education that it does not come close to sharing with any other state activity. This is the fact that in certain areas, Colleges and Universities need freedom, not merely as an administrative convenience to enhance their efficient co-operation, but as a source of creative energy, and as an indispensable means to all other achievements. For without freedom, productive teaching and research in the Western tradition are impossible.[6]

Comparable perceptions of university autonomy have been expressed by many writers, not the least among whom are Bok, Graham *et. al.*, Kerr and Gasset.[7]

The ideals of university autonomy and academic freedom have been largely adopted by universities in less developed countries (LDCs) where also the institutional forms of western universities have been introduced, often with a zeal which seems to equate the precision of the institutional copy with the

---

[5]Raymond Polin, "Freedom of the Mind and University Autonomy", in John W. Chapman The Western University on Trial (Berkeley: University of California Press, 1983), p. 39.

[6]Malcolm Moos and Francis Rourke, The Campus and the State (Baltimore: John Hopkins Press, 1959), cited in, Edward R. Hines and L.S. Hartmark, Politics of Higher Education Higher Education Report No. 7, (American Association of Higher Education, 1980), p. 19.

[7]See Derek Bok, Beyond the Ivory Tower: Social Responsibilities of the Modern University, (Cambridge: Harvard University Press, 1982); Andrew Graham *et. al.*, Neutrality and Impartiality - The University and Political Commitment (London: Cambridge University Press, 1975); Clark Kerr, The Uses of the University, Cambridge: Harvard University Press, 1982) and Ortega y Gasset, The Mission of the University (Princeton: Princeton University Press, 1944).

academic rigour and social relevance it is presumed the parent prototype represents.

With the extension of the western university in LDCs, the "ideal" of the university has also been transferred.[8] Universities, as dominantly conceived today, represent an international community of scholars, who implicitly or explicitly subscribe to the "ideal" of the university. And within this framework the necessity for university autonomy represents the linchpin on which the international academic community exhibits greatest agreement.

It is understandable, therefore, that any contravention of the hallowed principle of autonomy is invariably seen as a serious threat to the "idea" and the "ideal" of the university. Hence, the very legitimacy of government intervention in higher education is questioned.

Such intervention signals a "call to arms", not only by the local academics directly affected by the edict of some government, but also, if only in rhetoric, by the international academic community as well. Such intervention is seen to strike at the heart of the very nature of the university.

The following statement by Rosenfield is a good example:

> Universities in our societies (i.e., United States and Canada) must remain true to their essential natures and true to those principles that guarantee our academic freedom as well as all the other freedoms and liberties we cherish. That is to say, that we must recognize our obligations as not merely national and regional, they are also international. We must recognize that the world of true scholarship is indivisible and that no person or group, no nation, no state has a monopoly on truth, we must recognize that one of our legitimate functions is social criticism

---

[8]For discussion of the concepts of the "idea" and "ideal" of the university see John H. Newman, "Oxford" in The Idea of a University: Defined and Illustrated (Oxford: Clarendon Press, 1976) and Ortega y Gasset, The Mission of the University.

and, moreover, criticism that is aimed at society's renewal. We must recognize that the open society demands that we resist to like the stultifying effect of narrow nationalism and the constraints of artificially contrived political and ideological boundaries."[9]

And he went on to make the rather significant observation that:

If isolationism is dangerous in the political sphere, it is deadly in the world of the university.[10]

These observations of Rosenfield introduce two other salient dimensions of university autonomy *cum* academic freedom, both of which are crucial to a discussion of the legitimacy of government intervention in higher education, in such developing countries as Guyana and Tanzania. The first attests to a vested political interest in retaining accustomed Western conception of university autonomy and academic freedom. The second is fundamentally academic and testifies to an institutional interest in internationalizing standards and in the objective search for advanced knowledge. Within this framework, university autonomy and academic freedom are perceived as proxy indicators of the existence of such institutional standards, however defined.

On these observations, we cite below, the rationale which Rosenfield advances for international reaction to charges of "infringement" of academic freedom:

• The academic world is truly a transnational one.

• Lingering concerns over the behaviour of German universities during the rise and infamous reign of Nazism.

---

[9]Rosenfield, "Attacks on Academic Freedom in Foreign Countries", Tape Recording of Speech Delivered at OISE, 1985 - Call No. RT 1985 AV.

[10]*Ibid.*

- The facile distribution of information due to modern means of communication.

- The association of the absence of academic freedom with the absence of human rights.

- Human rights, including academic freedom, have become instruments of cold war in the lesser conflicts in the world, so the denial of academic freedom amounts to a political statement prejudicial to one of the two dominant political ideologies.

- The Western world wishes that the "standards" it possess be more generally shared by the rest of the world. It protests the absence of the standards in order to "encourage improvement" and "promote our own (i.e. Western) goals".[11]

Rosenfield also makes the point that to fail to respond to "infringements of academic freedom" is to be "complicit in the erosion of freedom which, once lost, may be lost forever.[12]

The discussion, thus far, has pointed up the "universal" interest in the question of university autonomy vs. government intervention. But Rosenfield's observation should also be stressed in that the university today cannot be neutral and apolitical (at least by implication of the ideas it generates) in its "search for truth". Such an observation brings into question Newman's Ivory Tower concept of the university[13] and the related concepts of autonomy and academic freedom which were justified in terms of the university's neutrality in the

---

[11]*Ibid.*

[12]*Ibid.*

[13]John H. Newman, The Idea of the University (Cambridge: Harvard University Press, 1976).

political life of its society.[14] Such an argument was advanced by Sir Robert Birley[15] and rejected by Wallerstein who contended:

> It is a political act for the university to support the Government in its normal functions. It is a political act for the university to be indifferent to the Government. It is a political act for the university to oppose the Government. However the university acts in relation to the Government, the university is engaged in politics. The significant question therefore is what political policy the university has or ought to have at any given moment.[16]

Given this unorthodox and provocative statement, it is rather tempting to continue our discussion in the general manner. But to do so would be to anticipate our arguments and in the process, deny the reader the evidence and analysis from two specific constituencies, Guyana and Tanzania, where the concept of university autonomy, as presently conceived, is, under pervasive and signal assault. We, therefore, turn now to these constituencies.

University Autonomy in Guyana and Tanzania

I said earlier that, generally speaking, universities in LDCs are institutional copies of some university type in the Western World. This fact is attested to by the intellectual community within the LDCs, the political leadership therein, and the growing number of their writers within the international academic community. This situation is true for Guyana and Tanzania where the University of Guyana and the University of Dar es Salaam, represent the only university in their

---

[14]For a discussion of this subject see Graham *et. al.*, Neutrality and Impartiality, especially pp. 49-195.

[15]Birley, The Real Meaning, pp. 5-6.

[16]Immanuel Wallerstein, University in Turmoil: The Politics of Change (New York: Atheneum, 1969), pp. 7-8.

countries.[17] The advent of political independence[18] brought to heightened discussion fundamental development contradictions in the educational system,[19] and the university became a pivotal institution in the post-independence development thrust.

Its ascribed tradition for "excellence" and "relevance" earned the university the pre-eminent position generating high level manpower skills to meet the development needs of the country. National and international support for the Human Capital Theory of Development[20] vindicated this emphasis on manpower development. But note the "excellence" and "relevance" claims which the University of Guyana and Tanzania enjoy we characterized as *ascribed* - not *achieved*. The first condition is a product of the status that these universities enjoy, as extensions of the "international community of scholars" referred to earlier in this paper. The second can only be a product of the work of the university within its own national environment. The capital test of "excellence" and "relevance" of the university: its capacity for

---

[17]Tanzania recently (1984) established a second university for the study of agriculture.

[18]Guyana gained its independence from Britain on May 26, 1966; Tanganyika its independence, also of Britain, in December 1961. It formed a political union with Zanzibar in 1964 under the name: The United Republic of Tanzania.

[19]At independence, only .03 percent of the 20-24 age group were enrolled in higher education courses in Tanzania. The corresponding ratio for Guyana was 1.1 percent. By 1981 these percentages had increased to 0.4 percent and 2.8 percent respectively. UNESCO, Statistical Yearbook, Table 3.2, (UNESCO, 1984).

[20]The Human Capital Theory of Development has its theoretical genesis in the work of Shultz (1961) and Dennizon (1961). Its principal contention is that "human capital", i.e., the complex of skills embodied in man, constitutes a major force in the development of the wealth of nations, one which is as important a component for success as "capital" (i.e., wealth, resources). Hence the development of educational services is not a luxury consumer item but a national investment.

pursuing advanced knowledge and resolving the needs and contradictions within its own society. Perhaps, too, such a contribution would <u>earn</u> the institution its status <u>within the contradictions of its own environment</u>, and thus vindicate its claims for autonomy and academic freedom.

Nyerere, the former President of Tanzania, expressed this in the following way:

> A university deserves its excellence if it identifies itself with society, if it serves the society. It should be in the forefront of the battle against poverty, misery, ignorance, injustice, inequality, servitude existing and persisting in a society. A university deserves the name of University [in Tanzania] if it is a <u>tool</u> for transformation, contributing ideas, manpower and service to further human dignity, equality and development of man.[21]

Nyerere went on to note that:

> Whether in a developing country or elsewhere, a university does not deserve the name (i.e., University) if it does not promote thinking. But our particular and urgent problems must influence the subjects to which thought is given, and they must influence, too, the approach. Both in university - promoted research, and in the content of degree syllabuses, the needs of our country should be the determining factor.[22]

Within this framework, Nyerere suggested some questions with which the University of Dar es Salaam should be concerned:

---

[21] Julius K. Nyerere, <u>Freedom and Unity</u> (London: Oxford University Press, 1966).

[22] Julius K. Nyerere, "The Role of the University" in <u>Freedom and Unity</u>, p. 181.

- What are the problems faced by Tanzania in a particular discipline?

- What are the obstacles which might prevent the achievement of a particular national goal, and how can they be overcome? and

- Is a particular policy conducive to the attainment of the basic objectives of Tanzanian society?

He went on to suggest that in order to answer questions such as these, the university and its students should "co-operate with the Government and the people". He sees no contradiction between these requests and the university's traditional role of an objective search for knowledge and truth. His expression of belief took the following form: "We expect these two things [i.e. "commitment" of the university to national goals and an objective search for truth] equally. And I don't believe this dual responsibility - to objectivity and service - is impossible of fulfillment."[23] Nyerere is not alone in his views. Professor R.C. Pratt, the first Principal of the University of Dar es Salaam College, then an affiliate of the University of East Africa, expressed similar ones:

> The University of East Africa must be a committed institution, actively relating our work to the communities it seeks to serve. This is in no sense, in contrast to, or in contradiction of, the intellectual objectivity and respect for truth which must also be an essential feature of a university. Commitment and objectivity are not opposites, are not in contradiction to each other. Rather the best scholarship is often a product of deep commitment[24]

It should be noted that very similar observations are expressed in Canada. For example, Betty Stephenson, a former Minister of Colleges and Universities in Ontario stated in 1983:

---

[23]*Ibid.*, p. 182.

[24]Professor R.C. Pratt, quoted in J.K. Nyerere, Freedom and Unity, p. 182.

We must be sure that the universities are able to respond to the needs of this province [i.e., Ontario], and this country [i.e., Canada] in graduate education ... I really doubt that solutions can be found in the traditional view that only by standing clearly and separately apart can universities realize excellence in learning. They must participate, influence and demonstrate leadership in society.[25]

She then went on to "warn" that higher education is expected to abide by the same rules as other sectors of society, "The value of the output of the institution will be examined in terms of its input into society."[26]

The overall significance of such statements as these for the question of government intervention in the university should not be lost, especially in so far as Tanzania and Guyana are concerned. Indeed, this perceived nexus between the role of the university and national development seems to legitimize government intervention in the university, in order to harmonize university activities and national educational and socio-economic goals. In Guyana, for example, the Government intervened to introduce National Service for its university students.[27] The same action was taken in Tanzania.[28] In Guyana in 1976, the Government intervened to introduce "free" education for all university students. Attempts were also made, though less successfully, to have the University of Guyana lower its academic minimum admission requirements and supplement the academic criteria by general requirements such as "community service". On the intervention of the Government the University of Dar es Salaam did adopt such hybrid admission criteria.

---

[25]University of Toronto, Bulletin, No. 7, 37th year, 7 November 1983, p. 2.

[26]Ibid., p. 1.

[27]National Service of one year for University of Guyana students was introduced in 1976. The initiative was the Government's. The academic community and student body were not very receptive to the idea but complied.

[28]National Service of one year was introduced in Tanzania in 1967.

In addition, the Tanzanian Government's adoption of the manpower requirements approach to educational planning had major implications for the exercise of university autonomy in that country. The National High Level Manpower Allocation Committee (NHLMAC) formed to oversee this development, makes this clear. Two are reproduced below:

- To determine *priorities* within the manpower needs, as forecast by the Manpower Division of the Ministry of Labour and Manpower Development.

- In the light of these priorities, to formulate and put forward such proposals as may appear to be desirable from time to time for alterations in, or additions to, the academic programs of institutions of higher education in Tanzania so that the pattern of outputs may, as near as possible, reflect the pattern of the nation's priority high level manpower needs."[29]

In other words, not only does the government, through MHLMAC, now exercise effective control over the prioritization of curricula activities in higher education institutions in Tanzania, but it has appropriated the right to make such "proposals" for changes in the University's academic program from "time to time" as "may appear to be desirable".

Conspicuous is the absence of university representatives on this committee. Its membership includes: as Chairman, the Principal Secretary to the President's Office, and the Principal Secretaries of the Ministries of Labour and Manpower Development, Education, Finance and Planning and Economic Affairs, and a senior representative of the Parastatal Sector.

---

[29]Government of Tanzania, Regional Seminar on Human Resource Development in East, Central and Southern Africa, Nairobi, Kenya, 25-29 March 1985, Commonwealth Secretariat, Marlborough House, Pall Mall, London, p. 15, (emphasis added).

The exclusive dependence of universities on public funds is not of itself a threat to the independence of the institutions and their ability to objectively study conditions and policies - particularly those which will not be favoured by their governments. It does, however, make them vulnerable.

The universities of Ontario draw their major annual income, directly via an enrolment related formula, from the provincial public purse. Those in Britain draw theirs in the form of direct block grants advised by a buffer body, the University Grants Committee (UGC). Yet there is no question that both sets of institutions are free to study and teach on matters and policies which run counter to the views of their governments of the day, and engage their energies in the pursuit of solutions to problems which are, apparently, of little concern to their societies.

What protects these universities, in spite of Dr. Stephenson's statement quoted above, is not a university tradition, but a limiting tradition of public administration. Within this tradition, university professors, students and administrators have confidence that, while they might be regarded as irrelevant, they will not be regarded as a political threat which has to be controlled or silenced.

Not only has the dependence on government funding of the University of Guyana and Tanzania made these institutions vulnerable to various forms of intervention, there is the danger that their objective views might well be viewed as political threats which must be silenced. "Silencing" does not have to take an extreme punitive form. It can take the form of failure to appoint, failure to approve promotion, failure to fund research. Therefore, there is a certain safety in pursuing "truth" by engaging in international guild controversies rather than those of one's immediate government.

Nevertheless, an annexation of the university's role to national development goals is hardly a sufficient condition to justify government intervention in the university. Rather, assuming that this nexus is valid, and that is my contention, intervention would be better predicated on whether the national university is sufficiently responsive to the initiatives arising from such a significant re-interpretation, as it were, of the "idea" of the university. Even in western countries, the university is no longer conceived of only as that "Ivory Tower". Nor is it any longer unquestionably accepted as necessarily being an "impartial" or "neutral" institution in its search for truth. These are matters for debate. But the debate is <u>within</u> the university community; the challenge comes from sub-groups of students and professors, not from governments. If the university's search for truth is now to be objectified in the attempts to correct the "abject misery of the people", the gross maldistribution of the nation's wealth and the gross underdevelopment of the national economy, the question remains what is to be the relationship between its (the university's) autonomous pursuit of these questions and the government's direction and control of these efforts.

The University of Guyana and to a lesser degree, the University of Dar es Salaam, like many universities in LDCs, have been slow to respond to these new demands.[30] They have not been the main players in redefining the "idea" of the university in a poor country where the institution must play a key role in national development. Perhaps this is merely an "institutional lag" conditioned by, among other things, institutional concerns over perceived and actual threats to their autonomy and academic freedom and concerns about their image and status in the international community of scholars.

These concerns are often quite legitimate. For example:

• In keeping with the "Musoma Resolution" of

---

[30]In the case of Guyana, this statement is validated in Clarence Perry, "The Organizational Effectiveness of the University of Guyana: A Case Study of an Emerging University in a National Development Context", 2 Vols. (Unpublished Ed.D. dissertation, University of Toronto, 1985). He concluded that: "Whatever approach used to assess the organizational effectiveness of the University of Guyana, the evidence reviewed ... suggests that it is not a well functioning University even when viewed from the traditional roles of Universities in a Western society, and it is not an effective instrument for the development of a poor nation (1:308).

1974[31] the Government of Tanzania *directed* that no student be admitted to the country's (then) only university, the University of Dar es Salaam, without first working for two years after graduation from secondary school. In addition the student must be recommended by his employer - which is to say the Government, since the Government is virtually a monopoly employer in Tanzania - who makes "satisfactory" performance an important basis of recommendation. What is significant here is that this initiative and its actual acceptance were effected without any consultation whatsoever with the university community. This policy was eventually scrapped in 1985 after it became conspicuously evident that it led to some basic contradictions in the system such as (1) a significant rise in the average age of the university student bodyd; (2) a significant decline in the enrolment of female students at the university; and (3) a serious shortage of students to take up available places in a number of faculties, especially the science, science-based technology, engineering, and medicine.

- The President of Tanzania is himself the Chancellor of the University of Dar es Salaam. The Vice Chancellor is a government appointee as well. Both of these positions have been instrumental in the introduction of government-directed changes at the university over time.

- All matters relating to university labour relations, planned construction, location of new facilities, etc. are the explicit responsibility of the Standing

---

[31]The Musoma Resolution constitutes, *inter alia*, a set of policy prescriptions determined by the National Executive of Tanzania's ruling political party, the Tanzanian African National Union (TANU), now renamed *Chama Chg Mapinduzi* (CCM) or the Revolutionary Party in TANU's *constitutional* role of *paramouncy over the Government*. This resolution "mandated" the Government to curtail the direct entrance of secondary school graduates into the University of Dar es Salaam.

Committee on Para-Statal Organizations (SCOPO). This is an autonomous government agency with no university representation.

- While Deans of departments may be nominated and approved by their peers, the ultimate decision to *appoint* is the prerogative of the Chancellor, the President of Tanzania.

Government intervention is also a fact of university life in Guyana. To cite two examples:

- By the intervention of the Government, the University Council was enlarged to facilitate "wider representation" of viewpoints. The result is that of the 33 members now constituting the Council, 23 are easily and widely recognized in Guyana, but especially within the university community, as political appointees, politically predisposed to support government-initiated changes in the university.[32] These include leading members of organizations directly affiliated with the ruling party/government and representatives of government-run organizations whose "heads" are themselves government appointees.

- The appointment of an internationally recognized Guyanese intellectual to the position of "Head" of the History Department of the University of Guyana is widely known, by the university community and the populace at large, to have been "vetoed" by the Government and consistently rejected despite genuine arguments by the university community. The appointment never materialized. The Government has never hidden its objectives to the political views of the nominee in question.

---

[32]The current secretary of the Council is also a government appointee at the University of Guyana.

Notwithstanding the character of some government intervention in university affairs in Tanzania and Guyana, what I am trying to demonstrate in this paper is that, in almost every instance, in these countries in the post-independence era the major innovation in the education and higher education systems originated from the political system not from within the university. Evidence is provided by the introduction of:

- free education for university students (Guyana and Tanzania),

- full time university attendance to replace the previously dominant part-time university program (Guyana),

- a Faculty of Education (from the Department of Education, Tanzania)

- a Faculty of Agriculture (Guyana, 1977),

- a Faculty of Engineering (Tanzania),

- limiting the student body to mature, qualified previously working students, sponsored by the Government, and

- the establishment of a special University for the Study of Agriculture (Tanzania, 1984).

In many ways, the political system has been well ahead of the university system in thinking about educational development and innovations. The tragedy is that there has been no strong university constituency to investigate and argue whether these politically based interventions are the best way to achieve the proclaimed national goals. The political preeminence may be explained by the fact that in the struggle for political independence that goal was intimately integrated with the struggle for greater educational opportunity - a "right" which had largely been denied the local people under the former colonial rule.

This affinity between the political leadership and the definition of how educational development is to occur has been largely strengthened over the post-independence years in an ongoing battle to free the economy of these countries from the "under-development economic and social dynamics" which restrain their development. The general public perceive this historical affinity between the political and educational systems as providing legitimacy to government intervention in their university. What such affinity cannot always vindicate, however, is the character, tendency and magnitude of such interventions.

It is my contention that the pervasiveness of Government intervention has reached such a stage as to contest the university tradition of educational leadership in terms of curricula and policy. In other words, while the universities in these two countries retain a *de jure* claim to institutional autonomy, that autonomy is increasingly being exercised in a *de facto* way by Government.

My view is that this trend has now become so well institutionalized, perhaps even routine, that government intervention in the university can no longer be seen as a deviation except from the international perspective. Moreover, if we accept the argument of one writer that the "autonomy of a university should be understood within the singularity of each national system", then it is difficult to escape the conclusion that the current inroads into university autonomy in these systems are probably irreversible and not necessarily a development to be deplored. They may still be accommodated within the international university academic community. However, such accommodation would require fundamental redefinition of the nature of the university. That is, in the name of the "idea" of the university, it may be necessary to limit institutional autonomy and academic freedom. To borrow a phrase from Sociology, such an accommodation would represent a "value stretch". The acquiescence to "government intervention", given its presumed irreversibility would involve acknowledging its presence but not, in theory, according it "legitimacy". To extend our analogy from Sociology, it would be comparable to acknowledging that an out-of-wedlock child exists but failing to give it legitimacy.

But there is a second, and we suggest, more rational alternative - one implicit in the persistence of Government intervention in both developed and developing countries. We refer to a re-interpretation of the notion of university autonomy. This is not as radical a suggestion as it may appear. Moreover, other basic changes related to the question of university autonomy, have already occurred. It is generally accepted that the "ideal" modern research university is a far cry from Newman's "Ivory Tower" and from Flexner's "college of scholars". Indeed, the fact that this conference is devoted to questions of the legitimacy of government intervention in higher education may well be symptomatic of such an ongoing re-interpretation effort. And on the related subject of academic freedom, it is well to remember the comment of Dr. Rosenfield:

> The doctrine that professors are immune to criticism or entitled to special deference in the political sphere, is deliciously attractive to teachers, but it has not the slightest chance of catching on. No free society can remain free and grant such a claim to any special group, be it professors or businessmen.[33]

To return to the question of a re-interpretation of the concept of university autonomy - does not the pervasiveness of government intervention in higher education indicate a tendency towards this possibility? Is not the dissolution of the concept of the liberal university irreversible? Has not a fundamental condition, the financial independence of the university, which nurtured the practice of university autonomy, been eroded even internationally? Is such a trend likely to be reversible? Are not most universities throughout the world largely, or completely, dependent upon their governments for funds? Should the usual accountability for the use of public funds not extend to universities?

Such questions are posed neither to support government intervention nor defend university autonomy. Rather, it is our intention to provoke the reader into thinking carefully about the question of the legitimacy of government intervention in higher education since we are all rather pre-disposed to reply to it in stark dichotomous fashion. This would be a betrayal of

---

[33]Rosenfield, "Attacks on Academic Freedom".

the university "idea", the "objective" search for the truth. And there is another compelling reason why the "second alternative" we noted above may be the rationale route to take. You will recall my earlier contention that the university, as traditionally conceived, involved both autonomy and academic freedom. These are Western educational traditions which have been internationalized through the extension of the Western university to developing countries. Since the institutions have been borrowed and did not grow out of the LDC's culture or traditions there seems to be a *prima facie* case for expecting these societies increasingly to question the "given" institutions, as their own growth matures.

Assaults on university autonomy in these countries are not unrelated to this growth of national consciousness. However, J.W. Chapman has given many examples of government intervention in Western countries.[34] Note, however, that this development - minus its intensity and, possibly, its character and tendency - is <u>not</u> limited to the developing world. In other words, there is evidence to show that the erosion of university autonomy is a universal phenomenon, even if it takes different forms in LDCs and in the West. Indeed, it is tempting to infer some degree of legitimacy to government intervention on the basis of this phenomenon alone. But the fundamental question surely has become, not one of legitimacy, but of *integrity*. Is there integrity in certain government interventions into the world, and conduct of, the university but not in others? Is this a question of the integrity of the institution or the integrity of the government - or perhaps of both? Should we expect governments to demonstrate integrity in their demands of the university? Should we expect the university, in turn, to demonstrate integrity in how it meets those demands and how it conducts its business? To focus on the question of integrity, has the advantage of:

- reminding the University - which may often be complacent or narrow in its outlook because of a former *laissez faire* exercise of university

---

[34] See J.W. Chapman, <u>The Western University on Trial</u> (Berkeley: University of California Press, 1983).

autonomy - that "autonomy is never granted or established once and for all; it must be continually won and protected".[35]

- allowing for the active exercise of discourse - the root of knowledge? - on issues of national significance.

Popper puts it this way:

> Although I am an admirer of tradition I am at the same time, an almost ardent adherent of unorthodoxy: I hold that orthodoxy is the death of knowledge, since the growth of knowledge depends entirely on the existence of disagreement.[36]

In the final analysis, our real concern should be, not the legitimacy of government intervention *per se*, but the definition of university conditions which will allow the institution to perform its traditional function, the objective search for truth.

In this connection, university autonomy seems to be in irreversible retreat, particularly in the LCD's. It seems to have been limited, but not necessarily invalidated by its origins. It has been inevitably conditioned by Western traditions which are not shared in the non-western world. Or, to quote another writer:

> Consider the wide range of customs and traditions of language and religion, of social patterns and of political culture, of economic development and ideological commitment. And, having so examined, considered and reflected, ask whether the categories of thought we may employ to address the question before us (i.e. Attacks on Academic Freedom in

---

[35]Polin, "Freedom of the Mind", p. 40.

[36]Karl Popper, "The Myth of the Framework" Occasional Paper (London: Association of Comparative Education, 1984), p. 2.

Foreign Countries) are indeed appropriate ones. We may indeed conclude that they are not.[37]

But having said this, we should be careful lest, in our concern over the "legitimacy" of government intervention and the persuasiveness of the relativist argument implicit in Rosenfield's observation, we fall victim to what Popper calls "The Myth of the Framework". In this context, that would mean acquiescing to varying standards for university autonomy depending upon the national context in which the university functions. This would be an abdication of what is, potentially, the most promising aspect of the notion of university autonomy. It is a laudable academic principle worthy of universal acceptance. We refer to the implicit notion that there is a universal standard in the university's objective search for truth, i.e., to subscribe to the notion that "the world of true scholarship [is] indivisible" since "no person or group, no nation, no state has a monopoly on truth."

If we accept the possibility that there is a universality of truth, then there can be truly universal principles and standards (such as university autonomy) which provide the objective conditions for the search for truth, and therefore scholarship is truly indivisible.

Indeed, it is my suggestion that the principle of university-government integrity become the point of departure in any re-interpretation of government-university relationships. To accept this is to accept Popper's argument that truth is not culture bound. He contends that, "One of the main components of modern irrationalism is relativism (the doctrine that truth is relative to our intellectual background or framework: that it may change from one framework to another)".[38]

---

[37] Rosenfield, "Attacks on Academic Freedom".

[38] Popper, "The Myth of the Framework", p. 4.

262

Conclusion

While we may rightly question the legitimacy of government intervention in higher education, our prerogative to do so should not be dictated by our concern for university autonomy *per se*. Indeed, as we have argued above, university autonomy, as presently conceived, is itself wanting. Rather, in the university's search for truth, its society would be better served if the discussion shifted to questions of the integrity of both the institution and of governments. Then government intervention could be established, and the relationship between the nature of the interventions and their effects upon the university's search for truth determined.

Our critique of government intervention in higher education should be primarily informed by a desire to assure the *existence* of conditions conducive to an objective search for truth. Traditional university autonomy is assumed to internalize and represent such conditions. But the reader will recall our arguments with regards to the limitation of university autonomy, as conceived today. It should also be noted that I have used the term *existence* in preference to "maintenance", "continuity" or "protection". Any such choice of word would implicitly invest the notion of university autonomy with a validity and currency it does not, in fact, enjoy. The use of the term *existence* is deliberate. Otherwise, it seems somewhat a-intellectual and contrary to an objective search for truth even to infer (or worse, deny) the closure of any state of knowledge, basic principle, or pivotal notion, to critical scrutiny and challenge. No state of knowledge, however good or useful, should become a "sacred cow". The use of the word existence is intended to make allowance for a zero-based critical analysis. In theory, at least, it accepts the possibility of an analytical mind-set free from a predisposition to accept, or reject, or otherwise compete or contrast conditions such as (a) university autonomy and (b) government intervention. Nowhere is it more important that such a mind set be developed than in nations such as Guyana and Tanzania which urgently need to arrest and reverse the under-development contradictions that plague their societies.

The university, for the foreseeable future, will either continue to be the pivotal institution in this process or it will become irrelevant and will wither and die. Hence, it is imperative that we establish the basic principles and conditions which will facilitate the university's task. After all, the service of man must constitute the whole purpose of the university's search for truth. It is my contention that government's intervention in the university will be judged to be legitimate or not only in so far as it promotes or negates, limits and frustrates the search for "truth".

Section III

Teaching and Breaching: U.S. Higher Education and the Constitutional "Wall Between Church and State"

by

Walter Hobbs[1]

The Bill of Rights contained in the first ten amendments to the Constitution of the United States begins with the twin provisions that "Congress shall make no law respecting an establishment of religion, or prohibiting the free exercise thereof..." In the jargon of constitutional analysis, these are known respectively as the Establishment Clause and the Free Exercise Clause. Together they comprise what Thomas Jefferson called a "Wall of separation between Church and State",[2] but the phrase has been popularly attributed over time to the two provisions generally.) This paper discusses several implications for U.S. higher education of that constitutional barrier to governmental involvement in religion, especially when government - in particular, the courts - intervene in academe to insure the integrity of the Wall.

The term intervention finds its roots, as do so many other words in the English language, in Latin: *inter*, meaning "between" or "among", and *venire*, meaning "to come". Literally, to intervene is "to come between or among". A moment's reflection reveals that the two possible meanings are drastically different, which again is not uncommon: to come between is divisive, and to come among is (ordinarily, though not always) associative - a joining in of sorts. The phrase, government "intervention" in higher education, typically conjures up the notion of intrusion by an unwanted third party, government, into the traditional relationships enjoyed by participants in the academic enterprise - plainly, a "coming

---

[1]Associate Professor, Higher Education, State University of New York at Buffalo, Buffalo, NY.

[2]Justice Hugo O. Black tells us that Jefferson was speaking specifically of the Establishment Clause as "intended to erect a wall..." Everson v. Board of Education, 30 U.S. 1, 67 S.Ct. 504, 91 L.Ed. 711 (1947).

between". It is important, therefore, at the outset of this discussion to sound the contrasting note; frequently in the United States government has joined with higher education, i.e., it has "come among" academe to exercise its considerable powers on behalf of the latter's interests and, often, its values.[3]

Another distinction is also in order. Academicians are inclined to view intrusions by government as illegitimate *per se*, and governmental support, on the other hand, as quite appropriate. However, even if such generalizations are essentially valid, they do admit of exceptions, i.e., of legitimate intrusions and of illegitimate assistance (no matter how helpful the latter may be). When one inquires, therefore, into the legitimacy of government intervention in higher education, one ought to be alert to four, not two, distinct possibilities: legitimate *vis-a-vis* illegitimate intrusions, and legitimate *vis-a-vis* illegitimate support. This examination of "the Wall" and higher education in the United States will serve to illustrate the matter. On occasion, courts tread on academic turf in the interest of vindicating either the constitutional prohibition against government establishment of religion and/or the constitutional guarantee of free religious exercise, and constitutionally informed persons cheer. At other times, the provision of government largesse to academic activities that are constitutionally ineligible to be funded from the public purse offends the reasonable person's concept of the rule of law. In such instances as these, any debate in the matter shifts from the issue whether specific government interventions in academe are legitimate or illegitimate, to the larger issue of whether the United States wants to retain its unusual constitutional doctrine of "the Wall". Unless and until that latter issue is joined and resolved, however, there is no question that under the present constitutional framework, some (not all) governmental intrusions are legitimate and some support is not.

Although the Wall is indeed unusual in the context of western civilization, it is not an anomaly in U.S. constitutional law. Separateness is no stranger to U.S. jurisprudence. The

---

[3]Cf., e.g., Keyishian v. Board of Regents, 385 U.S. 589, 87 S.Ct. 675, 17 L.Ed.2d 629 (1967).

separation of powers, for example (conveyed also by the term "co-equal [sic] branches of government"), is fundamental to an understanding of the constitutional vision of governmental jurisdiction. Congress, the legislative body of representatives of the sovereign people, promulgates social policy and enacts law to realize that policy in national life. The Executive implements that legislation, sometimes less enthusiastically and sometimes more so than was initially contemplated by Congress. And the Judiciary sits to review both the legislation itself and the implementation thereof to ascertain their constitutional validity. Yet the separation is never absolute, nor was it intended to be. The Executive may veto, rather than implement, the Congressional legislation. But the Congress may then override the veto, thereby compelling implementation (though not enthusiasm!). Judges are appointed by the Executive, but only with the advice and consent of the Senate (one of two houses in the bicameral legislature). Judges are life-tenured in their role of review of congressional and executive action, but the Congress has power to impeach and remove them for cause. The separation of powers, in other words, is unmistakable yet not unlimited, clear but not complete.

So it is with the Wall. The Constitution forbids government at every level (federal, state and local) to establish and/or infringe religious exercise. However, purism in the maintenance of the Wall is utterly impossible. Where a claimant, for example, might reasonably seek government services that are necessary to his or her free exercise of religious activity - say, fire protection for the local church - a critic might sensibly argue that government would be "establishing" religion were it to publicly fund such services to the devout.

The Court[4] has held that the operative criterion of appropriate government action is "neutrality":

> There is much talk of the separation of Church and
> State in the history of the Bill of Rights and in the

---

[4]Unless otherwise indicated, throughout this paper "the Court" refers to the U.S. Supreme Court, the highest Court to which disputes can be brought concerning federal issues.

decisions clustering around the First Amendment. There cannot be the slightest doubt that the First Amendment reflects the philosophy that Church and State should be separated. And so far as interference with the "free exercise" of religion and an "establishment" of religion are concerned, the separation must be complete and unequivocal. ... The First Amendment, however, does not say that in every and all respects there shall be a separation of Church and State. Rather, it studiously defines the manner, the specific ways, in which there shall be no concert or union or dependency one on the other. That is the common sense of the matter. Otherwise the state and religion would be aliens to each other - hostile, suspicious, and even unfriendly. ...

We are a religious people whose institutions presuppose a Supreme Being. We guarantee the freedom to worship as one chooses. ... We sponsor an attitude on the part of government that shows no partiality to any one group and that lets each flourish according to the zeal of its adherents and the appeal of its dogma. ... Government may not finance religious groups nor undertake religious instruction nor blend secular and sectarian education nor use secular institutions to force one or some religion on any person. But we find no constitutional requirement which makes it necessary for government to be hostile to religion and to throw its weight against efforts to widen the effective scope of religious influence. The government must be neutral. ...[5]

Eleven years later, the Court summarized its line of decisions requiring government neutrality in matters of church and state as follows:

The wholesome "neutrality" of which this Court's cases speak ... stems from a recognition of the

---

[5]Zorach v. Clauson, 343 U.S. 306, 72 S.Ct. 679, 96 L.Ed. 954 (1952), emphasis added.

teachings of history that powerful sects or groups
might bring about a fusion of governmental and
religious functions or a concert or dependency of one
upon the other to the end that official support of the
State or Federal Government would be placed behind
the tenets of one or of all orthodoxies. This the
Establishment Clause prohibits. And a further
reason for neutrality is found in the Free Exercise
Clause, which recognizes the value of religious
training, teaching and observance and, more
particularly, the right of every person to freely choose
his own course with reference thereto, free of any
compulsion from the state. This the Free Exercise
Clause guarantees. ...[6]

In handing down a decision in two cases consolidated under the
name Lemon v. Kurtzman, 403 U.S. 602, 91 S.Ct. 2105, 20
L.Ed.2d 745 (1971), the Court promulgated a three-pronged
test (gleaned from earlier decisions) by which to assess the
neutrality of any governmental action that is challenged as
violating either the Establishment and/or the Free Exercise
Clauses. All three of the Lemon criteria must be met; failure
on any suffices to invalidate the action. First, the action must
have a secular purpose; second, its principal or primary effect
must be one that neither advances nor inhibits religion; and
third, it must not foster an excessive government
entanglement with religion.

Lemon offers an illustration, in the context of the issues it
decided,[7] of the analysis by which it might be determined
whether the third prong of the test, "no excessive
entanglement", has been met. There the Court held that a
dedicated religious person, teaching children of impressionable
ages in a school affiliated with his or her faith and operated to
inculcate its tenets, would experience so great a difficulty in

---

[6]Abington School District v. Schempp, 374 U.S. 203, 83 S.Ct. 1560, 10
L.Ed.2d 844 (1963).

[7]Namely, whether a State may supplement and/or reimburse to church-
related elementary and secondary schools the salaries of teachers of secular
subjects.

271

remaining religiously neutral ("[d]octrines and faith are not inculcated or advanced by neutrals") that a comprehensive, discriminating, and continuing state surveillance would be necessary of (a) the school's financial records to determine which expenditures were for "nonreligious" purposes and which for "religious", and of (b) teacher performance for the requisite neutrality, to insure that restrictions required by the Establishment Clause are respected.

Colleges and universities, of course, present a somewhat different fact pattern from that of the elementary and secondary schools in that the student is an adult, not a person of "impressionable age". Consequently, different results may obtain when the three-pronged Lemon test is applied. A companion case to Lemon was Tilton v. Richardson, 403 U.S. 672, 91 S.Ct. 2091, 29 L.Ed.2d 790 (1971), in which at question was the constitutionality of federal aid to church-related colleges and universities in the form of construction grants for buildings and facilities used exclusively for secular educational purposes. The first prong of the test was not at issue - both parties acknowledged that the stated purpose of the enabling legislation[8] was to assist colleges "in their efforts to accommodate rapidly growing numbers of youth". As to primary effect (the second prong), the Court held that the trial record disclosed no evidence of violation by the recipient institutions who were parties to this case, of the statutory requirement that the grants be used to build facilities solely for secular and not religious functions; indeed, evidence showed that other church-related institutions had been required to return benefits for reasons of noncompliance[9] but these had not. The final consideration, therefore, was with the third prong, excessive government entanglement with religion. The

---

[8]Title I of the Higher Education Facilities Act of 1963.

[9]The Court held, however, that the statute was defective to the extent that it restricted use of the building for religious functions only during a twenty year period following construction, in which the U.S. retained a financial interest in the facility chiefly to permit enforcement of the restriction. Afterward, presumably, the building might be used for any purpose deemed suitable by the college. The Court declined to invalidate the entire Act on these grounds, but simply required correction of the statutory infirmity.

Court held that three factors substantially diminished the extent and the potential danger of such entanglement. First, college students are less susceptible to religious indoctrination than are younger students; college and postgraduate courses tend to limit the opportunities for sectarian influence by virtue of their own internal disciplines; and many church-related colleges are characterized by a high degree of academic freedom for both students and faculty. Second, the direct object of the aid provided by government was non-ideological, i.e.; facilities, unlike the teachers in Lemon, are religiously neutral. And third, the aid itself was a one-time, single-purpose grant without continuing financial relationships or dependencies. "The risks of government aid to religion and the corresponding need for surveillance are therefore reduced ... [and] cumulatively these three factors also substantially lessen the potential for divisive religious fragmentation in the political arena." Save for the enforcement provisions which required modification (cf. n. 7), the government grants to church-related colleges and universities for facilities construction were upheld.

Tilton sustained governmental efforts to aid church-related higher education, though Lemon rebuffed a similar attempt to assist church-related elementary and secondary education. Might the differing outcomes suggest that when higher education is the subject of litigation it is likely to fare well before the courts? Not always. Consider the case of Bob Jones University.

The Greenville, South Carolina institution was founded in 1927 to teach and propagate its fundamentalist religious beliefs. As a nonprofit corporation "organized and operated exclusively for religious, charitable, scientific, literary, or educational purposes",[10] it was granted tax-exempt status by the Internal Revenue Service.[11] Not only are organizations which enjoy such status relieved of liability to pay federal income tax

---

[10] Section 50(c)(3) of the Internal Revenue Code.

[11] The Internal Revenue Service (IRS) is the agency of the federal government created to administer tax law enacted by Congress.

themselves but, more importantly, individuals and corporations which contribute funds to the organizations can deduct the amount of their contributions (within given limits) from their otherwise taxable income. The latter is a major inducement by which nonprofit enterprises elicit financial support, and a virtual necessity to the economic viability of nongovernmental (i.e., not tax-supported) institutions.

From its inception, the University has contended as a matter of religious doctrine that the Bible forbids interracial dating and marriage. Until 1971, no blacks were admitted to studies, and from 1971-1975, only married blacks were admitted, and only if married within their race. Following an intermediate federal court's decision prohibiting racial exclusion from private schools,[12] however, the University permitted unmarried blacks to enrol. But maintaining its longstanding doctrinal position, it prohibited interracial dating and marriage on pain of expulsion.

In 1970 the IRS formally notified private schools throughout the U.S. that it had concluded, in light of a judicial decision prohibiting the Service from according tax-exempt status to private schools in Mississippi which discriminated in admissions on the basis of race, that it (the IRS) could no longer legally justify allowing tax-exempt status to any private school which practices racial discrimination at any level of education, nor that it could treat contributions to such institutions as "charitable deductions" for income tax purposes. Loss of its exempt status might well sound the financial death-knell for Bob Jones, and the University moved to defeat the Service's proposed revocation. For technical reasons, the challenge failed; in 1976, the IRS officially revoked the University's exempt status and, following additional technical manoeuvers, a lawsuit was instituted by the University against the IRS.

The trial court held, *inter alia*, that the revocation violated the University's rights under the Religion Clauses of the First Amendment, but the appellate court reversed the decision and

---

[12]McCrary v. Runyon, 515 F.2d 1082 (4th Cir., 1975), aff'd 427 U.S. 160, 96 S.Ct. 2586, 49 L.Ed.2d 415 (1976). Bob Jones University was not a party to the case.

the case went to the Supreme Court. There, despite the Court's own characterization of the University's belief as "genuine" that the Bible forbids interracial dating and marriage - as strong a candidate for protection under the Free Exercise Clause as one might imagine - the University lost.

The University's argument was that the IRS' policy cannot constitutionally be applied to schools that engage in racial discrimination on the basis of sincerely held religious beliefs. In response, the Court reiterated the oft-stated principle that the Free Exercise Clause constitutes an absolute prohibition against governmental <u>regulation</u> of such beliefs. But denial of tax benefits, despite the certainty of its substantial impact on the operation of private religious schools, will not in itself prevent those schools from observing their religious tenets. Similarly, though the Free Exercise Clause provides considerable protection for lawful conduct grounded in religious belief, there are significant exceptions to the general rule, for all burdens on religion are unconstitutional. In particular, the government may justify a limitation on religious liberty by showing that it is essential to accomplish an overriding governmental interest. For example, child labour laws prohibiting the sale of printed materials on public streets have been held valid against Jehovah's Witness children's participation in dispensing religious literature. As to Bob Jones University, the governmental interest at stake is compelling: the Government has a fundamental, overriding interest in eradicating racial discrimination in education[13] and that interest, said the Court, heavily outweighs whatever burden a denial of tax benefits places on the University's exercise of its religious beliefs.

Thus far the score is 1-1, <u>Tilton</u> for the university, <u>Bob Jones</u> against. In the vocabulary of the remarks which introduced this discussion, <u>Tilton</u> illustrates government "joining with" church-affiliated higher education in advancing institutional interests, and <u>Bob Jones</u> discloses government "coming

---

[13]"Racially discriminatory schools exert a pervasive influence on the entire educational process, outweighing any public benefit they might otherwise provide." Norwood v. Harrison, 413 U.S. 455, 93 S.Ct. 2804, 37 L.Ed.2d 723 (1973).

between" an institution and its central religious values. It will be left to the reader to decide whether to applaud or to decry the respective outcomes, that is, to ponder which, if either, is legitimate "intervention".[14] A new development, however, has recently emerged and needs to be taken into account if one is to have a full view of U.S. higher education and the Wall separating church and state. The Wall seems not so much breached as suddenly and grandly bypassed.

From 1973 to 1977, a student religious group named Cornerstone regularly sought and received permission to conduct its meetings in campus facilities of the University of Missouri at Kansas City. In 1977, however, the group was informed it could no longer meet in University buildings, given a regulation adopted by the governing Board in 1972 prohibiting the use of University grounds or buildings for purposes of religious worship or religious teaching. The students brought suit to challenge the regulation on grounds, *inter alia*, that the University's discrimination against religious activity and discussion violated their Free Exercise

---

[14]For myself, I find Tilton's result reasonable, at least with respect to the several institutions that were the challenged parties in that case, for the record seems plainly to show that the colleges carefully met the criteria of the Higher Education Facilities Act. But I entertain reservations about the reasoning of the Court concerning the extent to which the Act met the Lemon criteria, for a continuing scrutiny by government so long as the building may stand to insure that the facilities are never used to serve a religious function, requires both a relationship with the schools and a constant exercise of judgment as to what is and what is not "religious", that in my view are exceedingly excessive entanglements. As to Bob Jones, this paper is not a proper forum in which to examine the hermeneutic validity of the doctrinal stance the University proudly heralds, so suffice it simply to say I dissociate myself completely from their substantive position, and I do so as one personally and knowledgeably committed to a biblical perspective on reality. Nevertheless, I am troubled by the Court's easy dismissal of the implications of the burden that denial of tax exempt status in the service of a compelling governmental interest places on the University's sponsors' constitutionally "protected" free exercise of religion. I'm reminded of Martin Niemoller's plaintive confession: "They came for the Jews but I was not Jewish, so I did not cry out. They came for the Catholics but I was not Catholic, so I did not cry out. They came for the Protestants. I cried out, but there was no one left to listen."

rights and their freedom of speech.[15]

The trial court held that the regulation was not only justified, it was required. It was not the students' Free Exercise rights that were trampled by the allegedly offensive policy, but rather the Establishment Clause that would be violated by provision of the State University's facilities for religious use. The court rejected the argument that the University could not discriminate against religious speech on the basis of its content. To the contrary, the court found religious speech entitled to less protection than other types of expression.

The appellate court reversed the decision. It held that the Establishment Clause does not bar a policy of equal access to University facilities open to groups and speakers of all kinds, including religious. And the Supreme Court affirmed.

Although the Court applied the Lemon test in its analysis of the dispute, the critical feature of the Court's reasoning seems instead to be its focus on the content of the speech for which protection was sought, not on the tension between Establishment and Free Exercise. As is usually the case, the characterization of the fundamental legal issue was "outcome determinative". Having concluded that the issue was "free expression", the Court's course was clear: it has long been established principle that freedom of expression is to be upheld unless the most compelling of circumstances warrant placing limits on speech, and even there the limits must be the least onerous feasible.

The first and the third prongs of the Lemon test were plainly met: both the trial court and the appellate court had held that an open-forum policy would have a secular purpose and would avoid governmental entanglement with religion. But the University argued (and the trial court agreed) that allowing religious groups to share the public forum to express their religious sentiments would have the "primary effect" of advancing religion in contravention not only of the federal

---

[15]Freedom of speech is also guaranteed by the First Amendment: "Congress shall make no law ... abridging the freedom of speech".

Establishment Clause but of the narrower counterpart Missouri constitutional prohibition as well. The Supreme Court thought that that argument misconceived the issue. The question was not whether a religious forum would be created in violation of the federal, let alone the State's, Establishment Clause. Inasmuch as the University had opened its facilities for use by student groups, the question was whether it could now exclude particular groups by reason of the content of their speech.

To pose the question thus was to answer it:

> [The students'] First Amendment rights are entitled to special constitutional solicitude. Our cases have required the most exacting scrutiny [when] a State undertakes to regulate speech on the basis of its content. ...[T]he State interest asserted here - in achieving greater separation of church and State than is already ensured under the Establishment Clause of the Federal Constitution - is limited by the Free Exercise Clause and in this case by the Free Speech Clause as well. In this constitutional context, we are unable to recognize the State's interest [in vindicating the Missouri constitution's more stringent Establishment provision] as sufficiently "compelling" to justify content-based discrimination against [the students'] religious speech.[16]

Lawyers are fond of asking whether dissimilar results can be reconciled, i.e., whether two or more cases that seem to pose conflicting legal principles can be rationally explained and merged. Widmar and Bob Jones University are candidates for just such an analytical exercise. The first gives great weight to one party's (the students') right to share with others a forum in which to express themselves freely without regard to the

---

[16]Widmar v. Vincent, 454 U.S. 263, 102 S.Ct. 269, 70 L.Ed.2d 440 (1981). The Court went on to reaffirm previous holdings that permit restrictions on speech in the interest of reasonable "time, place and manner" regulations designed to prevent interference with the institution's pursuit of its primary educational tasks.

religious content of that expression. The second, by contrast, inflicts a heavy price to pay (loss of tax-exempt status) for the right to stand upon a religious view that even the Court acknowledges is genuinely held.

The difference appears to be attributable chiefly to the fact that the students sought to participate in the free and unfettered expression of views in the marketplace of ideas, whereas Bob Jones University sought to maintain a practice which, no matter how genuinely "religious", is today plainly repugnant to the values and ideals of the sovereign people as promulgated by their representatives.

The comparison is instructive. In both cases, government (through the medium of the courts) "intervened" in academe. Reasonable persons may well disagree whether either case represents a legitimate such intrusion. But this much is clear: the Wall constructed by the Establishment and Free Exercise Clauses of the U.S. Constitution to separate Church from State was neither impregnable nor unavoidable. Indeed, at times it was unarguably breached. The Wall is, however, a most formidable barrier, one that must be carefully assayed and measured if it is to be a protector of cherished values - academic as well as other - and not merely a hurdle to be negotiated in a legal proceeding.

The disposition of academic issues not yet taken to the highest court (and which may never reach that body, absent a controversy of sufficient gravity to warrant such review) can at best be only guessed at. Would a church-affiliated college be compelled to accept as foreman of a building project funded in part with government monies a person who is an outspoken atheist? Would a decision reached within a doctrinal framework but contrary to law (e.g., dismissal of an employee whose pregnancy was terminated by legal abortion) be invalidated? The most confident prediction one might hazard is that such issues would almost certainly be debated in the shadow of the Wall. More than that is difficult to know. Surely, determining in advance of such litigation the character and legitimacy of whatever governmental intervention may arise is simply out of the question. As Widmar, following upon Tilton and its progeny, makes clear, the U.S. Supreme Court is not easily anticipated.

State Formulas for Funding Higher Education: Trends and Issues

by

Jane Adams Lamb[1]

The funding of public universities and colleges in America has historically been a matter left to the states, an issue resolved in a climate of respect for higher education and of compromise based on different political realities. Examination of their complex budget documents for higher education shows that no two states justify the dollars spent for higher education in exactly the same way. Yet within these differences, one can identify similarities and trends that reveal not only expenditure patterns, but also philosophical patterns which affect the public institutions. If the predicted influences on higher education in the eighties - enrolment decline, increasing government intervention, declining state resources, and increasing emphasis on quality and accountability[2] - are occurring, their effects will be evident in the budget documents.

The primary tool used for the allocation of state funds for public higher education in the U.S. is the formula, a descriptive compilation of apparently objective mathematical relationships (or "formulas") that relate historic or projected

[1]Associate Professor, Department of Social and Health Resources, University of Nevada - Reno, Reno, NE.

[2]See Carnegie Council on Policy Studies in Higher Education, Three Thousand Futures: The Next Twenty Years for Higher Educatiaon (San Francisco: Jossey-Bass Publishers, 1980); Sloan Commission on Government and Higher Education, A Program for Renewed Partnership: The Report of the Sloan Commission on Government and Higher Education (Cambridgeg, Mass.: Ballinger Publishing Company, 1980); and V.A. Stadtman, Academic Adaptations: Higher Education Prepared for the 1980s and the 1990s (San Francisco: Jossey-Bass Publishers, 1980).

cost to work load to yield an estimated future funding need.[3] This study examined state budget request documents in order to identify changes that were occurring in budgeting methods. Differentiation between "formula" and "non-formula" states was often difficult. As Meisinger suggests, "the definition of a budget formula is a debatable issue among both practitioners and researchers alike".[4] For purposes of my study, states were counted as "formula states" if the response specifically described and/or labelled an objective mathematical budget process with institutional measures "a formula". Data were collected on the structure of these budget formulas used in 1985 to generate budget requests or allocations to public higher education by conducting a mail survey of the higher education coordinating bodies in forty-eight states. In Wyoming and Vermont the request was made directly to the university system. Copies of the budget formulas, or budget guidelines used in each state, were solicited. In addition to the budget documents requested, questions were asked about the percentage of the formula request actually funded, unexpended funds, items outside the formula, and methods for rewarding quality or measuring performance.

Responses were received from forty-two states. Of these forty-two, twenty-seven sent descriptions of a budget or allocation formula for four-year colleges and universities. Three additional ones sent data on formulas for community colleges only. Subsequent phone calls confirmed that three of the eight nonrespondent states used budget formulas, but sufficient

---

[3]See Paul Brinkman, "Formula Budgeting: The Fourth Decade" in Larry L. Leslie (ed.), New Directions for Institutional Research: Responding to New Realities in Funding (San Francisco: Jossey-Bass Publishers, 1984); Francis McKenzie Gross, "A Comparative Analysis of the Existing Budget Formulas Used for Justifying Budget Requests or Allocating Funds for the Operating Expenses of State-Supported Colleges and Universities" Unpublished Ph.D. dissertation, University of Tennessee, Knoxville, 1973; and Francis McKenzie Gross, Formula Budgeting for Higher Education: State Practices in 1979-80, Working Paper Series (Boulder, Colorado: National Center for Higher Education Management Systems, 1982).

[4]Richard J. Meisinger, Jr., State Budgeting for Higher Education: The Uses of Formulas (Berkeley, California: University of California Center for Research and Development in Higher Education, 1976), p. 23.

information to formulate an adequate description of them was not available. Thirty-one states, a combination of formula and nonformula ones, sent some level of response to the four questions.

A comparative analysis of the structure of current state budget or allocation formulas was then carried out from the state documents, letters and other information. Specific aspects of the formula process and formula structure were examined, particularly those that recent literature had identified as changing. The structure and complexity of the present formulas were then compared to the formulas described by Dr. Francis Gross in his similar surveys of 1973 and 1979.[5] In this comparative analysis the following factors were examined: the number of states using formulas, the base factors utilized, the computational methods, the level of differentiation within formulas, the complexity of the formulas, and the geographic distribution of states using formulas.

Description of Formula Budgeting

Thirty states were using formulas in the preparation of budget requests for state funds for four-year public colleges and universities and/or in the distribution of allocated state funds within the higher education system. There was no automatic linkage between the budget preparation criteria and process and the allocation criteria and process. Four states described a formula used for allocation only. Two states described two separate formulas - one for the budget request and one for grant allocation. The remaining twenty-four states reported formulas used for the budget request only. The parties participating in both of these processes (requesting and allocating) varied from state to state. The formulas were designed and sanctioned by the university system itself, the higher education coordinating body of the state, the governor and the legislature, or by various combinations of the above.

Evidence of interest in budget formulas was evident from the number of state studies, with resulting changes, that had

---

[5] Gross, "A Comparative Analysis"; and Gross, Formula Budgeting.

occurred since 1980 (fourteen) and the number of studies underway in 1985 (six). Yet, with all the changes occurring, formulas continued to be structured primarily by the functional classification areas that define the Educational and General portion of the budget (instruction, research, public service, academic support, libraries, student services, institutional support, and operations and maintenance of plant). Instruction and operations and maintenance of plant were the two categories most often included within the formulas.

Base factors that drove the formula (in order of frequency of use) were portions of current or past budgets, student credit hour production, FTE[6] enrolment, square feet/acreage, head count, FTE faculty/staff positions, and value of inventory. The most frequently used base was the budget itself, either the previous year's budget or some portion of the present proposed budget, continuing the emphasis of an incremental approach to budgeting and masking the importance of the base factor driving the other portions of the budget. If FTE enrolment, head count, and student credit hour production were considered jointly, then the number of students within the educational system became by far the greatest factor in determining the budgeted amount. Thus, one must conclude that the states do not appear to be abandoning enrolment-driven formulas in times of stability or decrease in the numbers of students.

Yet a variety of methods were being used to mitigate the power that the level of current enrolment had upon the final formula figure. Use of head count, especially in Student Services, occurred in fourteen states. Buffering or decoupling was described in some portion of the formula in sixteen states. Capping of enrolment was mandated in the budget documents in only two. Buffering describes the various devices limiting the responsiveness of the budget to enrolment changes by defining the amount of change that will be taken into account. Examples are multi-year averages, limits on allowable or recognized growth or decline, and corridor or threshold limits. Under typical corridor or threshold approaches, a range of enrolment is established, and only changes outside this range

---

[6]Full time equivalent.

will affect funding. Decoupling involves removing the linkage to enrolment altogether in as many parts of the formula as possible.[7] Marginal costing was being used in only four states, whereas a combination of fixed and variable costs appeared to some extent in almost every formula. Six states used fixed and variable costing in every portion of their formula. The inclusion of summer school hours in the FTE or SCH[8] count appeared to be increasingly popular.

The three computation methods which Dr. Francis Gross described in 1973[9] continue to cover the variety of calculations within formulas. The rate per base factor unit (RBFU) is the specified or given rate or factor multiplied by some institutional descriptor or base factor. The percentage of base factor (PBF) refers to a given percentage of some other functional classification or budgetary portion. The base factor position ratio with salary rates (BFPR/SR) establishes a ratio (e.g., faculty to students, faculty to support staff, staff per square foot, faculty to student credit hours) on which to calculate the needed full time equivalent teaching positions to be multiplied by given salary rates. The BFPR/SR method was used most often in budgeting for instruction. The simpler RBFU or PBF were used more often overall. The RBFU was the most common approach used to calculate budgets for Operation and Maintenance of Physical Plant.

The use of data from "comparable institutions" was identified as a new item in many formulas. Although the southern states had previously used the standards of Southern Region Educational Board (SREB), more respondents now cited formulas using national standards from "prestigious" institutions. The establishment of higher dollar factors, better student/faculty ratios, and more generous salaries within the

---

[7] Dennis P. Jones, Higher Education Budgeting at the State Level: Concepts and Principles (Denver, Colorado: National Center for Higher Education Management Systems, 1984).

[8] Student contact hours.

[9] Gross, "A Comparative Analysis".

formulas was attributed to, and justified by, data from "comparable institutions".

The amount of the formula request actually funded by the state legislatures varied from 73 percent to 100 percent in 1985. If the average over the last five years is compared with that percentage, every formula state respondent had experienced an improvement in this percentage in the 1985 funding period. Both New Jersey and Washington cited the low percentage of past funding as a contributing factor in their decision to abandon formula budgeting.

Twelve states reported they did not have to return unexpended funds at the end of the fiscal period, but only five of these were budget formula states.[10] Georgia's 1982 Study on Public Higher Education recommended that the university system be allowed to keep unexpended funds as a management incentive.

The portion of the budget included in the formula varied from state to state with an apparent movement to increase the items under formula calculation. States like Kentucky and Oregon which recently wrote new formulas moved in the direction of including more items. The identification of "decision items" within the budget structure that highlight funding beyond continuation levels appeared frequently. Equipment replacement and upgrading now are appearing in formulas.

In comparing formulas from 1973, 1979, and 1985, several findings emerged. Fourteen states that were using formulas in the 1973 Gross study had continued to use a formula approach since that time.[11] Seven states[12] had been using formulas in 1973 and also in 1985, but may have had a discontinuous

---

[10]California, Minnesota, Mississippi, New Mexico, and Tennessee.

[11]Alabama, Arkansas, Colorado, Florida, Georgia, Louisiana, Mississippi, Missouri, Ohio, Oklahoma, Pennsylvania, South Carolina, Tennessee, and Texas.

[12]Maryland, Minnesota, Nevada, New York, South Dakota, Virginia and West Virginia.

history of use. They were not recorded as using formulas in 1979. However, due to limitations of the 1979 study, these states probably had been using formulas continuously since 1973. If so, this would bring the total of states using formulas continuously for at least twelve years to twenty-one. Over these twelve years, four states[13] were identified as having discontinued the use of budget formulas, and nine[14] as having begun to use them. Illinois, Michigan and Nebraska were identified in 1985 as using a formula only for their community colleges.

Over the period 1973 to 1985 the "building blocks" of formulas - the base factors, the formula factors, and computational methods - appear to have remained structurally very similar, but their content has changed. Head count was not reported in use as a base factor in any formula in 1973. By 1985 it was the prime measure of choice for student services, but student credit hour production and FTE enrolment remained the main factor for use in other budget areas. The extent to which FTE enrolment, SCH production, and head count were used in 1985 appears as great as the use of the first two in 1973. In other words, the influence of enrolment on the size of grant an institution derives from the formula has not directly diminished in the past twelve years. What had changed was the process used to arrive at the base enrolment number. Head count, summer school enrolments, buffering, and decoupling were now mitigating the effect of decreases in numbers. Square footage/acreage appeared in all three studies as the base factor of choice for physical plant operation and maintenance. No clear shifts in the use of the three computational methods can be seen.

The presence in the formula of weights to differentiate costs on the basis of academic disciplines, institutional differences, and student or class levels changed little according to the data of the three studies, except for two areas. In 1985 there was an

---

[13]New Jersey, North Dakota, Washington and Wisconsin.

[14]California, Connecticut, Idaho, Kansas, Kentucky, Massachusetts, Montana, New Mexico and Oregon.

increase in the use of differential weights for the various academic areas in the instruction and academic support budget categories and a decrease of the use of weights for institutional distinctions in the operation and maintenance of physical plant budget.

The complexity of the formulas was examined by use of the following complexity factor:

Number of functional classifications

plus

Number of base factors above number of functional classifications

plus

Number of weights applied to each base factor

plus

Number of formula factors above number of base factors

Applications of this complexity factor showed that four states had increased the complexity of their formulas from 1973 to 1985, and two had decreased it. The two who showed a decrease in complexity were Colorado and Florida, two states that have recently revamped their formulas with new emphases. Florida capped enrolment and is emphasizing quality, and Colorado has constructed a model that is not tied directly to enrolment.

In 1973, 1979 and 1985 more formula states were reported from the Southeast than from any other region of the country. The gain in number of formula states by the West from one in 1973 to five in 1985 was the only sizeable change in geographic distribution.

Evidence of Quality Reward or Measurement

Twenty-one states[15] reported some technique which was

---

[15]Alabama, *Arizona*, California, Colorado, Connecticut, Florida, Georgia, Idaho, *Indiana*, Kansas, Louisiana, Massachusetts, Missouri, Montana, *New Jersey*, Ohio, Tennessee, *Utah*, Virginia, West Virginia and Wisconsin.

interpreted in their state as indicating special funding for quality. The other states may also have these, but, if so, in their responses they did not interpret them as "systems for rewarding quality or measuring performance for budget purposes". South Carolina reported a proposed quality improvement initiative program which was intended to provide incentive funds as "seed capital" for program improvement. Of the twenty-one states referred to above, five were non-formula states. These have been indicated by the use of italicized print.

Ten types of quality improvement programs were identified from the responses:

Categorical one-time grants Grants given for a specific purpose to a specific area with no promise of continuation funding. The establishment of an endowment is an example of this type of quality incentive.

Percentage of budget total The addition of a certain percentage of the total operating budget to create incentive monies for quality improvement. The method by which these funds are distributed to campuses may be one that uses preset criteria or competition.

Designated area Funding specifically earmarked for particular academic disciplines to upgrade the quality of their offerings. An example of this type of grant is special funding to upgrade computer or engineering education in order to attract "high tech" industry to a state.

Competitive grants Monies awarded to campuses or disciplines competing within the system with proposals to upgrade quality.

Program review Required periodic review of academic programs that is in some way linked either to continuation funding or to enhancement funding. This is often viewed as a type of "quality control".

Student testing An outcome measure of quality based on required testing of students on a designated instrument. Funding may be tied to the performance of students on the test or simply to the participation level of campuses in the testing program.

Other stated outcomes In addition to, or in place of, student testing, any measure of quality that emphasizes outcomes or performance. For example, in community colleges, the measurement used was job placement.

Student scholarships The state funding of merit (not need based) scholarships to attract and keep academically talented students in state and in public education, interpreted by some states as a quality improvement measure.

Centres of excellence The creation and funding of centres specifically designed to foster excellence and focus on quality issues.

Staffing The establishment and funding of chairs or reward systems designed to attract and keep quality faculty.

States reported the use of categorical one-time grants most often (ten states) as the tool for funding for quality. Examples of such grants were funds to "augment library holdings" in Alabama and funds to carry out "short-term focused strategies as defined by the Regents" in Georgia. Nine states were using a given percentage of the budget as "set aside" monies that could be used for quality enhancement.[16] The designated purpose of these funds differed from state to state. For example, the objectives ranged from curriculum innovation and new program development (Florida) to the establishment of Centres of Excellence (Colorado). Funds for designated areas, identified by six states, often overlapped these first two categories. Tennessee committed the largest percentage of resources and had a tiered system of various measures of quality by which funds were distributed. Competitive grants were discussed in seven states as tools to reward excellence with additional funding. The model ranged from competition within designated topics (such as curriculum or administrative efficiency) or within campuses (a set amount per campus to be awarded competitively).

---

[16]Alabama - two percent; Colorado - two percent; Connecticut - one percent; Florida - one percent; Georgia - one percent; Missouri - variable by campus; Ohio - one percent; Tennessee - five percent; West Virginia - one percent.

Program review, student testing, and other stated outcomes were directed toward product or outcome measurement. Nine states used program review, three used student testing, and five used other outcome measures. In all of these cases no base funding was affected by specific performance measures, only enhancement funding. Program review was often in place as part of a program budgeting tool. For example, Oklahoma changed from a budget functional basis to an educational program basis for its entire budgeting process.

Four states emphasized scholarship programs (called Eminent Scholars Programs in Florida) to retain the brightest students in the state in public education as a way of upgrading overall quality. Four states identified the establishment of centres of excellence, and five states included the establishment of special "chairs" or faculty salary bonuses as incentives to the creation of quality.

Whether these funding mechanisms are considered part of the formula or not appears to be relatively unimportant in terms of their effect. Some states place them in the narrative description of their formula, and some states specifically identify them as "outside the formula". In either case, they are established funding policy included in the budget documents and apparently as objective as any part of the formula in shaping the allocation of resources.

Conclusion

The use of formulas does not appear to be on the wane, as was sometimes anticipated in the light of decreasing enrolments. Rather, states are searching for alternative ways of coming up with flexible funding mechanisms within the formula itself. Formula budgeting appears to be alive and well, increasing in complexity, and the favoured budgeting method for the allocation of state funds to higher education. At the same time, however, states are building into their formulas potential sources of accountability that may carry with them greater political control of the higher education enterprise. In defining the quality to be rewarded, or in setting standards through the formula, state lawmakers are expanding their role in the decision-making process.

The importance of descriptions of quality enhancement measures in budget documents described in this research lies not in their complete reflection of all the programs that are occurring around the country, but rather in the interpretation by state higher education officials that these moves reflect an emphasis on quality through the use of the budget. The formula budgeting process has influenced and shaped higher education in unexpected and sometimes undesirable ways and will continue to do so in the future.[17] For example, formula budgeting and funding based on the number of students has encouraged growth and rewarded universities and colleges that admit students regardless of their qualifications and keep students regardless of performance. Ideally, decisions about the components within the formula, or the factors within any budgeting technique, should be based on sound educational philosophy, not just on cost analysis and political negotiations.

If the traditional enrolment-driven formulas reward and encourage access and growth, the addition of enhancement dollars appears designed to reward and encourage quality and competition. The selection of the criteria for excellence will be critical in determining the direction that higher education moves. They should be decided with special concern for the mission of public colleges and universities and awareness of the incentives that are built into funding decisions. In rewarding quality, the measure is not as easy to derive as the FTE students or head count of enrolment. The primary base factors being used are still input measures (such as salary, outstanding faculty, volumes in the library, the brightest students, equipment, particular programs, etc.), not output measures. Only six states described and rewarded student testing or other stated outcomes. With increased output measures could come accountability tied to funding, a governmental intrusion not seen before in higher education.

---

[17]Richard H. Allen, "New Approaches to Incentive Planning" in Larry L. Leslie (ed.), New Directions for Institutional Research; and Richard H. Allen and James R. Topping, Cost Information and Formula Funding: New Approaches (Boulder, Colorado: National Center for Higher Education Management Systems, 1979).

An emphasis on quality enhancement is being used in some budget documents to "sell" increased funding for higher education to state legislatures. The danger in this approach is that within a few years, the demand for demonstrable results for the money spent will be heard. Goals for a state's public higher education system to be ranked in the upper-quartile range nationally for salaries or student/faculty ratios are being established. With more and more states trying to reach these goals, increases in funding in every state offset each state's movement up the scale. Even student performance on standardized tests is being used to indicate quality improvement. But the tenuous linkage between the amount of dollars spent and the quality of the education[18] may cause problems in the years ahead for higher education leaders who promise too much for the dollars given.

In addition to identified quality enhancement dollars, the 1985 formulas appeared to be moving in similar directions that may indirectly reward quality. The use of data from comparable institutions to raise funding levels of formula factors, the inclusion of more items under the formula, the structured mechanisms within formula budget instructions for special requests, and the increased number of factors reflective of differences in role and mission with particular emphasis on distinguishing among academic disciplines - all these have the potential to reward less for quantity of students and more for traditional academic programs that may enhance quality. In 1985 there was an air of competition in many budget documents not seen in 1973. Evidence of this ranged from the emphasis on merit scholarships to capture and keep the brightest students in state, to the creation of prestigious faculty chairs to reward nationally-recognized faculty.

The linkage between increased enrolment and increased funding is fading, even in formula states,[19] but the states have

---

[18]Howard R. Bowen, The Costs of Higher Education (San Francisco: Jossey-Bass Publishers, 1980).

[19]Larry L. Leslie and Garey Ramey, "State Appropriations and Enrolments", Journal of Higher Education 57, (January/February, 1986), 1-19.

not abandoned enrolment as a driving factor in formulas. The changing definition of enrolment to reflect other work load realities (summer school and head count) is enabling institutions to justify increased budget requests even if their enrolments are declining. The higher percentages of funded requests may testify to the effectiveness of communication about the needs of higher education. The emphasis on quality, rather than quantity, has undoubtedly assisted in this communication with state legislatures. Whether this funding trend reflects, or helps to shape, such educational issues as access (who should be given the opportunity to enter college) cannot be determined, but the linkage is certainly present.

States appear to be changing formulas frequently, not only in response to changes in public higher education, but also to shape public higher education in particular ways and to sell increased support to state legislators. If the decisions being made about the factors that drive the formula are harbingers of the direction of public higher education, then we can expect quality, accountability, and competition to be the driving forces in the years to come.

Higher Education Associations in Washington: Influencing Government Intervention

by

Harland G. Bloland[1]

Higher education in the United States is such an important and increasingly central segment of the society that there is no way for the national government to avoid intervening to influence the system. We in higher education have attested to this importance, and encourage people to believe it. We use it to justify our existence. The significance of higher education has meant that in the U.S. the federal government and the higher education system have always had a close and continuing relationship. Therefore it is not a question of intervening or not intervening. It is rather a dispute over how much, on what basis, in what context, over what issues and with what in mind.

As the federal-higher education interaction has increased and the relationships deepened, a number of organizations and instruments have been constructed to monitor, control and, in general, manage it. One such linking structure is the higher education association which represents whole institutions. This kind of association is important because of its broad base of representation, its connection with a wide variety of information sources, and its ability to organize with other associations in a decentralized system to coordinate communication and activities which influence policy making.

Institutional representation (universities and colleges) is significant in interest group theory generally, because, as Robert Salisbury has pointed out, institutions now dominate interest representation in Washington. Who and what they represent is ambiguous. How do the associations representing colleges and universities articulate the demands of individuals and groups within the institution - the faculty, students, trustees, or administration? It is not clear who speaks for the

---

[1]Professor of Higher Education, School of Education and Allied Professions, University of Miami, Coral Gables, FL.

institution. Questions of legitimacy may arise.[2]

Although there is a large number (estimated 450) of associations in Washington representing a wide array of postsecondary interests, the most active, visible participants which represent institutions is a group of six higher education associations. Their membership consists of most colleges and universities in the United States. The group includes: the National Association of State Universities and Land Grant Colleges (NASULGC), the American Association of State Colleges and Universities (AASCU), the American Association of Community and Junior Colleges (AACJC), the Association of American Universities (AAU), the Association of American Colleges (AAC), and the National Association of Independent Colleges and Universities (NAICU). The major umbrella association is the American Council on Education (ACE).

Although they do a great many other things, the most important activity of these associations is to act as interest groups positioned between their members and the federal government (particularly Congress and the bureaus that implement policy). Since memberships overlap, and therefore their interests are sometimes duplicated, each association has primary identification with a major sector of the higher education enterprise, one which often put it at odds with the other associations. Thus, NASULGC, which is identified with the great land grant universities, looks closely at federal legislation affecting research, graduate education, low tuition, and public education generally. It is joined in its advocacy of public education and the egalitarian spirit of low tuition by AASCU, but AASCU has less interest in research and graduate education. AACJC, which represents community colleges, is also a low tuition advocate, but it concentrates on the first two years of undergraduate education and on ways to respond quickly to community needs. It is less interested in legislation about research and graduate studies. AAU represents the 56 most prestigious graduate, research dominated universities in the U.S. and Canada. It has no strong position on the

---

[2]Robert H. Salisbury, "Interest Representation: The Dominance of Institutions", American Political Science Review, Vol. 78, No. 1, (1984) pp. 64-76.

public/private issues which the other associations must confront, because it has high percentages of both types of institutions among its members. AAC has retreated from its former position of representing private institutions and now concentrates on liberal education. Therefore NAICU is the basic organization around which most of the private, independent colleges and universities cluster, seeking aid for their cause in federal policy. Overall, ACE, the umbrella association, attempts to reconcile the opposing interests within the community, and to orchestrate a coordinated, united front on behalf of higher education to Congress and the executive branch.

This paper analyzes the situation in which these associations find themselves and the milieu in which they struggle to give voice to the needs and wants of higher education in the U.S. Their actions and perspectives are placed in a context that interprets how, why, and when they can have some impact on government intervention, and when and in what circumstances they have difficulty in acting (or reacting) effectively.

Part of the explanation for action and reaction is found in the sheer complexity of the changing environment of Washington, a milieu that provides both opportunity and constraint for the associations. Some of their situation must be interpreted in the context of issues that are extremely difficult to resolve, based upon legislation that was passed some years ago, and which becomes more and more difficult to deal with as time goes on. A good example would be the problem of equitably distributing federal funds for student aid. I shall discuss the associations and their actions in the context of types of public policy that influence the ease and difficulty of problem solution.

The use of policy types to help analyze policy arena relationships, political orientations and activities, has as its most notable modern day exemplar, Theodore Lowi. His review in 1964 of American Business and Public Policy: The Politics of Foreign Trade[3] touched off a debate over whether

---

[3]Raymond A. Bauer, Itheil de Sola Pool and Lewis A. Dexter, American Business and Public Policy: The Politics of Foreign Trade (New York: Atherton Press, 1964).

policies caused politics or *vice versa* that continued among political scientists for the next two decades. Without attempting to resolve that debate, I shall relate the policy taxonomy, developed and modified by Lowi and others, to the associations in their efforts to combine two very difficult tasks: (1) representing the interests of their particular sector of higher education, (e.g., private or public) and (2) cooperating with other associations, often from opposing sectors, to represent the interests of higher education as a whole.

According to Lowi, policies are of three types, each engendering a whole set of politics and ways of groups relating to each other, with different sets of policy circumstances. Focusing on the policies that government and interests generated, his schema included: distributive, regulative and redistributive policies. This classification has been useful in organizing thinking about policy even as the argument of policy *vs.* politics has continued.

As Lowi first defined these categories, he viewed them as power arenas, each with its own, "characteristic political structure, political process, elites, and group relations".[4]

Distributive Policies

For Lowi, distributive policies

> ... are characterized by the ease with which they can be disaggregated and dispensed unit by small unit, each more or less in isolation from other units and from any general rule ... loser and recipient need never come into dire confrontation.[5]

This meant that higher education as a policy arena does not compete with agriculture for the same funds. You can give some money to education and some to agriculture and neither

---

[4]Theodore J. Lowi, "American Business, Public Policy, Case-Studies, and Political Theory", World Politics, Vol. XVI, No. 4 (July, 1964), pp. 677-715.

[5]*Ibid.*, p. 690.

need be aware or interested in the other's policy claims. It is a form of patronage in which resources are divided and divided again, so that none of the major participants feel totally deprived; and it reduces conflict.

Regulatory Policies

These are not capable of endless disaggregation as are distributive policies. These policies make direct decisions about who will be deprived and who will not. They apply to individuals or organizations, but decisions are made on the basis of a general rule. They cannot be continuously divided, as is the case with distributive policies. This is viewed as a problem in higher education when regulatory policies (e.g., those related to health and safety, age of retirement for faculty and administrators, affirmative action programs, anti-discrimination laws) are applied to institutions. Universities regularly plead that higher education is different from business and government. Although they agree in principle with many regulatory policies, because of their uniqueness, they also believe they must be treated differently (distributively). They should be in charge of their own regulation (self-regulation). In this they are not very different from other groups' desires, but the arguments they use are often interesting and unique - and in some cases may be plausible. These policies engender more conflict in higher education than do the distributive policies.

Redistributive Policies

These resemble regulatory policies in that large categories of individuals and organizations are affected. But their impact is much greater. These policies may deal with social classes (the rich, middle class, and poor); they may affect major status groups (minorities, women, the young and old) differently; they commonly involve not how property is to be used, but who owns the property. Income tax is often aimed at redistribution. So is affirmative action. However, it is not so much the final policy outcome, but its anticipated results which engender strong conflicting responses among people.[6]

---

[6]*Ibid.*, p. 691.

Lowi later (1967 and 1972) reformulated and refined his categories, and a number of other writer have built upon his initial insights. Salisbury added the notion of self-regulatory policies (1968), and other contributors include Froman (1968), Hayes (1981), Lowi (1967, 1972). This paper draws upon the work of Randall Ripley and Grace Franklin who have developed the original Lowi scheme into a four-fold policy typology. Their scheme still includes distributive and redistributive policies (although much refined over the years), but divides regulatory ones into protective regulatory and competitive regulatory policies. And they apply these categories not only to the making of policy through legislation, but to the implementation process as well.

The use of the concept of policy types is helpful in understanding the role of the six associations in Washington, because the ways in which they relate to each other, to their constituent members, to Congress and the bureaucracies are influenced greatly by the perceptions these principal actors hold of the kind of policy being formulated. In the case of redistributive policies Lowi makes a special point of saying that perception of what might happen engenders strong conflicting political positions and activities even when the policies don't actually fundamentally redistribute. In general he and others who have contributed to this literature tend to reify the policy types. They over-concretize the policy environments, assuming that participants readily and accurately perceive which policy type is under discussion, and they act on the basis of this given environment. In response to other notions about concepts of enactment and negotiation of reality (Weick, symbolic interactionists, etc.), it is the contention of this paper that these policy types are essentially viewpoints which the principal actors have and upon which they act, and thus create the policies. The views of the actors may change drastically so that at one point they believe that they are in a distributive policy arena, but later come to view their situation as regulative or redistributive. Then too, the actors have preferred policy orientations. They attempt to define and redefine the policy process so that they can then act as if one policy type is dominant rather than another. While Presidential and/or Congressional activities may be aimed at putting into effect a certain policy type (to distribute, to regulate, and/or to redistribute), other actors in the policy arena may be interpreting those actions as creating or sustaining different policy types. Moreover, they may present a sense of powerlessness and drift stemming from perceptions of larger uncontrollable forces at play (e.g., inflation, threat of war). These may modify outcomes so that what was intended as distributive easily becomes regulative or redistributive without anyone intending or desiring that it be so.

It is important to realize that the whole notion of types of policy orientation arose, to some extent, in reaction to the conflict in political science over the roles of interest groups in U.S. politics. Were interest groups to be regarded as central of politics in the U.S. or were they largely irrelevant? After several decades of defining interest groups as the centre of politics, the Bauer *et al* book[7] seemed to cast them at the periphery. One of Lowi's contributions was to suggest that their importance depended upon the type of policies being considered, and could change over time, even on the same issue.

Next I shall examine Washington's higher education "community", that is, the six major associations which constitute the core of the higher education institutional representation in the nation's capital.

The Community and the Policy Types

For the community, the most favourable of all circumstances is one in which they all agree upon a policy and it can be explained to a sympathetic Congress and administration. When that occurs, they are successful and the desired policy goes forward. In such circumstances the arena is often called a "subgovernment". Less flatteringly, it is referred to as an "iron triangle". What does this mean? As Ripley and Franklin define them, "iron triangles" are the groups of people who effect most of the routine decisionmaking in an area of policy.[8]

---

[7] Bauer *et. al.*, American Business and Public Policy.

[8] Randall B. Ripley and Grace A. Franklin, Congress, the Bureaucracy, and Public Policy. (Homewood, Il: Dorsey Press, 1984), p. 18.

A typical subgovernment is composed of members of the House and/or Senate, members of congressional staffs, a few bureaucrats, and representatives of private groups and organizations interested in a policy area. Usually the members of Congress and staff members are from the committees or subcommittees that have principal or exclusive jurisdiction over the policy area dominated by the government.[9]

Higher education's somewhat permeable iron triangle includes the House Committee on Education and Labor (particularly the Subcommittee on Postsecondary Education), the Appropriations Subcommittee on Labor, Health, Human Services and Education, the staffs of those committees and the chief counsels of the chairs of these committees, the Senate Committee on Labor and Human Resources (and its Subcommittee on Education, Arts and Humanities), and the Senate Appropriations Subcommittee on Labor, Health, Human Service and Education. In addition, there is the Secretary of Education, the Assistant Secretary for Postsecondary Education, the heads of some of the research bureaus, the executive secretaries and government relations officers of the community of associations, and a shifting group of prominent university presidents.

In the case of higher education, the subgovernment for many circumstances may be more of an ideal than a reality. For, as Ripley and Franklin point out, a functioning subgovernment tends to deal with matters that are routine, "... policy that is not currently embroiled in a high degree of controversy".[10] For the associations, routine tends to turn into the non-routine, as Congress tries to formulate and the bureaux to implement legislation that will have an impact upon higher education.

The subgovernment, distributive policy process operates well when the community, through discussion, negotiation,

---

[9]*Ibid.*, p. 10.

[10]*Ibid.*

compromise, and cooperation, can present a single voice to Congress. If the proposed policy does not encroach upon another major policy domain it is in the realm of distributive policymaking. Then, given a congressional committee and subcommittee structure that is actually attempting to do something for higher education, much of the policymaking which occurs will be successful. It will not be very widely publicized. It will be relatively noncontroversial. Congress intends a distributive policy process to take place when it calls upon the associations to stop going their individual ways and present some coherent, united policy proposals. This happens more often than one would suspect, given the general climate in which higher education has been formulated in the postwar years.[11]

Of special note is the proposition that Congress tries to deal even handedly with the private and public institutions - particularly in the area of student aid. When policy is formulated that the representatives of the two sets of institutions feel has been fair, particularly when Congress wishes to distribute some benefits to higher education, the noncontroversial distributive subgovernmental situation prevails. In fact, the community feels it is being successful. However, this type of peaceful distributive policy is disturbed when the "low-profile" activities are opened up to outsiders. This may happen in several ways, all of which modify substantially the environment. First, "... if the subgovernment participants themselves disagree on some point fundamentally, this disagreement may become publicized and stimulate attention and intrusion from non-members of the subgovernment".[12]

This occurs frequently on questions of student aid - whether it should be distributed on an equal basis or on the basis of tuition costs. Such a question calls into consideration some very basic

---

[11]See Lawrence E. Gladieux and Thomas R. Wolanin, Congress and the Colleges. (Lexington, Mass.: D.C. Heath, 1976.)

[12]Ripley and Franklin, Congress, the Bureaucracy, and Public Policy, pp. 10-11.

issues concerning the purposes and status of private and public institutions. It brings to the surface the fundamental divergence on egalitarianism *vs.* quality in higher education. It attracts interested persons and groups far beyond the subgovernment. The newspapers, television, magazines, and public figures will begin to react to the issue, expanding it beyond the controllable boundaries of the subgovernment. I shall return to this question later in terms of its overtones of redistributive policy and the conflict that is engendered by this definition of the issue.

Second, interest on the part of the President of the United States, a change in the composition of the Senate and/or the House could result in the spotlight being turned upon the policies of a previous administration that were congenial to the current subgovernment policy process. Thus, the entry of the Reagan administration in Washington, and the Republican majority in the Senate, created a situation in which there was, from the associations' point of view, a rising tide of negative interest emanating from the White House and Congress. Chester Finn, the current head of the Office of Educational Research and Improvement (successor to NIE), wrote an interesting article on the probable demise of the "liberal consensus" which he described as characterizing education policy from the end of World War II. The old loyalties and comfortable subgovernments could no longer count on reciprocal protection.

Third,

> ... a new issue that attracts the attention of outsiders can be introduced into the subgovernment's jurisdiction. The new issue can upset normal decision making if it is more important or different in character from the issues the subgovernment is used to dealing with, especially if the issue involves regulation of private activities or redistribution of wealth to one group at the expense of another.[13]

---

[13]*Ibid.*, p. 11.

For the community, the conflict that started in the late 1960s and gathered momentum in the seventies centred upon the increasing regulation of higher education activities. OSHA, civil rights legislation and affirmative action all threatened the smooth functioning of the subgovernment. They thrust what were essentially regulatory politics upon the subgovernment, making its ability to control policy much more uncertain. In general, when events, persons or circumstances intrude upon the subgovernment's formulation and sustenance of distributive policies, the associations as interest groups, become less effective, so they have a stake in organizing and maintaining distributive policy arenas. This means there is a real need to limit the number of participants in the policy process and to limit the number of issues that must be dealt with.

Ripley and Franklin divide regulatory policies into two types, competitive regulatory and protective regulatory.

Competitive Regulatory Policies

They aim at

> ... limiting the provision of specific goods and services to only one or a few designated deliverers. Some of the potential deliverers who want the business win; some lose ... This type of policy is a hybrid, which subsidizes the winning competitors and also tries to regulate some aspects of service delivery in the public interest.[14]

This policy orientation occurs in higher education particularly with the awarding of research funds to universities. This research is in the public interest, as defined by the federal government - research for defense purposes, to increase the yield of agricultural products, to eliminate poverty, to underwrite medical research, research to fight delinquency, research on drug abuse. Competitive regulatory policy requires individuals, departments or institutions to compete

---

[14]*Ibid.*, p. 26.

for the funds to undertake such research as the government wishes to have carried on. The regulatory part occurs because the activity is subject to the oversight of Congress and its agencies. There is the threat of recalling funds. There are monitoring and reporting regulations which involve constant activity if the funds are to be renewed. These can generate considerable conflict between the bureaucracies and the institutions of higher education. There is hostility toward the number and types of regulation, the timing of fund allocations, and the levels of permitted overhead payments. Recently there has also been conflict disrupting relations among institutions, and between the associations and congress, for example over the process of allotting funds for coal gassification research to an institution, not on the basis of the normal peer review process, but as a result of direct appeal to, and lobbying of, Congress to grant the award. This created considerable upheaval among the major research universities. It represents a case of how competitive regulatory policies can become highly controversial.

Protective Regulatory Policies

This policy type, and the programs that accompany it, are "designed to protect the public by setting the conditions under which various private activities can be undertaken. Conditions that are thought to be harmful (air pollution, false advertising) are prohibited; conditions that are thought to be helpful (the publication of interest rates on loans) are required".[15]

Such policies cause conflict because they cannot be divided endlessly in the way that distributive policy benefits can. A set of rules and regulations is established that is supposed to apply to (and confer benefit on) whole classes of persons and activities. The concomitant prohibitions, limitations and commands to act create strong reaction among the classes they are supposed to apply to. In higher education, the most important recent protective regulatory policies have been in the areas of discrimination, with regard to hiring practices, promotion and tenure policies, health and safety requirements, and so on. Affirmative action was certainly intended to be

---

[15]*Ibid.*, p. 27.

redistributive. Higher education institutions, as well as the associations, believe it should be redistributive - but on their terms. Their case is not against redistribution as such but upon the locus of decision making for protective regulatory policy.

The Higher Education Act as Distributive and Redistributive Policy

In 1965, Congress passed the Higher Education Act, the intent of which was to set in motion a redistributive policy using federal funds to students and institutions of higher education to effect the intended change. The purposes and effects of that law now look more distributive than redistributive, but one major purpose of that act was to encourage less affluent young people to study, thus enhancing equal educational opportunity through the provision of financial aid to students. The major redistributive section of the bill was a program of educational opportunity grants. These aimed at helping individuals whose financial needs were exceptional to go to college with the inclusion of a work-study program and subsidized loans, targetted at low and middle income families. All economically marginal groups seemed to be covered. However, the actual amount of money made available was relatively modest, and much of the bill was devoted to a number of categorical programs for other purposes, many of which assisted institutions, e.g., aid to developing institutions, college construction grants.

A much larger conflict arose when reauthorization of the Higher Education Act came before Congress in the early 1970s. The associations, reflecting the wishes of many college presidents, favoured a shift to direct institutional aid. This proposal was written into the 1965 law, but without appropriations, even as there was growing sentiment within Congress and other interested parties for changes in the act to greatly enhance the opportunities for needy students to go to college. The universities were certainly not opposed to student aid. But, in terms of policy perspectives, the association community was seeking a distributive law, in which substantial funds would also go directly to their institutions to be used as the institutional leaders thought appropriate. Such a policy would reduce the public visibility of the funding allocation and enhance the significance of the subgovernmental decision-making process.

The law that was eventually passed, the Higher Education Amendments of 1972, was clearly a bold move on the part of Congress to establish a redistributive policy. Its most important part was a reaffirmation of student aid over institutional aid, and its transformation from aid for equal opportunity to entitlement. This was a change from the opportunity of a qualified student to gain a college education to a right of a qualified student to attend college.[16] The scholarship program of the 1965 act was retained, but the major increase in funding was for the neediest students.

Once the law was passed, the institutions of higher education quickly accepted the new mandate and worked to regularize the federal/higher education relations by re-establishing, to a large extent, a distributive, subgovernmental set of relationships to deal with the changed circumstances. This was possible because all institutions of higher education benefitted greatly from the new student aid. Congress and the associations worked diligently and successfully to make certain that neither private nor public education would feel discriminated against in the student aid entitlement programs. However, just beneath the surface of community cooperation and unity was a problem that would later emerge and build into a deeply, divisive aspect of the association relations. This was how to treat the independent and public institutions with equal fairness in the allocation of funds to students, when there were ever widening differentials in tuition charges between the private and public schools. The question of fairness was posed as equal benefits *vs.* need benefits. If students were granted equal benefits, i.e., the same amount of money to enable them to attend college, many would have to select the less expensive public institutions. If, however, the money was allocated as a percentage of tuition costs, then more funds would go to

---

[16]Advisory Commission on Intergovernmental Relations, "The Evolution of a Problematic Partnership: The Feds and Higher Ed" in The Federal Role in the Federal System: The Dynamics of Growth. (Washington, DC: ACIR, U.S. Department of Education, National Institute of Education, Educational Resource and Information Centre, 1981), p. 25.

students who attended private institutions since the larger grants could offset their much higher tuition charges.

The 1972 Amendments Act was the high water mark in recent years of Congressional efforts to generate redistributive policies that would provide more opportunities for the less affluent to attend postsecondary institutions. By the mid 1970s, there was a growing sense that middle class families were not benefitting enough from the federal student aid programs. While this engendered some Congressional support for tuition tax credit legislation, neither the Carter administration nor the community were enamoured with this means of effecting redistributive policy. To the associations, tuition tax credits looked to be skewed in favour of private colleges and universities. Therefore, their solution was to promote a distributive policy. They asked for more money both for poor students and for middle class students. For Congress and the Carter administration this had sufficient consensus, so the Middle Income Student Assistance Act was passed in 1978. Although the name strongly suggests redistributive policy, in fact, by asking and receiving more funds for new groups, it is a distributive policy *par* excellence. Its passage indicates that the subgovernment relationships were working well. And the reauthorization bills of 1976 and 1980 were also instances of distributive policies working fairly smoothly. Financial aid to students was extended and fine tuned.

The Emergence of Accentuated Federal Regulatory Policy

Although the federal government always regulates as it promotes the public good, the passage of the various laws aiding postsecondary students, constructing facilities, and stimulating research had brought a welcome infusion of funds with what appeared to be a minimum of regulation. However, with the passage of the 1972 Amendments visible government regulation took a sharp upturn. The 1972 Act itself was heavily influenced by groups and perspectives which were external to the higher education establishment. The trend toward federal action to promote equity and encourage opportunity for those who had previously been excluded, meant there was greater federal willingness to intervene sharply in higher education policy and to press strongly for accountability, i.e., to create procedures which would ensure that the policies were implemented as intended.

In addition, a series of regulations emerged from social action legislation which directly affected higher education, although higher education was not the specific target of the legislation. These laws and regulations included: the Equal Pay Act of 1963; Equal Employment Opportunity-Tile VII of the Civil Rights Act of 1964 and its amendments; Affirmative Action - the Executive Order 11246 of 1965; Age Discrimination - amendment to the Employment Act of 1967; Occupational Safety and Health Act of 1970; Environmental Protection Regulations; the Rehabilitation Act with its sections on Access for the Handicapped.

These across the board regulations applied to business, government agencies, and other places of employment, as well as to higher education institutions. But there were additional regulations that were directed specifically toward higher education, e.g., the Educational Rights and Privacy Act (Buckley Amendment), which dealt with how student records should be treated.

This rapid increase in protective regulatory policies touched off strong negative reaction from college and university presidents and their association representatives. For a period of time, relief from what the institutions perceived as excessive government regulation superceded the quest for funding as the first priority for higher education in Washington. The most prestigious, graduate, research-oriented universities were the most outspoken critics of the new regulatory atmosphere. President Derek Bok of Harvard, President Muller of Johns Hopkins and others spoke eloquently of the negative effect of federal regulation.

Four issues were especially salient. First, the affirmative action provisions and extensions of the Equal Pay Act seemed to threaten the traditional academic merit system of rewards and standards, and to threaten academic freedom through the creation of extensive federal monitoring systems and the collection of elaborate data on employment procedures and policies.[17]

Second, the costs to universities and colleges of complying with federal regulations were viewed as excessive and increasing. The American Council on Education reported that compliance costs for federally mandated programs added between one and four percent to institutions' operating budgets.[18]

Third, institutions were concerned that academic priorities were being distorted by the demand for federal conformity and that institutional resources, time, and energies were being exhausted by the burdens of regulation.

Fourth, higher education representatives were especially incensed by the practice of requiring entire institutions to conform to the federal regulations when the regulations seemed to pertain only to a particular federally funded program. Thus, for example, federal support for physics meant there must be federal regulation of admissions to the art school.

There has been considerable unresolved debate concerning whether or not the regulations were in fact unfair and excessive, especially in relation to an assertion that higher education is neither a kind of business, nor a typical government bureaucracy. The argument is that higher education is unique, and it needs greater autonomy in order to fulfill its aims and its responsibilities to society.

Since the aims and purposes of federal, protective regulatory policies were focused on concepts of justice, fairness, and equal opportunity, goals that the institutions heartily endorse, the higher education spokespersons argued that their institutions were the most responsible, appropriate and sensitive monitors of these social aims. Therefore, self regulation was the best means of assuring that social justice would be served on the campus. The Washington association community conducted

---

[17]*Ibid.*, p. 36.

[18]*Ibid.*, p. 38.

studies, publicized higher education concerns, and orchestrated prominent presidential statements on the burdens of regulation. By the mid 1970s, Congress, the incumbent administration and the agencies had begun to ease the burdens of the perceived high level of federal regulation. In a basic way these federal regulatory policies actually offered the means for the associations to cooperate and present a coordinated, unified approach to government. Despite the fact that the policies affected the university and college sectors differently (research-oriented and private institutions were the most disturbed by the regulatory policies), all institutions identified with the idea of autonomy and self regulation. Therefore there was the basis for real cooperation among the associations.

New Forms of Government Intervention

No matter what the U.S. federal government does, it greatly affects higher education. Both government involvement and government non-involvement can become major instances of intervention. Thus, when Ronald Reagan was elected President of the United States and brought to the White House a philosophy and set of policies aimed at reducing government involvement in a wide range of domestic activities, including federal involvement in higher education, the effect was that of massive intervention in the higher education enterprise.

As the Reagan administration took aim at all domestic programs other than those related to defense, and successfully introduced proposals to reduce those portions of the federal budget, the higher education community quickly shifted priorities, from protesting against government regulation to attempting to preserve federal funding of higher education, particularly the student aid programs. In the first year of the new administration a spirit of good citizenship and fairness prevailed, and there was not much hard lobbying directed toward exempting higher education aid. However, all domestic programs were under scrutiny and would be cut, including higher education. For 1983 the administration budget contained proposals that would have slashed Pell grants by 40 percent and eliminated a series of other established higher education programs. This was indeed a threat that brought the disparate sectors of higher education together in an all out effort to preserve the federal government's fiscal presence in postsecondary education. It not only brought the associations together but generated a massive grass roots campaign organized by the Washington community to influence Congress to stave off the impending Draconian losses. The grass roots campaign was a success. A sympathetic congress, temporarily at least, saved the student aid programs.

However, much larger events and circumstances were impinging upon the subgovernment of higher education, now somewhat in disarray, modifying substantially the environment in which it operates. The huge and increasingly out of control federal debt encouraged Congress to pass the Graham, Rudman, Hollings Act. This law seemed to shift responsibility and accountability for federal fiscal policy out of the hands of Congress, dumping it into a decision-making device that would trigger across the board cuts when federal spending exceeds income.

Perhaps, even more drastically, Congress became enmeshed in an odd redistributive policy action through the passage of a tax reform bill that looked singularly beneficial to both the very rich and the poor, or at least those poor who have some potentially taxable income. For higher education, the impact of this reform is unknown. Probably it will have a bad effect, at least on institutional fundraising. One highly praised aspect of the reform was that it would eliminate a host of tax breaks that benefitted some groups, businesses and individuals, and not others. It was argued that this would be accompanied by generally lower income tax rates. In terms of higher education, the effect of the reform might well be to discourage gifts to universities and colleges that had previously been tax exempt. This at a time when the administration was urging government to do less directly for higher education since it should (and could) be responsible for its own funding - both private and public institutions having discovered the great benefits accruing to private fundraising. Endowments could be increased, institutional autonomy enhanced, new programs started, new faculty hired and buildings and equipment added.

Within the higher education community itself the signs of disequilibrium were abundant. The strong imperative to suppress differences which had accompanied the need to present a unified front and preserve the structure of the student aid programs in the early 1980s had persuaded the private sector associations to compromise far too much on the question of how student aid should be distributed. By the mid-1980s they felt that they had made a bad deal. One might say that they had been encouraged to participate in distributive policy formation, but they now realized that this had had a very unfavourable redistributive result. With the Reauthorization Bill (unresolved at the writing of the paper), the central political problem for the higher education associations and their constituents is that a climate of uncontrolled redistribution policy pervades Washington. And the redistribution process is taking place without much thought for its consequences for higher education. Whether the associations cooperate with each other and present a united front, or whether each tries to obtain its own needs by its own efforts, seems to make little difference. The forces external to higher education now seem much stronger and capricious in terms of their effects on higher education, and we have evidence of the extreme impact the U.S. federal government in its efforts to solve some of the fundamental problems of society.

The Drunkard's Streetlamp? Contexts of Policy Change in U.S. Teacher Education

by

Catherine Cornbleth

and

Don Adams[1]

There is a story of a drunkard searching under a street lamp for his house key, which he had dropped some distance away. Asked why he didn't look where he dropped it, he replied, "It's lighter here!"[2]

The calls in the U.S. for school reform which were heard in 1983-84 were followed by changes in state education and teacher education policy and in 1985-86 by further calls for the reform of preservice teacher education. Of interest in this paper are (a) the extent and nature of the recent calls for teacher education reform and state level teacher education policy changes and, particularly, (b) the contexts in which the changes are being made. What factors in the policy environment seem to account for the current attention to teacher education and emerging policy reformulation? What are likely future policy directions?

At one level, both the commission reports calling for teacher education reform and the changes in state teacher education policy to date can be seen as responses to the school reform reports which cited the poor quality of teachers and teaching as a principal cause of a "rising tide of mediocrity". Examination

---

[1]Associate Professor, Departments of Instruction and Learning and of Administrative and Policy Studies, School of Education, University of Pittsburgh; Director, International and Development Education Program and Professor of Education, Economic and Social Development, University of Pittsburgh, Pittsburgh, PA.

[2]A. Kaplan, The Conduct of Inquiry (San Francisco: Chandler, 1964), p. 11.

of the state policy changes in their structural and socio-cultural contexts, however, suggests a more complex interpretation. The apparent context is not necessarily the effective context that actually shapes policy change. Anticipating the outcomes of our analysis, we suggest there are multiple, interacting contexts for the changes in teacher education policy; where the light is bright is not necessarily where satisfactory explanations are to be found.

Although U.S. teacher education has been the subject of continuing critique, exhortation, and debate, little attention has been paid to questions of policy and context. Consequently, the present analysis is an exploratory one, drawing upon work in other areas such as theory of education systems. For example, we adapt Archer's conceptual framework[3] to organize our inquiry and first consider the recent history and situation of teacher education (structural conditioning) and the various calls for teacher education reform and emerging policy changes (social interaction). Context as we conceptualize it is broader than Archer's structural conditioning; it also encompasses extrasystemic demographic, social, political, and economic

---

[3]From a macro-sociological position strongly influenced by Weber, M.S. Archer in Social Origins of Educational Systems (University edition) (London: Sage, 1984) offers an account of the emergence of national educational systems and their subsequent change (specifically England and France) characterized by a three-phase cycle of structural conditioning, social interaction, and structural elaboration. The structure of the education system is seen to condition but not determine the actions of individuals and groups within it. Social interaction is a function of both structural conditioning and extrasystemic influences. The structural elaboration or system change resulting from social interaction then conditions subsequent social interaction. Within this framework, we see teacher education as a subsystem of the national education system that is subject to influences from the structural conditioning and social interaction of the larger system as well as its own internal relations and dynamic. We also note that the boundaries of the education system in the U.S. are not well defined. In fact, they seem to shift with the time, place, and issue of interest. Thus, our conception of context as encompassing but not limited to systemic factors or structural conditioning and our attention to relevant social interaction (e.g., commission activity) that spans the education system and its environment.

conditions, traditions, and ideologies.[4] Finally, we briefly speculate on the contexts of future changes in teacher education policy.

Teacher Education in the U.S. Education System

Contemporary U.S. teacher education lacks a clearly differentiated and coherent mission, and its precarious location within higher education results in vulnerability to external pressures. These conditions emerged from teacher education's historical experience of competing expectations and divided control.[5] We shall briefly sketch some outlines of that history with particular attention to structural factors which shaped teacher education policy and practice.

Teacher education programs encompassing both academic subject areas and professional education studies leading to the baccalaureate degree did not become widely institutionalized in schools, colleges, or departments of education (SCDEs) in colleges and universities until the first quarter of the 20th century. Earlier, teachers had been prepared in so-called normal schools, which appeared in the early 19th century along with "normal departments" in urban high schools and local or state supported teacher institutes for inservice training.[6] It was not until the post-World War II period that we find the majority of U.S. elementary and secondary teachers with at least a baccalaureate degree level of education. Today, most

---

[4]Cf, J. Meyer and B. Rowan, "Institutional Organizations: Formal Structure as Myth and Ceremony", American Journal of Sociology, Vol. 83, No. 2 (1977), pp. 340-363.

[5]See, for example, M.L. Borrowman, The Liberal and Technical in Teacher Education (New York: Bureau of Publications, Teachers College, Columbia University, 1956); J.E. Lanier, Research on Teacher Education, Ocassional Paper No. 80 (East Lansing, Mi: Michigan State University, Institute for Research on Teaching, 1984); and A.G. Powell, The Uncertain Profession (Cambridgeg: Harvard University Press, 1980).

[6]D. Warren, "Learning from Experience: History and Teacher Education" Educational Researcher, Vol. 4, No. 10 (1985), pp. 5-12.

school teachers have a master's degree, or its equivalent in graduate credit hours.

Since the mid-19th century teacher education reform efforts have been directed toward increasing the length of teacher preparation in academic, professional, and practical (i.e., on-site or school-based) studies. This increased preparation has been accomplished largely by mandate, particularly through the states' requirements for teacher certification. Through the 1930s, "creating and strengthening the institutional framework of teacher education superseded concern about its quality".[7] Structural growth was perceived as qualitative improvement.

In the 1980s, the institutions providing teacher education face competing and often conflicting expectations with limited resources and autonomy. The more than 1200 SCDEs are housed in colleges and universities where they are often underfunded and looked down upon by arts and sciences faculties and other professional schools. They are constrained by state program approval and teacher certification requirements, buffeted by changing market conditions, and expected to serve schools as they are. Teacher educators continue to struggle to obtain scholarly acceptance and respectability within the university and professional status outside. They also attempt to meet state and market demands and to provide leadership for school improvement.[8]

Among the structural or systemic factors shaping teacher education, one might cite: the organization and relationships of SCDE faculty and administrators within SCDEs and within their colleges or universities; local area schools and teacher and administrator associations; the state government including the state education agency, state board of education, governor, and legislature; accreditation agencies such as NCATE (National Council for the Accreditation of Teacher

---

[7]*Ibid.*, p. 10.

[8]See, for example, H. Judge, <u>American Graduate Schools of Education: A View from Abroad</u> (New York: Ford Foundation, 1982).

Education); professional associations of teacher educators, educational researchers, other education specialists, and academics; and the national government including executive agencies such as the Department of Education, Congress, and the federal judiciary.[9]. This number does not include government agencies, foundations, or locally oriented and SCDE affiliated groups.] Given the number of SCDEs and the diversity of interests represented across 50 states, both the control and the responsibility for teacher education are multifaceted and uneasily shared.

Teacher education, like elementary and secondary education in the U.S., is a state responsibility. The states' influence upon teacher education programs has been strong and direct, primarily through their power to approve SCDE teacher preparation programs and to certify teachers. In this period of national concern about schooling, the states have played an active role. Although there are discernible trends in current state actions, there appears to be no common teacher education reform agenda and no single predominant interest group.[10] The plurality of competing interests and influences on teacher education policy seems likely to continue.

Calls for Reform

School Reform Reports

The 1983-84 school reform reports, of which the National Commission on Excellence in Education's A Nation at Risk[11]

---

[9]In February 1986, AACTE published a directory of more than 150 organizations related to teacher education (Directory of Organizations Related to Teacher Education, [Washington, DC: American Association of Colleges for Teacher Education, Eric Clearinghouse on Teacher Education, 1986].

[10]See R.L. Jacobson, "National Groups Starting to Jockey for Position in Movement to Reform Education of Teachers", The Chronicle of Higher Education, 5 June 1985, pp. 14-15.

[11]National Commission for Excellence in Education, A Nation at Risk: The Imperative for Educational Reform (Washington, DC: U.S. Government Printing Office, 1983).

was the most widely publicized, directed attention not only to curriculum and standards, school leadership and management, but also to teachers and teaching. While low pay and lack of incentives were cited as factors discouraging able people from entering or remaining in teaching, the perceived weakness of teachers and teaching was attributed primarily to the poor quality of present teacher preparation programs.

To improve teacher education, the school reform reports urged establishment of high standards for program admission and completion, including competence in an academic discipline and demonstration of effective teaching performance. These standards are to be maintained jointly by SCDEs and state certifying agencies who will administer the required tests. Mandatory testing is to assure undefined quality.

Teacher Education Reform Reports

The 1985-86 teacher education reform reports can be seen, in part, as responses to the earlier school reform reports.[12] While the 1980s have seen various calls for reform of teacher education,[13] none has generated the attention and response of the recent commission reports. Three reports are of interest here because of their national scope and audience.[14] In order of appearance they are: AACTE's A Call for Change in Teacher

---

[12]The National Commission for Excellence in Teacher Education's Call for Change in Teacher Education (1985), for example, is explicitly offered as a response to the National Commission on Excellence in Education's Nation at Risk (1983).

[13]For example, B.O. Smith's A Design for a School of Pedagogy (Washington, DC: Department of Education, 1980).

[14]Other reports include C.E. Feistritzer's The Making of a Teacher (Washington, DC: National Center for Education Information, 1984); the Southern Regional Education Board's Improving Teacher Education: An Agenda for Higher Education and the Schools (Atlanta: Southern Regional Education Board, 1985); and the California Commission on the Teaching Profession's Who Will Teach Our Children?: A Strategy for Improving California's Schools (Sacramento, Ca: California Commission on the Teaching Profession, 1985).

Education[15]; The Holmes Group's Tomorrow's Teachers[16]; the Carnegie Task Force on Teaching as a Profession's A Nation Prepared: Teachers for the 21st Century.[17]

None of these teacher education reform commissions was a national government sponsored group such as the National Commission on Excellence in Education that produced A Nation at Risk. Two of the three were initiated from within the profession (AACTE, The Holmes Group) and one included only deans and professors of education from "major research-intensive universities" (The Holmes Group) rather than representatives of SCDEs, teachers, government, and business as had been the case with the school reform commissions. Only the Carnegie Forum Task Force can be considered an outsider to teacher education. Chaired by an IBM vice-president and chief scientist, the 14 member commission included six current or former state or national government officials (three with education posts), four business, corporation, or foundation executives, and one teacher educator (the dean who chaired The Holmes Group). Interestingly, both of the insider initiated commissions received financial support from private foundations (Carnegie Corporation of New York, Ford, Hewlett, Johnson, Lilly, New York Times) and the U.S. Department of Education (from then Secretary Terrel Bell's discretionary fund). Despite the internal initiation of two of these three commissions, the range of interests and sources of funding represented can be interpreted as illustrating teacher education's dependence on others for support, direction and credibility.

---

[15]AACTE, National Commission for Excellence in Teacher Education, A Call for Change in Teacher Education (Washington, DC: American Association of Colleges for Teacher Education, 1985).

[16]The Holmes Group, Tomorrow's Teachers: A Report of the Holmes Group (East Lansing, Mi: The Holmes Group, 1986).

[17]Carnegie Task Force on Teaching as a Profession, A Nation Prepared: Teachers for the 21st Century (Washington, DC: Carnegie Forum on Education and the Economy, 1986).

Six categories of recommendations can be distinguished in the teacher education reform reports:

1. higher standards and competency testing for prospective teachers (AACTE, Carnegie, Holmes)

2. redesign of teacher education programs (AACTE, Carnegie, Holmes)

3. improvement in conditions of teaching (AACTE, Carnegie, Holmes)

4. differentiation of teacher roles (Carnegie, Holmes)

5. accountability for teacher education (AACTE)

6. increased resources for teacher education (AACTE)

The recommendations in each category vary in intended audience or action site (e.g., SCDEs, state governments) as well as degree of specificity. While there are similarities across the reports, there are also important differences (particularly in categories 2 and 4). It is noteworthy that the recommendations extend beyond teacher education *per se* to the conditions of teaching in elementary and secondary schools (category 3) and the organizational structure, i.e., roles and relationships, of schooling (category 4); the retention and performance of better or more highly qualified teachers prepared by SCDEs requires that they be supported in their teaching, and granted status and responsibility commensurate with their expertise.

Higher standards and competency testing All three reports call for higher academic standards for admission to teacher education programs and for graduation and/or certification. Standards are to be maintained by means of competency testing. Entry standards should focus on general education and communication skills. Competency assessment at graduation or certification should include demonstration of effective classroom teaching.

The new standards and assessments, presumably, are to be instituted and carried out jointly by SCDEs and the states. In addition, Holmes proposed creating Professional Teacher Examinations, and Carnegie proposed establishing a National Board for Professional Teaching Standards which would set standards and assess and certify teachers who meet them.

Having survived the more selective admission process proposed in these reports, candidates would enter more coherent and rigorous, as well more practice oriented, teacher education programs than now exist in most SCDEs.

Redesign of teacher education programs All three reports are in agreement with the AACTE in calling for an "exacting, intellectually challenging integration of liberal studies, subject specialization from which school curricula are drawn, and content and skills of professional education". Carnegie and Holmes also call for strengthening liberal studies and academic specializations, which generally are not the responsibility of SCDEs, and note that both arts and sciences and professional studies must be redesigned to prepare candidates for Professional Teacher Examinations or Board certification.

Extended, supervised field experience is recommended by all three reports. In addition to student-teaching prior to graduation and certification, AACTE called for a state mandated induction period or internship of at least a year. During this time, provisionally certified teachers would have a reduced teaching schedule and participate in professional development activities jointly provided by the school district, experienced teachers, and colleges-universities (including SCDEs). Holmes called for clinical experience at multiple sites, preferably at designated Professional Development Schools. Such schools would participate in a "structured partnership" with the SCDEs characterized by shared teaching, cooperative supervision, and collaborative research. Carnegie called for paid internships and residencies, preferably in designated "clinical schools" analogous to teaching hospitals.

The major difference among the reports with respect to the design of new teacher education programs is that Carnegie and Holmes, but not AACTE, would have the states and/or colleges-universities abolish undergraduate degrees in education and make a bachelor's degree with an academic major the requirement for admission to a graduate, professional education master's degree program.[18] Whereas Holmes looks to its member institutions to take the lead in making the desired changes, Carnegie looks to SCDEs in collaboration with school professionals, supported by college-university leadership and state incentives such as recognition of Board certification in teacher compensation plans. Finally, both AACTE and Carnegie recommended state encouragement and support for experimental teacher education programs, particularly those that involved major structural changes and new relationships within the schools.

Improvement in conditions of teaching All three reports, especially Carnegie, presented strong arguments that the recruitment and retention of more capable teachers is dependent on substantial improvement in the conditions under which teachers work in elementary and secondary schools. SCDEs can prepare better teachers, but teacher education by itself cannot improve classroom teaching and learning. The recommendations in this category directed states and local school districts not only to raise teachers' salaries but also to

---

[18]A "minority" report signed by nine of the 17 members of the AACTE commission called for a fifth year program requiring a bachelor's degree with an academic major for admission. While not advocating an end to undergraduate teacher education, the AACTE recommendations would seem to require extension of the typical four-year program. It should be noted that, in this guise has emerged once more the old controversy between "concurrent" and "end on" patterns of teacher pre-professional preparation. Since this is a Canadian audience many of you will know that the concurrent program by which students simultaneously undertook liberal academic studies and professional teacher studies was the common British pattern for elementary school teacher education, and the end on pattern was in general use for would-be secondary school teachers. We understand that this pattern is still the common one in Ontario for secondary school student teachers (they enter as three-year general or four-year honours graduates a one-year diploma type B.Ed. program). And after the McLeod Commission recommendations, in the late 1960s and early 1970s, when the Teachers Colleges of Ontario were closed, for elementary school student teachers the new university programs provided both concurrent and end on patterns. The McLeod Report also recommended the creation of interesting programs for university graduates, which would be jointly administered by the SCDEs and the big metropolitan school boards in the province. We understand this innovation was tried for several years but by the mid-70s no such programs remained.

provide them with time, space, materials and technology, support services, and autonomy, i.e., with participation in decision-making commensurate with their professional responsibilities. In other words, there was a call to treat teachers as professionals and hold them accountable for student learning. Carnegie and Holmes also recommended revision of the structure of teaching, which would require changes in the present division of authority between teachers and administrators, and reallocation of resources from "administrative overhead" to instruction (see next section).

Differentiation of teacher roles Both Carnegie and Holmes recommended the restructuring of teaching. The former proposed distinguishing and certifying "Lead Teachers" with "proven ability to provide active leadership in the redesign of the schools and in helping their colleagues to uphold high standards of learning and teaching". The latter proposed a three-tier system of Instructors, Professional Teachers, and Career Professionals. Career professionals (estimated at 20 percent of the teacher force), having "proven their excellence in teaching and in their own education [usually by having a doctorate], and in examinations", would assume roles similar to clinical professors in medicine. Professional teachers (the majority) would have demonstrated "competence at work, in rigorous professional qualification examinations, and in their own education" - the latter being a master's program which includes a year of supervised teaching. Instructors would be temporary (licensed for up to five years), beginning teachers, usually with an academic bachelor's degree, who have passed tests in their subject area, communication skills, and "rudiments of pedagogy". Their teaching would be "supported and supervised" by career professionals. This proposed restructuring calls on the Holmes Group members to provide the appropriate graduate programs for professional teachers and career professionals and, in conjunction with assessment specialists, to provide the various competency examinations, and calls on the states to offer the different teaching licenses.

Accountability for teacher education By not directly addressing the question of accountability, Carnegie and Holmes seem to leave accountability with SCDEs and the states. However, they proposed, in effect, to hold SCDEs (and perhaps also the states) accountable through the voluntary teacher examinations and certification which are to be developed. The Holmes Group further commits its member SCDEs "to establish accreditation standards that reflect our five major goals". AACTE, in contrast, explicitly endorsed the *status quo* by recommending that "teacher education programs should continue to be located in colleges and universities", that "certification and program approval standards and decisions should continue to be state responsibilities in consultation with the profession", and that voluntary national accreditation (specifically, NCATE) should be strengthened.

Resources for teacher education Here, AACTE called on college-university and SCDE administrators to provide sufficient resources for the recommended teacher education program improvements, and on the states and federal government to support "the further development, dissemination, and use of research information in education and teacher education".

Together, the teacher education reform reports move considerably beyond earlier school reform reports' call for higher standards and competency testing for admission to teacher education programs and for graduation. Although standards remain prominent, attention is directed not only to controls but also to structural change and substantive program improvement. The Carnegie and Holmes reports are more innovative and less deferential to both the states and the 1200+ SCDEs than is the AACTE report. They would, for example, put out of business the more than 600 SCDEs which do not offer graduate degrees. Holmes looks to its own members to initiate the desired changes, including examinations and accreditation. Carnegie plans to establish a voluntary National Board for Professional Teaching Standards and invites teacher involvement and support. All the reports point to the interdependence of higher education, teacher education, and school teaching, and the resulting need for coordinated reform strategies. Whether there will be such a "second generation" of education reform in the late 1980s, what Carnegie calls "a renewed education agenda", remains to be seen.

State Level Policy Changes

In the United States, of all governmental levels, it is the states that have the most influence on teacher education. States certify and/or license teachers (a clear distinction between certification and licensure is not made in most states) and set the requirements for licensure. One such requirement is the satisfactory completion of a state-approved teacher education program at a college or university in the state (with special provisions for out-of-state applicants). Direct federal government involvement in preservice teacher education has been marginal and sporadic, primarily consisting of occasional small grants to support teacher education research or experimental programs. At present, the federal role with respect to teacher education is one of exhortation for higher standards to be achieved by means of competency testing for admission to teacher education programs and again for program completion or certification.[19]

Given the states' role in teacher education and their active role in education policy-making generally in the 1980s, as compared to the previous two decades,[20] continuing changes instate policy with respect to teacher education can be expected. At this point, we will summarize recent changes (1983-85) and emerging directions; in our concluding section, we speculate on future prospects.

Whereas state education policy in the 1970s and early 1980s sought to improve teaching largely by standardizing and

---

[19]D.L. Clark and T.A. Astuto, The Significance and Permanence of Changes in Federal Education Policy 1980-1988 (Bloomington, In: University Council for Educational Administration, Policy Studies Center, 1986).

[20]T.A. Astuto and D.L. Clark, The Effects of Federal Education Policy Changes on Policy and Program Development in State and Local Education Agencies (Bloomington, In: University Council for Educational Administration, Policy Studies Center, 1986); and M.W. Kirst, "State Policy in an Era of Transition", Education and Urban Society, Vol. 16, No. 2 (1984), pp. 225-237.

regulating it,[21] attention now seems to be shifting to enhancing the quality of teaching and the conditions of teachers' work.[22] Recognition of the limits of regulation-incentive policies is spreading, and structural changes in schooling and teacher education are being considered. For example, in the 1970s and early 1980s, changes in teacher education typically required additions to existing programs - more field experience, courses on the teaching of students with special needs, and using research to improve teaching effectiveness. Recent changes and those now under consideration are more far-reaching, although not widespread. They include SCDE-school partnerships and internships for new teachers.

Recent state education policy changes have varied in scope, substance, and specificity. Our account of them draws heavily on reports prepared by Education Week[23] and AACTE's State Issue Clearinghouse,[24] supplemented by media accounts and, in the case of Pennsylvania, by State Board of Education documents. The AACTE report addresses nine areas of state teacher education policy: standards, incentives, irregular certification routes, program curricula, capacity building for SCDEs, research/data/evaluation, SCDE faculty development, resources for practitioner inservice, and evidence of maintenance of equity. The Education Week report includes two categories relevant to teacher education: teacher careers and compensation, teacher training and certification. As of late 1985, according to AACTE, most state activity was in the areas of standards, incentives, and irregular certification Our

---

[21]L. Darling-Hammond, Beyond the Commission Reports: The Coming Crisis in Teaching (Santa Monica, Ca: The Rand Corporation, 1984).

[22]E.B. Fiske, "Efforts at Changing Schools in U.S. Entering New Phase", New York Times, 27 April 1986, p. 19.

[23]"Changing Course: A 50-State Survey of Reform Measures", Education Week 6 February 1983, pp. 11-30.

[24]AACTE, Teacher Education Policy in the States: 50-State Survey of Legislative and Administrative Actions (Washington, DC: American Association of Colleges for Teacher Education, 1985).

interest here is in AACTE's standards and program curricula and Education Week's teacher training and certification categories (because they directly address teacher education), and we focus on three states: California, New York and Pennsylvania (CA and NY, because they have long required extended teacher preparation, and PA, because it is neither a leader nor a laggard in teacher education - and because it is our current home).

Standards Standards for entry to teacher education programs and for certification, according to AACTE, are still rising. As of spring 1986, 30 states were requiring competency tests for new teachers, and 10 states were considering such tests.[25] The standards and accompanying tests address basic (i.e., communication) skills, general knowledge, subject area knowledge, professional knowledge, and/or teaching performance.

In 1981, the CA legislature made basic skills tests mandatory for teacher certification. Also, effective 1988, all teachers would be required to "become familiar with the uses of computers and technology science in classrooms".[26] In 1982 (effective 1984), the NY board of education made examinations a mandatory requirement for teacher certification and licensure. In 1984, the board specified tests of basic skills, general and subject area knowledge, and professional knowledge, which were incorporated into the "Regents Action Plan". In 1984 (effective 1987), the PA board of education adopted the governor's proposal for tests of prospective teachers' basic skills, general and subject area knowledge, and professional knowledge prior to certification. The board also approved the governor's proposal requiring "background checks" of all school employees, including prospective teachers, based on state police and child abuse records.

---

[25]The States not reporting action on competency tests for new teachers in the Education Week survey were Alaska, Colorado, Idaho, Maryland, Michigan, New Jersey, North Dakota, Oklahoma, Utah, and Vermont; Massachusetts had rejected but was reconsidering competency tests.

[26]AACTE, Teacher Education Policy, p. 9.

Establishing higher standards and competency tests is consistent with the traditional standard-setting and enforcement role of the states as well as with current federal policy preferences. Prior to passage of the Elementary and Secondary Education Act in 1965, state departments of education had primarily been regulatory agencies. Although in the past two decades the state role has expanded, it remains primarily regulatory.

Teacher education programs Beyond raising the entry and/or exit standards, it is difficult to determine how many states have instituted changes in teacher education programs. AACTE reports that, as of fall 1985, two-thirds of the states had "raised standards" for SCDE programs. Several changes have been mandated in CA, and others are under consideration. In 1983, the legislature made it mandatory (SB 813) that SCDE methods instructors have teaching experience, amounting to 25 percent of one semester, in a public school at least once every three years. The CA Commission for Teacher Certification now requires that at least two-thirds of prospective teachers' undergraduate or graduate subject area studies be directed to what is taught in high school courses. According to the AACTE survey, the CA Teacher Credentialing Commission "has defined statewide standards for teacher education that require programs at any institution to be equal to or above standards for other professional programs at the same institution".[27] Under consideration is a joint proposal of the Chancellor of the CA State University (CSU) system and the Superintendent of Public Instruction to provide planning grants to groups of CSU faculty (academic and SCDE) and school districts for effective integration of academic studies and teacher preparation with classroom experience. NY is reported to be considering major teacher development programs, but no policy changes were reported to the AACTE or Education Week survey.

In May 1985, the PA department of education announced that revised standards for SCDE program approval had been adopted by the state board of education and would become effective in 1987-88. New provisions in the PA general

---

[27]*Ibid.*, p. 9.

standards include: general education comprising at least one-third of the bachelor's degree and including arts, humanities, natural and social sciences; field and clinical experiences not later than the sophomore year or the prospective teacher's first year in the teacher education program; a minimum of 12 weeks of full-time student teaching (previously, there had been no minimum and practice teaching ranged from six to 16 weeks across the 88 PA SCDEs); preparation of the cooperating teachers who supervise student teachers, including observation and evaluation training; and accommodation of nontraditional (i.e., other than full-time undergraduate) students.

Induction According to AACTE, state provision of support and evaluation systems for new teachers is increasing. As of fall 1985, 14 states had created induction programs and 21 states were considering them.

In 1983, the CA legislature created a "mentor teacher" program. This provides for volunteer mentor teachers, selected on the basis of "exemplary teaching", to work with other teachers especially those who lack regular certification. By late 1985, the program had been implemented in Los Angeles. Under consideration is a joint proposal of the CSU chancellor and the superintendent of public instruction for a pilot program involving CSU faculty and urban school teachers to support first year teachers (currently, 50 percent of first year teachers drop out of teaching in some CA urban areas).

Neither the AACTE nor the Education Week surveys reported policy changes in NY with respect to induction of new teachers.

In 1984, the PA board of education adopted the governor's proposal (effective 1987-88) for a one year internship for new teachers. This "structured induction period" is to be established by the employing school districts to provide a mentor relationship between each new teacher and an "induction team" that may include college-university faculty.

Induction programs extend teacher preparation and ease initiation to school teaching. As with standards and testing, the extent to which changes in teacher education programs and the creation of induction programs have the intended effect of improving classroom teaching and pupil learning remains to be seen. In any event, changes in the substance and structure of teacher preparation programs, including closer working relationships with the schools, seem to be the emerging trend in state teacher education policy.

Interestingly, no action was reported by CA, NY, or PA in the ACCTE categories of capacity building for SCDEs or research/data/evaluation, and only CA had taken action with respect to SCDE faculty development. Also, of the three, only CA had created its own teacher education commission. Jointly initiated by the legislature and superintendent of public instruction (and Hewlett Foundation funded) the California Commission on the Teaching Profession issued its first report and recommendations in November 1985 (see footnote thirteen).

Contexts of Policy Change

What has been described thus far, and more, can be viewed as the context for state teacher education policy change to date and the potential context for future change. Our purpose here is to conceptualize context in a way that distinguishes effective from nominal context and that contributes to our understanding of recent changes and anticipated future ones.

Recognizing that context is widely acknowledged but largely uncharted territory - not unlike the "new world" of 15th century European maps and perhaps for good reason - we proceed with caution. The complexity and elusiveness of the notion of context, at least in the case of the U.S. education system, makes it difficult to "pin it down" and link empirically to particular policies. The resulting tendency to decontextualize discussion of educational policy, however, limits our analysis and understanding of both policy and policymaking. The task we have set for ourselves, therefore, is to sketch a conceptual framework, based on the current U.S. teacher education reform experience, that will help inform empirical investigation and explanation of context-policy relationships.

Conceptualizing Context

By nominal context we mean whatever is "out there" that might influence policy making - in other words the environment at large. Context is more than the source of demands upon a system; it also is a source of constraints, priorities, and norms that shape the action of the system. In addition to demographic, political, economic and social conditions, each event or cluster of events (e.g., a set of school reform reports) is potential context for subsequent events (e.g., teacher education reform reports, state policy changes). Within the education system, each layer (e.g., national, state, district, local) can be seen as potential context for those nested within it (e.g., state, SCDE).

Effective context, in contrast, refers to those aspects of the nominal context that actually influence policymaking by attracting policymakers' attention and directing their actions. For example, during the past decade, the activity of religious right in U.S. society and politics has been part of the nominal, but not the effective, context of change in teacher education policy. While the religious right has been effectively influencing health care, judicial selection and many other policy areas, we have no evidence of its impact on teacher education policy. Our examination of the effective context of change in state level teacher education policies suggests two major features: (1) the effective context is both structural and socio-cultural; and (2) it varies over time and with the issue, the stage of policymaking, and the local situation within the national milieu.

By structural context, we mean the established roles and relationships, including operating procedures and norms, of the teacher education subsystem and the national education system of which it is a part. In a sense, the system is the structural context. The education system, in Archer's[28] language, conditions interaction with and within it. As a subsystem of the national education system, teacher education is subject to the structural conditioning and social interaction of the larger system, as well as its own internal relations.

---

[28] Archer, Social Origins.

332

Three features of the national education system of the U.S. seem particularly relevant to teacher education policy. One is that its boundaries are neither well defined nor stable. Some observers seriously doubt that education in the U.S. can be said to constitute a system. A second is that the system boundaries are highly permeable, providing relatively easy access to interested groups. The tradition, if not the practice, of local, public control of education serves to encourage efforts of all manner of external groups to try to influence the contours and course of schooling. The third feature is the location of teacher education within the U.S. education system. While there is some federal influence and support, teacher education is a state responsibility both *de jure* and *de facto*. Within the states, teacher education uneasily straddles basic (elementary and secondary) and higher education agencies where, typically, it is a concern of both and the priority of neither.

The loosely bounded and permeable nature of the national education system, together with the precarious location of the teacher education subsystem, makes education generally and teacher education in particular highly susceptible to external influences. We characterize these influences as the socio-cultural context. If the U.S. education system was more tightly bounded and/or less permeable, socio-cultural influences would be less prominent.

The socio-cultural context includes the larger environment of the society, external to the education system, particularly those extrasystemic demographic, social, political, and economic conditions, traditions and ideologies, and events that appear to influence teacher education policy. We recognize that clearly separating internal-structural from external socio-cultural context factors is difficult and may not always be possible given the nature of the U.S. education system. The teacher education reform reports, for example, span structural and socio-cultural contexts. The Holmes and AACTE reports were internally initiated. The AACTE commission was composed of representatives of various groups including business and government. The Carnegie Forum Task Force was externally initiated and constituted. Since our purpose is not categorization but identification of policy relevant context factors, the distinction remains useful in guiding inquiry. At the least, it directs our attention beyond, as well as within the system. The distinction also is important, as we suggest in the next section, insofar as the effective policy context appears to vary with the stage of policymaking: socio-cultural context factors appear to be more salient to agenda setting, structural factors to policy formation.

It is our contention, therefore, that the effective context of state level changes in teacher education policy is not only multifaceted, it also varies over time and with the issue, the stage of policymaking, and the local situation within the national milieu. Variability, like the importance of socio-cultural factors, seems to be a function of the national education system and teacher education's location within it. Variation is evident in the presence of particular context factors, their relative strength or intensity, and their interaction (e.g., aggregation, conflict). For example, the past 40 years have witnessed alternating emphases on equity and excellence in education, with an accompanying assumption of incompatibility. Demographic changes and imbalances in teacher supply and demand within and across the states provide another example.

How context is identified can be seen as another source of its variation. For example, are effective contextual factors those perceived and reported by policymakers or those which an observer would identify as apparently influencing policymaking? Empirically linking policy and context is neither simple nor straightforward. Lacking access to the inner workings of state policymaking, we will focus on the apparently influential aspects of the broader or national milieu when considering the effective contexts of the agenda setting and policy formation stages of educational policymaking.

Contexts of What?

Given our distinction between nominal and effective context and our contention that effective context varies over time and with the stage of policymaking, we shall separately consider the effective contexts of state level agenda setting and subsequent policy formation which resulted in teacher education policy changes during the past three years. *Policy change* encompasses new goals or new means of reaching existing ones. *Agenda setting* refers to the process whereby needs, problems, and issues are brought to the attention of policymakers who decide which will be addressed. It includes constituency building as well as identification and definition of problems and determination of priorities. *Policy formation* refers to the action taken on identified problems, i.e., the response or solution offered, which may involve redefinition of a previously identified problem to a more manageable form.[29]

The effective context of agenda setting for teacher education policy change, 1983-85, appears to have been primarily socio-cultural. Teacher education has been an issue on state policy agendas as a result of (a) the coalescing interests of teacher educators seeking status, school reformers seeking improvements in teaching and learning, and business and government leaders seeking to restore public confidence in their institutions, and (b) the impetus provided by the school reform reports and the economic and political conditions to which they pointed.

As previously noted, the school reform reports identified the poor quality of teacher preparation as a serious problem. They called for improvement by means of higher standards and competency testing for admission to, and completion of, programs of teacher education. Required would be demonstration of knowledge in an academic discipline and of effective teaching performance. Higher standards and testing were to increase the quality of teacher education and teachers, and thus of teaching and learning in the schools, in order to ward off national economic disaster and political-military vulnerability.

What is important about the school reform reports is not so much their seemingly rational call for higher standards and competency testing for new teachers as their function as a catalyst for change. Given the nature of the U.S. education

---

[29]To make the present analysis manageable, we do not examine the contexts of subsequent stages of policymaking such as implementation and evaluation nor do we distinguish among different issues, local situations, or state policy actors (e.g., governors, legislators, state boards and departments of education), their differing agendas and roles, or the varying contextual influences on each.

system, would-be reformers must gain the attention and support of a range of publics across the 50 states. As a consequence, nationwide change efforts have, historically, taken the form of reform movements with an evangelical religious character rather than less flamboyant legislative and administrative or bureaucratic improvement efforts.[30] Those who view American society as crisis-ridden fail to recognize the stability that underlies public debate. The school reform reports served to crystallize and expand a constituency for teacher education reform by gaining wide media exposure and capturing public and policymaker attention with cries of crisis. There are striking similarities among these school and teacher education reform reports in their language of crisis and hope. Crisis language has become an integral part of everyday political and social life in the U.S.[31] Calls for reform simultaneously signify dissatisfaction, impatience, and optimism. Crisis and urgency, exhortation and hope are dramatically communicated in language intended to shape belief and mobilize action for spiritual renewal as well as for national economic and defense strength and security through educational reform.

Consistent with this interpretation of the function of the school reform reports is A. Wise's (personal communication, June 13, 1986) view that lack of public confidence in education and teachers, rather than the intrinsic quality of teacher education, provided impetus for the recent suggestions for teacher education reform. In this climate, teachers are identified as both a cause and a solution. Examining what he calls the "conservative restoration" in U.S. society and schooling, 1969-84, Shor takes a more critical stance.[32] He contends that the "excellence" movement has been an effort to restore public

---

[30]J. Meyer, "Reform and Change", IFG Policy Notes, Vol. 5, No. 4 (1984), pp. 1-2.

[31]See M. Edelman, Political Language: Words that Succeed and Policies that Fail (New York: Academic Press, 1977).

[32]I. Shor, Culture Wars: School and Society in the Conservative Restoration 1969-84 (Boston: Routledge and Kegan Paul, 1986).

confidence in institutions generally and to deflect attention from erosion of the "American Dream", i.e., declining economic opportunities for all but a favoured few. Restoring a common curriculum of "new basics" for students (and the equivalent for teachers), he suggests, is "tantamount to restoring authority itself"[33] without offering immediate benefits in return. Insofar as agenda setting to date has not directly confronted substantive teacher education quality issues, it is not unreasonable to view agenda setting as responding to underlying and largely unarticulated political priorities.[34]

In addition to socio-cultural context factors, the structural location of teacher education has been a factor in putting teacher education on state policy agendas. Lacking status and numbers that could translate into political power, teacher educators and SCDEs are vulnerable to criticism and imposition. They are a relatively easy target for policymakers compared to the more than two million practicing teachers and 18,000 school districts.

Turning from contextual factors that appear to have put teacher education on state policy agendas to those that might account for the problems identified and given priority for action, we again find socio-cultural influences predominant, particularly the school reform reports and demographic changes. In the absence of the school reform reports, it is highly unlikely that many states would have considered raising teacher education standards or requiring testing. While California and New York imposed teacher testing in 1981 and 1982 respectively, prior to the reform reports, most states, Pennsylvania is a good example, did not do so until later. Not only did standards and testing make the agenda of state governments, but 30 states now (spring 1986) require competency tests for new teachers and ten others are considering them.

---

[33]*Ibid.*, p. 120.

[34]Cf. C. Cornbleth, "Ritual and Rationality in Teacher Education Reform", Educational Researcher, Vol. 15, No. 4 (1986), pp. 5-14.

No other policy changes designed to improve the quality of teacher preparation have been so widely considered or adopted across the states. In second place are the induction programs for new teachers, which have been created in 14 states and are under consideration in 21 others. Although induction programs were advocated by the teacher education reform reports, and earlier by professional associations, as a means of improving the quality of teaching, demographic factors are probably the major motivation for their consideration at this time. Of concern to school officials and state policymakers alike are current shortages of certified teachers and the high dropout rates among new teachers in some urban areas, particularly in California. There are approximately 2.2. million teachers currently in the U.S. By 1992, an estimated 2.6 million teachers will be needed, but only 1.6 million will be available if current enrolment and retirement trends continue.[35] One way of making up the projected one million shortfall would be to hire teachers who lack regular certification and provide on-the-job support and education through induction programs. Induction programs can, therefore, be seen as justifying the hiring of persons who do not meet teacher certification requirements as well as an effort to improve, support and retain newly certified teachers.

Of the structural context factors that might account for the teacher education problems being identified and given priority for action, the federal government policy preferences appear most salient. Federal policy preferences may be interpreted as sanctioning, if not actually encouraging, higher standards and competency testing while discouraging such other initiatives as experimental teacher preparation programs by neglect and failure to provide resource incentives.

The contextual influences on agenda setting to date may well serve to constrain potential reform of U.S. teacher education. Receptivity to teacher education reform has been enhanced by the school reform reports, but their specific recommendations, combined with demographic pressures and federal education policy preferences, would seem to limit rather than expand policy options. Whether the more recent teacher education

---

[35]See, for example, Darling-Hammond, Beyond the Commission Reports.

reform reports succeed in expanding the policy agenda remains to be seen.

The effective context of teacher education policy formation, 1983-85, overlaps the agenda setting context and includes the agenda setting process (see Figure 1). Although socio-cultural factors remain important, structural factors gain prominence. In the agenda setting process, proposed solutions to identified problems are evaluated in terms of what is deemed to be feasible as well as what is desirable. Attention is apt to be given to such factors as the policymakers' jurisdiction, traditional practice, and the legacy of prior changes as well as the immediate considerations of incentives and disincentives for particular changes, available or obtainable resources to support change, and the degree of consensus behind one or another proposal. In the course of these evaluations, previously identified problems may be redefined to make them more manageable. As one kind of problem is translated into another, usually more manageable form, both problems and solutions tend to become routinized. For example, the identified problems of teacher quality and teacher education quality have been defined in terms of standards by the school reform reports, and by state policymakers at least in part because standards are consistent with their traditional regulatory function. They can be mandated and monitored with relative ease and visibility. By defining the issue as "standards" policymakers can give the impression of "doing something" to restore public faith, without making major changes in the system or risking opposition from important constituencies. For the most part, the costs of standards and testing are imposed on outsiders, e.g., on students who are applicants to programs and on graduates who are prospective new teachers. Teacher educators and SCDEs are powerless to object to such external controls.

The context of state policy formation is not necessarily constraining. At times, it provides impetus for innovation. This is especially true when socio-cultural influences for change are strong and the state governor or legislative leaders take an active interest in reform. For example, the new PA standards for SCDE program approval announced in 1985, the only major revision of standards applicable to all teacher education programs in fifteen years, was first proposed in

Figure 1

Contexts of State Teacher Education Policy

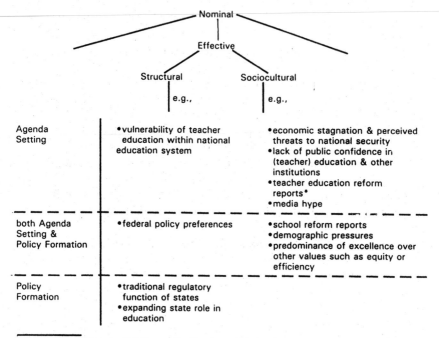

	Structural e.g.,	Sociocultural e.g.,
Agenda Setting	• vulnerability of teacher education within national education system	• economic stagnation & perceived threats to national security • lack of public confidence in (teacher) education & other institutions • teacher education reform reports* • media hype
both Agenda Setting & Policy Formation	• federal policy preferences	• school reform reports • demographic pressures • predominance of excellence over other values such as equity or efficiency
Policy Formation	• traditional regulatory function of states • expanding state role in education	

*may but as yet have not influenced policy formation

1980-81. Opposition, primarily from teacher and teacher education associations, modified the proposed changes and delayed their implementation. However, the widespread attention to education during the past three years, including the governor's "Agenda for Excellence", seems to have spurred compromise on both the substance and procedures of revision - at least none of the groups involved wanted to be seen as blocking reform. In this case, the climate created by the calls for reform facilitated action on an item already on the state policy agenda.

In sum, the factors in the policy environment that seem to account for the current attention to teacher education and emerging policy reformulation are both structural and socio-cultural, and they appear to have little basis in any direct assessment of teacher education or teaching (see Figure 1). The structural vulnerability of teacher education makes it a prime target of criticism, and to some extent, a scapegoat for other problems. The expanded state role in education generally over the past decade suggests that further policy activity is likely with respect to teacher education. The effective socio-cultural context of reform in teacher education policy was seen to include perceived political-military threats to U.S. national security, popular disaffection with domestic institutions and leadership, economic stagnation resulting in declining global competitiveness and erosion of the "American Dream", and demographic changes which portend a severe shortage of school teachers will develop within the decade - all this as well as the school reform reports' calls for change which have acted as a catalyst. Within this national (and increasingly international) milieu, schools, teachers, and teacher education have been targetted as both a source of national problems and their solution.

Interestingly, the contexts of policy change, at least thus far, do not seem to include technological and knowledge factors. Change in teacher education, for the purpose of improving schooling, is not being sought as a result of research generated knowledge or technological discoveries. Nor does there seem to be any particular desire to reduce costs by increasing efficiency in the education of student teachers or in the teaching in schools. Furthermore, recent teacher education policy changes do not contain provisions for evaluating their effectiveness. In other words, research is not being used for agenda setting, policy formation, or policy validation.

Given that the largely socio-cultural context of agenda setting tends to be less tied to the *status quo* than the more structurally influenced context of policy formation, perceived problems are likely to be redefined and acted upon in ways that are system maintaining rather than reformist. The 1983-85 state-level teacher education policy changes have hardly been revolutionary. In part this is because drastic changes were not sought; but also it is because state bureaucracies are essentially conservative. In contrast, the 1985-86 teacher education reform reports call for more extensive changes. In our concluding section of the paper, we will speculate on the contexts of future policy changes.

Future Prospects

If recent history and the foregoing analysis are any guide, the contexts of future changes in teacher education policy will be increasingly structural and conservative, despite the far-reaching recommendations of the recent reform recommendations and their urgent appeal to economic, political and demographic needs. The contexts will be increasingly structural because the three major teacher education reform commissions have issued their reports. There are no other teacher education reform groups on the horizon. Now it is the turn of policymakers to do their part. Although the three commission sponsors are continuing to work toward their goals outside the arena of government, and this might provide some pressure and impetus for state (or federal) policy change, a "wait and see" stance seems the state policymakers' more likely response, for reasons to be considered below. The contexts of future policy change will be increasingly conservative in part because structural influences have been, and likely will continue to be, more conservative than socio-cultural ones.

There are three additional contextual reasons for our conservative projection which should be recognized, and there are two countervailing factors that might precipitate more substantive policy change. One reason for conservatism is fatigue; policymakers and their publics are apt to tire of education problems soon and shift their attention to other areas, returning teacher education to its SCDE and professional association caretakers. It may be that teacher education reform has just been one in a series of "issue-attention cycles" which Kirst characterizes as "an intense flurry of activity" followed by "a period of gradual loss of media attention and routinization of policy in terms of traditional patterns"[36] when it becomes apparent that the identified complex problems cannot be quickly or easily resolved. A second, related, ground for conservatism is policymakers' quite understandable reluctance to risk major change when there is reason to expect that the demand for change will fade. In this context, the tactic is to delay or only approve modest changes rather than reforms that may offend important constituencies and/or prove unworkable. Finally, two of the three recent calls for teacher education reform have come from SCDE representatives. SCDE faculty and administrators lack status, numbers, and acknowledged expertise; their recommendations to their universities and state policymakers probably will not be taken seriously unless they are supported by influential outsiders. Furthermore, they also may be seen as self-serving since, after all, they are the ones to be reformed.

Two socio-cultural context factors that could have the effect of counteracting projected policy conservatism are the Carnegie involvement and the demographic pressures. The Carnegie Forum Task Force is composed of high status outsiders, not the establishment of teacher education. It appears to have already generated bipartisan political attention (e.g., its proposals were on the agenda of the August 1986 conference of state governors) and aroused some corporate and foundation interest in supporting the implementation of its recommendations. These indications of widespread support may be as much a function of Carnegie's substantial role in the reform of medical education early in this century, and the expectation that Carnegie can do the same for teacher education, as of their actual recommendations. Whether or not one subscribes to self-fulfilling prophecies, such positive attention and tangible support might well precipitate significant policy change. In addition, the demographic pressures already noted will be a

---

[36]Kirst, "State Policy in an Era of Transition", p. 236.

spur for action. This may result in some serious scrutiny of the recommendations for differentiated staffing as a means of avoiding the mass hiring (and eventual tenuring) of persons who would not even meet current teacher certification standards - as happened in the 1950s and 1960s. Moreover, the time is ripe for such policy change. The present configuration of demographic and other contextual factors is unlikely to recur in the foreseeable future.

In conclusion we note that streetlamps provide something to hold on to, as well as provide illumination. This exploration of the contexts of policy change has ventured both where the light is bright (and support is available) and where it is rather dim (and support is not readily at hand). The extent to which we have been stumbling in the dark remains to be seen by those who would pursue investigation and explanation of context-policy relationships in teacher education and other areas.

Government Investment in Research Universities for Economic Development

by

Maureen McClure[1]

As global economic competition heats up, national governments will be pressed to cast about for more productive public investments. Much ado has been made about the relationship between the high tech successes of Silicon Valley and Route 128 and their university connections. While some success is evident, the great bulk of university based research has not been clearly linked to economic growth. Public policymakers who look to universities as a source for economic growth should proceed with caution, especially in the short term. Current research university incentive systems may not be adequate to support the diversified research base necessary for both regional and national development. Research universities should be wary of research partnerships for economic development because of the high risk of government intervention. Without carefully negotiated policies, universities may find they have danced too far down the road of dependence on the piper's development tune.

From a government perspective, current *ad hoc*, agency driven policies are inappropriate for coordinated strategic planning for investment in economic growth. System reform will require that public policymakers see themselves as <u>investors in</u> and not <u>managers of</u> economic development. Policymakers considering investment in university research for returns in the form of economic development should consider three constraints to effective strategic planning: (1) the technical constraints of property rights, (2) the political constraints of haphazard, crisis oriented planning, and (3) the organizational constraints created by differing incentive structures.

---

[1]Assisstant Professor, Administrative and Policy Studies, School of Education, University of Pittsburgh, Pittsburgh, PA.

In the U.S. the links between support for university based research and sustained national economic growth are haphazard at best. Federal policymakers have shied away from a commitment to explicit, sectoral planning for economic growth. Little is known about the complex relationships between investments in university research and regional or national capital formation.

University Research: Property Rights and Incentives for Production

Economic development built on traditional private and state capital is primarily generated through trading on the ownership of property rights.[2] The owner benefits from rights derived from exclusive consumption of a good, for example, a quarter. One must possess these exclusive benefits before entering private markets to voluntarily exchange them for other goods and services, say a candy bar. Private markets work best when those property rights are clearly defined and limited. A candy manufacturer can define property rights fairly simply: possession of a piece of candy. University researchers cannot exclude others as easily as the candy manufacturer, they must share their property with others. University researchers cannot package public information like a piece of candy for exclusive consumption.

University based r&d consequently has different characteristics from traditional market goods. It is quite liquid, easily stored and transported. Property rights are not easily captured: research is easily leaked to others without payment. As communications technology grows, so does the leakage potential. Ease of diffusion, under the conditions of market exchange, therefore, can become a liability rather than an asset.

University based research also functions as a "joint" or "intermediate" product and thus it is difficult to track, either as

---

[2]W.C. Stubblebine, "Property Rights and Institutions" in The Economics of Legal Relationships edited by H.G. Manne (St. Paul: West, 1975), pp. 11-22.

an input or as an output.[3] As an input within the university, it is generally considered a joint product with teaching and service, although many university researchers engage in limited teaching or service. The productive outputs of research are also difficult to trace. For example, an individual or an organization may derive substantial benefits from a university sponsored journal article, but those gains may not be traced to the author of the research. Neither the researcher nor the university, and more importantly not even the sponsor, will benefit directly from this increased wealth.

This ease of diffusion of university research systematically leads to underinvestment in unregulated private markets. Private investors are generally unwilling to subsidize research that produces large indirect (public) benefits but small direct (private) benefits. The traditional public finance argument calls for government subsidy up to the point of an implied "natural" equilibrium of public and private benefits.[4] Unfortunately, national governments are too small to capture fully the returns on their investments, because the capital created by information accrues to academic disciplines and not to geographical boundaries; it is produced by international "free riders", and encouraged by traditional university dissemination. Free riders choose not to invest in academic research because they have access to its benefits without sharing its costs. The free rider problem underlies a perennial tension between the university commitment to open publication and corporate and governmental reluctance to subsidize university research that can be shared with national and international competitors.

For example, if U.S. taxpayers subsidized long term health research at a major U.S. research university, and a West German pharmaceutical company developed products based on

---

[3]D.A. Garvin, "An Economic Analysis of University Behavior", Unpublished dissertation, Massachusetts Institute of Technology, 1979; and E. James, "The university department as a non-profit labor cooperative", Photocopy, files of H. Cline, University of Rochester, 1978.

[4]E.K. Browning and J.M. Browning, Public Finance and the Price System. (New York: MacMillan, 1977), pp. 21-53.

that research, the West German government would indirectly benefit from the pharmaceutical company's taxable profits. Economists refer to such market leakages as "externalities". Indeed, in the late nineteenth century, the German chemical industry was built on British basic research.[5] For a variety of reasons the British were unable to translate their research into economic development.

Traditionally, U.S. federal policymakers have eschewed formal, coordinated strategic planning for economic development. However, while bureaucratic, central planning may be ineffective, benign neglect could well be equally inappropriate. The economic links to university research must be forged through formal policy; they cannot be assumed.

The traditional public finance solutions of national public intervention in the form of subsidies may actually exacerbate leakage. For example, the U.S. government poured billions of dollars into health-related research over the last few decades, more than all other countries combined.[6] Out of that mass subsidy, a fledgling biotechnical industry is beginning to emerge. But what remains to be seen is the public return on its investment of tax dollars. Both research universities and professors acting as private entrepreneurs, with economically rational expectations, have legally entered into offshore licensing agreements. This may lead to further leakages in national investments, leaving fewer taxable dollars to trickle back into federal coffers if development occurs offshore. U.S. taxpayers will, in essence, have subsidized their economic competitors.

Of the three general types of university based research (basic, applied and prototype development), basic or grant related research is, in the main, the least useful for economic development because property rights are not easily attached.

---

[5]S. Rose and H. Rose, Science and Society (Harrmondsworth, Middlesex, England: Penguin Books Ltd., 1970), pp. 28-36.

[6]M. McClure, "Constraints to Mid-Range Planning for University R&D" (Unpublished thesis, University of Rochester, 1983), p. 9.

Yet it constitutes the core value and incentive structures of the traditional research university. It produces a greater share of social or international capital in part because it is "law seeking". Because outcomes are not easily measured basic research sponsors are more likely to capture returns in different ways: altruism or political and social legitimacy. This is predictable where public sponsor returns are not tied to outcomes. Basic researchers trade freedom from private market discipline for dependence on political sponsors seeking returns in the form of re-election. This occasionally allows empirical, law-seeking basic research to be somewhat unfettered. The congruence of public sponsor and basic researcher expectations, however, is likely to be rare. Neither the basic researcher nor the public sponsor have incentives to invest in property rights formation. Indeed, basic research activity seeks instead to be untainted by such concerns.[7]

Francis Bacon called this type of research *experimenta lucifera* or light bearing knowledge.[8] Sponsors traditionally invest with the understanding that humanity, not themselves, will receive the primary returns. Basic research is the most highly prized in the university, perhaps because its funding grants are usually the least restrictive. There are, however, no free lunches, even for academic pipers.

Due to its relative ease of diffusion, however, basic research contributes to development through the generation of international capital. Its great weakness in building individual, organizational or national capital becomes its great strength in the international arena. In a health related field, for example, university research which leads to better information about the causes, risks and costs of a disease may lead to policies enacted internationally that, over the longer term, lower international health care costs. Public information that is easily diffused can provide a significant return on a public research investment and thus be valued by those

---

[7]L. Thomas, "The Value of Basic Science" in Rochester Review, University of Rochester (Summer, 1981), p. 34.

[8]Rose and Rose, Science and Society, p. 14.

seeking to increase the quality of a generic commonweal. One could not design less suitable processes to lead directly to national economic development.

This is not to say that basic research only fuels international development; rather, basic research claims humanity as its primary beneficiary. Basic research focused in specific areas related to the formation of property rights can make indirect contributions. Most corporate sponsored basic research follows these lines. An initial strategic plan is designed, and then basic research is chosen to fit the strategic goals. Publicly sponsored basic research loosely follows this model. Congress decides to "do something" about a perceived social problem and allocates research funds to specific agencies. Such decisions are rarely tied to careful investment policy and almost never tied to economic development. The persons charged with funds allocation, almost by default, have a great deal of discretion. Vague goals and minimal followthrough to measure investment return can create an extensive federal patronage system.

Applied or contract research is by definition more contextual; it is meant to contribute to the solutions of a sponsor's problems. Bacon referred to this type of research as *experimenta fructifera* or fruit bearing knowledge. As research becomes more contextual, property rights are more easily attached to its findings. Applied research can be better used to produce a "comparative advantage" than basic research, although there is often a great deal of overlap between the two. Most publicly sponsored contract research falls in this category. While it suffers from some of the same problems as basic research, it is more clearly defined to fit agency goals. This type of research is generally a more efficient choice for federal agencies. When project control is more focused in agencies, fewewr discretionary resources are available to the researcher and the university. Contract research has lower value and prestige in the university. There is a constant tension between sponsors looking for contextual solutions to specific problems and university researchers who are rewarded for generalizable outcomes.

Prototype development is the least "law seeking" because it is the most contextual. Prototypes are the solutions to particular problems. They are designed to create distinct goods or services that can be exchanged in the market. Property rights are easily attached to prototypes. Interestingly, this kind of research did not form part of Bacon's conceptual framework. Prototypes are the most direct route to development, but they are the least valued and rewarded by traditional university incentives and honours.

Until the linkages to public economic development are more clearly described, university research faces a funding heritage that claims only a serendipitous relationship to property rights. This leads to high levels of risk and uncertainty relative to proprietary r&d. With its propensity to lead and its emphasis on long term, diffuse payoffs, university based research may not prove attractive to either public or private investors seeking direct returns to development. The current structure of policy within the public sector and the universities may impede rather than encourage investment for development.

Funds for U.S. Research: Haphazard Economic Growth

In the U.S. most university research is supported by public "mission oriented" sponsors. The missions of federal agencies were not designed to be coordinated with either public or private economic development, although they have been held tacitly to development agendas. Without explicit policies to require federal agencies to demonstrate how their investments contribute to economic growth, major slippages can occur. One case of uncoordinated investment is the federal sponsorship of health related research, primarily through the National Institutes of Health. Funding greatly increased during the 1960s when Congress, unwilling to institute a national health insurance program, chose r&d funding as a demonstration of a good faith public investment.[9] Considerations of economic development were tangential at best. Within a few years, universities, not government laboratories, became the primary recipients of health related funding. (Most major medical

---

[9]S.P. Strickland, "The Integration of Medical Research and Health Policy" Science 173(4002), 17 September 1971, pp. 1093-1103.

research centres, however, did not proportionately increase their output of medical doctors. Instead, they expanded the number of Ph.D.s engaged in medical centre research.[10]) Of the total number of research scientists and engineers employed in universities during the late seventies and early eighties, sixty percent of them were appointed in the life sciences.[11] Unfortunately, the private sector did not increase its sectoral investment to keep pace with public growth. Consequently, by the nineteen eighties, almost eighty-five percent of the nation's life scientists were federally supported, either in universities or federal laboratories.[12]

The organization of university r&d continued to exacerbate a related political problem. University researchers' need for many full time graduate assistants created an expansive growth rate, leading to an oversupply of doctoral students in the life sciences. These trained specialists, having had extensive public support, later had difficulty finding jobs in the private sector. Many faced years of postdoctoral experience at very low rates of return on the public's and their own investment in training.

Congressional oversight may have left the private sector unable to absorb as large a share of federal cutbacks as the Reagan administration had hoped.[13] This inability may well be repeated with the current shifts in research funding toward defense. While these federal missions are important, future research investment levels should address the questions of their contribution to national economic development. How does investment in the missions of federal agencies lead to a regeneration of the nation's tax bases? Are there more efficient ways for the U.S. government to invest in university research?

---

[10]*Ibid.* .

[11]National Science Board 81-1, Science Indicators, (Washington, DC: National Science Foundation, 1982).

[12]National Science Board 82-2, University-Industry Research Relationships (Washington, DC: National Science Foundation, 1982).

[13]M. McClure, "Constraints to Mid-Range Planning, p. 219.

Funding in the past has not relied on cross-sectoral strategic planning. As a result, current policy needs focus in three major areas. First, federal research policy has, *de facto* focused on agency missions, with few coordinated strategies for economic growth. Second, beyond the defense and health sectors, with their respective low economic development potential, there has been little coordinated sectoral planning for university research leading to national economic development. Third, the U.S. national economy is comprised of distinct regional economies that are masked by national aggregate measures; future policy should explicitly consider the long term effects of federal policies on regional as well as national economic development.

Public Investments in Universities for Development: Organizational Conflicts

Public research policy has operated under the myth that investment in basic research leads to public dissemination and eventually through a serendipitous process, to national economic growth.[14] The myth is flawed partly because it ignores the problem of property rights discussed earlier. A basic research structure that champions open and collegial dissemination tacitly assumes that development occurs through an international accumulation of information. However, this premise runs counter to governmental notions of domestic capital formation. Moreover, the "organizational culture" of governments and universities do not directly nourish economic development. The U.S. government funds actual or perceived future political crises; it does not fund according to coordinated, sectoral, strategic plans. Its investment is primarily a response to political stakeholders; it is not a result of efforts to regenerate the tax bases. These policies are short term; they generate irresponsible, inefficient, boom-bust cycles in university research funding. Finally, public policymakers place a higher value on compliance than performance, assuming that research is a consumption good and not an investment; they do not develop allocation mechanisms to track resource flows and economic growth returns adequately and to demonstrate their linkages.

---

[14]Thomas, "Value of Basic Science".

There are important distinctions between public and private research investments in capital formation. Public capital is derived from taxation. Private capital is formed in the markets of exchange. It cannot be assumed that the boundaries for these arenas or markets coincide. The former is bounded by geography; the latter is constrained by demand and supply. Theoretically, federal agencies support the development of national public capital for its citizens; corporations support the development of private capital for their investors. Private and public sector efficiencies are not synonymous. They may even work against each other. Multinational corporations have interests that differ from those of state and federal governments. For example, it is rational for governments to invest in research at national universities that will lead directly to national economic development but will have minimal international leakage to economic competitors. Defence is a primary illustration. On the other hand, it is rational for private interests to invest in offshore university research which will lead to exclusive returns to their investors, regardless of the origin of the investment or the return.

Consistent with their basic research ideals, the major research universities provide the greatest prestige to international contributions. The vast majority of university r&d funding in the U.S., however, comes from federal agencies to support specific missions. Yet, the real economic growth potential is at the regional level.[15] It would appear, therefore, that prestige and productive potential are inversely related. While the development goals of these separate levels are not necessarily antithetical, neither are they necessarily coincidental. We do not yet know how national, public investment in research universities produces a national, public return in the form of economic development.

---

[15]E.M. Hoover, An Introduction to Regional Economics (New York: Alfred A. Knopf, 1971), pp. 251-295.

Research that leads to Economic Development: Regional Focus

Major university research investment policy also requires further clarification of the relationships among (1) r&d import capital (resource flow), (2) r&d capital formation, and (3) regional and national economic growth.

"R&d import capital" simply measures the resources that flow into a particular university from external investment sources and are invested or consumed by the university and its regional economy. For example, MIT and Harvard attracted enormous amounts of federal tax dollars into the Boston area over the last fifty years.[16] Likewise, the San Francisco Bay area greatly benefitted from federal research subsidies of Stanford and Berkeley. California and Massachusetts alone imported over 40 percent of the federally sponsored university research funds over the last several decades.[17] Federally sponsored university research has both directly and indirectly contributed to the regional economic development created by Route 128 and Silicon Valley. This long term funding has created an implicit U.S. government investment policy whose impact should be assessed so that the regional capital import aspects of national research funding policy can be made more explicit. For example, if this regional growth results from intensive federal investment, then it may be anomalous and may not be an appropriate model for regional development in other parts of the country.

"R&d capital formation" is concerned with the accrual of returns to university research investments. Capital can accrue regionally, nationally or internationally. Capital formation measures the creation and production of knowledge, skills and their consequent technology. It is difficult to separate development stemming from imported regional resource flows from development generated by capital formation. For

---

[16]National Science Foundation 81-311, National Patterns of Science and Technology Resources (Washington, DC: 1981).

[17]McClure, "Constraints to Mid-Range Planning", p. 63.

example, an increased federal resource flow into a region may boost its economy without producing capital to sustain development. The imported subsidies attracted by the university would have a multiplier effect similar to the presence of a military base. The economy is sustained only in a dependent relationship; if the subsidies are cut, growth declines.

If, on the other hand, investments in research result in capital formation, this new capital generates its own independent resource flows. The reduction of federal resources would not necessarily lead to a decline in growth. In the best of all possible worlds, the investments of federal resources would lead to sustained regional development with positive national spillover effects. The returns to national investments in research universities would be measured in two stages: first, the national return on knowledge generated by the research itself, and second, the national return on public research that results in regional tax base growth. We should try to distill the federal resource flow from the capital formation effects because of their divergent implications for policy. Where federal r&d investment results primarily in a regional wealth transfer with little spillover to national development, investment returns accrue primarily at a regional rather than national level. Without measurable capital formation, these regions could become dependent on federal subsidies, especially if they allow federal subsidies to displace their own development investment. Under these conditions, federal investments could conceivably produce negative national returns.

The federal government should assess the relative national risk and return to investment in university research, development and transfer in regions. It may want to turn over a larger share of economic development responsibilities to regional consortia. To avoid negative returns, it could encourage the states to play a greater role in supporting the infrastructure required to compete for federally funded r&d. Federal and state coordination would be necessary to reduce "zero sum" regional transfers. Decentralized, coordinated, sectoral strategic planning may generate effective policies without a cumbersome regulatory bureaucracy. Federal and state policymakers would see themselves as investors in, not managers of, economic growth. But, this is an unlikely prospect in the near term because the U.S. public bureaucracy has been structured by policies that measure compliance, not performance. Policies have focused on the distribution and consumption of resources rather than on the assessment of returns to the tax base.

Governmental accounting systems are not designed for strategic planning for development.[18] Public data collection now offers little useful information about research investments and their returns to economic growth.[19] Regulatory policies that monitor research processes instead of assessing post-audit outcomes may impede the development of information capital. In the past, the *ad hoc* federal policies for investment in university based r&d have been monopsonistic because the U.S. federal government is, by far, the largest single buyer of university research. At the agency level oligopsony exists - seven agencies account for over ninety percent of the funding. This gives agencies bargaining leverage with the research universities. The result is that internal university research policies are not necessarily consistent with the institution's best interests. Universities spend more of their resources in agency compliance than in the strategic management necessary for internal planning integrity. This induces poor management practices in the universities and leads to a narrow perspective that confuses means and ends. Universities interested in building links between r&d and tax base renewal should reassess current federal funding policies. Where those policies clearly intervene in the long term strategic planning of the institution, they should be publicly called to task until they are changed. Universities should seek state level and corporate support in these efforts.

What should the role of federal research investment be in r&d policy? There have been strong arguments for a more

---

[18]M. McClure and I. Abu Duhou, "Prototype Costing at Research Universities: Is It Possible?", Paper presented at the American Educational Research Association, Division J, San Francisco, April 1986.

[19]M. McClure and D. Plank, Educational Statistics for Educational Policy: A Political Economy Perspective (Washington, DC: National Council on Educational Statistics, 1985), pp. 3-7.

extensive federal planning role in the coordination of development policy. Discussion has centered on industrial policy toward "sunrise" and "sunset" areas of the manufacturing sector.[20] Given the current rickety policy structure of agency based investment in research, coordinated planning is unlikely. Until there is first a shift toward a policy paradigm of investment in development, future federal allocations for research will continue to focus on distribution instead of production. This distribution focus has stunted federal investment policy. The U.S. has never evolved a sectoral perspective in which agencies are coordinated around a common goal of development. (This is not a call for centralized planning; rather it is recognition of a problem that warrants serious discussion.)

The Future: Implications for Policy

In the past, relatively little attention was paid to policies regarding tax base regeneration. Much of the public policy literature focused on agency missions and distributional issues. Growth was assumed, creating sponsors and researchers, unfettered by development issues. However, given the increasing uncertainty of a world political economy, the future of the American tax base is no longer assured.[21] Regeneration policy requires more investment-minded sponsors and entrepreneurial/creative researchers. If public investments do not produce returns sufficient at least to offset the effects of population growth, capital depreciation and inflation, the nation's future tax base will have difficulty regenerating. Currently, most public research is channeled into agencies which pay limited attention to development. Future federal research funding policy can ill afford the

---

[20] See R.B. Reich, The Next American Frontier, (New York: New York Times Books, 1982); B. Bluestone and B. Harrison, The Deindustrialization of America, (New York: Basic Books, 1982); S. Bowles, D.M. Gordon and T.E. Weisskopf, Beyond the Wasteland, (Garden City, NY: Anchor Books, 1984); and I.C. Magazine and R.B. Reich, Minding America's Business, (New York: Vintage Books, 1982).

[21] See M. Feldstein, The American Economy in Transition, (Chicago: University of Chicago Press, 1980).

inefficiencies caused by the present laxity. Coordinated sectoral policy should focus on economic growth beyond the policy arenas of federal agency missions, and the research universities should be central to this reform. With effective coordination, their presence can enhance both regional and national development.

An excellent research university, for example, is capable of attracting high quality students into a region. If they stay, their presence could make significant contributions to its creative development. Such universities can help attract business and industry; they can contribute to the quality of life in the region by directing their resources into policy arenas. However, the universities must not only clearly define their competencies but also recognize their limitations and avoid promoting themselves as economic panaceas. They must be wary of demands placed on them by national and regional leaders seeking direct university involvement in short term policy quests that tax the institution's research capacity unduly. This type of service requires support in the form of long term commitments to even resource flows. Universities should decide for themselves what they are willing to contribute. Interventionist planning policies would be particularly inappropriate, although they currently exist *de facto*.

One way of beginning reform would be to recast some share of research funding in terms of its contribution to the maintenance and growth of identified tax bases. This would entail mapping out "tax base to tax base investment cycles", tracking the flows of resources from the loci of investments to the loci of returns. Data would be collected to trace both public and private capital formation at regional and national levels.

Since the relationship between economic development can be an extraordinarily subtle and complex process, investment policies should encourage not only closer public and private sector cooperation, but also intragovernmental cooperation and flexibility, especially at the regional level. While much laudable effort is already occurring in these areas, more explicit policy attention will be required.

Policymakers interested in economic development could begin by subsidizing more systematic university based data collection to track the effects of capital import and formation on regional and national economies. A regional model may well provide a more appropriate unit of analysis than a national one. The role of federal r&d policy might eventually shift to the support of coordinated regional development rather than the management of a national industrial policy. From this position federal policymakers could encourage public and private sector cooperation within and across regions.

Research universities with adequately designed policies can serve as centres for this type of syncretic development. With proper infrastructure support, they could provide high quality information and analysis to a variety of stakeholders. The university's longer term perspective would help forge coalitions and lend credibility to development efforts and, because of its traditional commitment to cosmopolitan academic values, the university could provide a forum for reasoned discourse across interest groups.

The federal government could help support these efforts by sponsoring high quality, timely, accessible and comparable data bases. Federal r&d policymakers could sponsor projects that would help federal agencies make their data collection more appropriate for tracking economic development returns. Universities could receive long term capital support to help coordinate intragovernmental and private sector data base systems, and their policy research centres could help track and interpret regional and national development efforts.

State and local policymakers have strong incentives to support university research infrastructures (primarily because of their capital import potential).[22] Too often in the recent past, state governments have focused almost exclusively on the potential of research to create jobs in the near future. A more balanced portfolio of investments would include short, mid and long term returns to regional tax bases.

---

[22]J. Freeman, Conversation, University of Pittsburgh, April 1986.

The universities themselves should consider more diversified human capital portfolios that are more efficiently linked to funding. Few, if any, can afford to keep pace with the technological requirements of advanced research and maintain large numbers of tenured professors in disciplines where research funding dried up years ago. Too often, excellent researchers are left without support because the winds shifted in Washington. Externally, the research universities should take a stronger leadership role in the reform of research funding by encouraging more responsible coordination of economic development policies, leading to more stable funding commitments. For example, public endowment of research universities during surplus periods would help balance diminished resource flows during recessions. Their internal promotion and compensation policies could be linked more responsibly to funding. Stronger efforts to endow research support could support the best researchers in both public and private institutions.

Until the links and limits between university r&d and future tax bases are more clearly charted, policymakers and researchers may be left to the whims of the piper's paymasters.

The Imperial Role of the Empire State in Higher Education: Five Cases from New York in the 1970s

by

Richard C. Lonsdale,

Judith S. Glazer,

David C. Levy,

and

Lynn D. Walsh[1]

Introduction

If a case can be a photograph of a slice of time in the interaction between organizations and government, then a series of cases may be viewed as a film strip of that interaction. It's not exactly a moving picture, but through multiple exposures it can show a much more dynamic image than any single exposure. And the sequence of shots may enable us to extract a higher order of understanding of the interaction, somewhat along the lines of a meta-analysis.

In this context five cases are presented, all from New York State. Four of them portray the interaction of two or more institutions of higher education (IHEs) with various agencies and levels of state government. The fifth depicts the state's highest court adjudicating a dispute between two of its top educational governing boards. All five cases grew out of crises. The first two were financial crises; the third was interorganizational; the fourth was philosophical, involving adherence to a political dogma long beyond its point of utility or truth; and the fifth a to-the-bitter-end territorial struggle. Three cases were the subject of doctoral dissertations

[1] Professor of Educational Administration and Higher Education, New York University; Associate Dean of the School of Education and Human Services, St. John's University; Dean, Parsons School of Design, New School for Social Research; Associate Vice President for Academic Affairs, State University of New York College at Old Westbury, NY.

completed at New York University under the guidance of the senior author; the other two were prepared by the senior author from the literature, from interviews, and from experience.

The various roles of the state government interacting with public and independent institutions of higher education are the focus of these cases, although that was not necessarily the conceptual focus of the three dissertations. The cases are arranged in chronological order from 1969 to 1978. The first case shows Parsons School of Design, then about to go bankrupt, achieving an "affiliation" with the New School for Social Research, with the state playing a benign but passive role. The second case shows a large independent institution (New York University) rescued from the brink of bankruptcy by an emergency state law, signifying the most active of state participation. The third case shows the State University College at Westbury in the centre of the struggle between public and independent IHEs on Long Island, with the Board of Regents, under heavy political pressure, finally acceding to a compromise in the controversy. The fourth case shows the long build-up to the decision by the Board of Higher Education of the City University of New York (CUNY) to terminate an entrenched policy of "free tuition" for resident, matriculated, undergraduate bachelor's degree candidates, and to institute a uniform tuition policy in response to New York City's fiscal crisis. The final case shows the state Court of Appeals deciding against the State University of New York (SUNY) and in favour of the power of the Board of Regents to discontinue weak doctoral programs.

This introduction ends with a brief word about the system of institutional-governmental relations in higher education in New York State. New York has a highly centralized structure and process of governance for higher (and also for lower) education. In a very real sense, the state legislature is the foremost educational governing body, and it is actively involved in carrying out that role. A joint session of the legislature (without the nomination by, or concurrence of, the governor) elects the Board of Regents. This board exercises broad policy-making power over all institutions of education in the state, public and independent, most of the professions, and all libraries and museums. It appoints the State Commissioner of Education, who serves at its pleasure as its executive officer and as "President of the University of the State of New York", the corporate name for all education in the state.

Public higher education is provided through SUNY (the State University of New York) and CUNY (the City University of New York). Some 64 institutions comprise SUNY; 19 make up CUNY. SUNY was formed in 1948, CUNY in 1961. Most of the 135 independent (private) institutions predate the formation of both public systems of higher education, although some individual institutions in the public systems were founded well back in the nineteenth century. With the consent of the senate of the state, the governor appoints the members of the SUNY Board of Trustees. The governor and the mayor of New York together appoint the members of what is now called the Board of Trustees of CUNY. All academic programs must be registered with and approved by the State Education Department (SED), which also has the right of review of these programs. New York provides more financial support to independent institutions than any other state in the U.S., while, of course, also funding the two public systems of higher education. Figure 1 illustrates many of these relationships.

The Case of the Parsons School of Design

The description of this case, which climaxed in early 1970, is based upon the dissertation of David D. Levy, completed in 1979.[2] It shows New York state in the role of counselor and friendly, but passive, supporter of two IHEs engaged in the process of combining through affiliation as a way to avoid the bankruptcy of one of them. The coupling took place when, in February 1970, the independent New School for Social Research in New York City accepted the plea from the independent Parsons School of Design, also in New York City, for an "affiliation" form of merger. The decision averted the extinction of Parsons, led to its reinvigoration, and has resulted in a combined institution that has proved to be stronger and more diversified in every way. The events leading to the crisis and the affiliation were dramatic.

---

[2]David C. Levy, "An historical study of Parsons School of Design and its merger/affiliation with the New School for Social Research", Unpublished doctoral dissertation, New York University, 1979.

SOCIETY
(demand for education, values, attitudes, beliefs, manners and customs,
inhibition or receptivity to change, etc.)

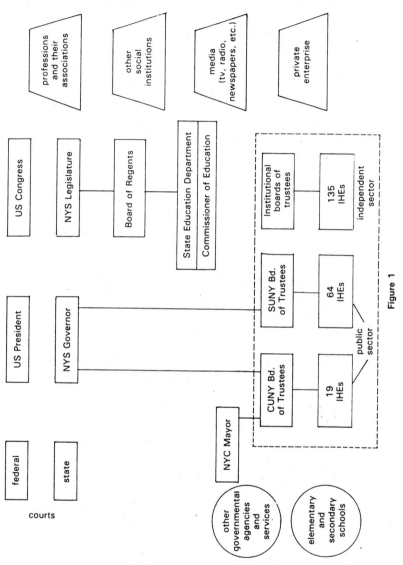

A systems representation of higher education in New York State.

Figure 1

WORLD AND NATIONAL TRENDS
(including macro-decisions and micro-decisions)
(population, energy, international relations, employment, GNP, professions, etc.)

After several years of shaky financial conditions in the late 1960s, the Parsons School of Design faced the prospect, in December, 1969, of having to close because of insolvency. There were a number of prior conditions and developments which had led to that state of affairs.

1. The board of trustees had permitted successive annual deficits to occur in the late 1960s, at least one of them on the order of about 27 percent of the annual operating budget. These deficits were partly met by dipping into the institution's small endowment.

2. A benefactor, Arthur A. Houghton of the Corning Glass Corporation, who had been a primary source of support of the school during the preceding years, let it be known that that year he was phasing out his contributions.

3. The school had failed to acquire permanent facilities and was occupying space in mid-town Manhattan, which was an expensive drain on the annual operating expenses.

4. The school had only a three-year undergraduate program and the administration had been slow to develop it to the level of a bachelor's degree. That development not only would have attracted more students but would also have enabled them to tap external funding from private and state sources.

5. The school had failed to raise its tuition to levels comparable with the tuition of its main competitors, thus foregoing significant income for an institution almost wholly dependent on tuition for its operating revenue.

6. The faculty was made up mainly of adjunct instructors and professors (in one year to the extent of 75 percent of the total) and all were paid on the basis of a "sessional rate", not an annual salary, so it may be said that the institution's policy was to strive for a "cheap payroll". But the

size of the instructional staff was extravagant. The faculty had been permitted to grow some 79 percent from 1960-69 during a period of at first steady and then declining student enrolment.

7. Administrative costs had also been permitted to escalate.

8. Fund-raising efforts came too late.

9. There had been no real attempt to develop an evening division which would have been a new and, possibly, major source of income.

Even with all this:

> Strange as it may seem, under the circumstances, it came as a great shock to those members of Parsons' administration who were privy to financial policy matters that the chairman of the Board had concluded by mid-December of 1969 that the school faced a crisis so major as to warrant the immediate consideration of the suspension of activity and the closing of the school by the end of the spring 1970 term or sooner.[3]

Having faced up to the possibility of this calamity, the board of trustees authorized the school's president, vice-president, and legal counsel to seek advice from the New York State Education Department. On December 19 the three officers met at Albany with the chief of the SED office of higher education and with a representative of the higher education management services.

The discussion at that meeting concentrated on procedural mechanisms for dismantling the school. According to Levy's account - and he was present at the meeting in his capacity as vice-president of the school -

---

[3]*Ibid.*, p. 175.

It must be noted here that the State Education Department staff was extraordinarily cooperative and expressed its deepest concern for Parsons' plight. They made it clear that they would do whatever they could to help preserve the school in some form, merged or otherwise. Towards this end they immediately suspended requirements previously imposed, such as the expansion of library facilities, as a prerequisite to the granting of the Bachelor of Fine Arts degree (which program was planned for implementation the following fall).[4]

The Parsons representatives presented to the two SED officials a list of five institutions with which Parsons might possibly merge. Of these five, the SED men recommended the New School of Social Research as the most likely prospect.

The Parsons board of trustees met on December 22 to hear the report of the Albany visit, and approved exploring a possible merger with the New School. Representatives from Parsons met with officers of the New School on December 30 to discuss the possibility of a merger. There followed intensive analysis by the administration of the New School of the pros and cons of joining the two institutions. And after only six weeks, the board of trustees of the New School, on February 10, 1970, approved the Parsons affiliation. The decision was announced by the senior officers of both institutions to the Parsons faculty at a special meeting on February 19. That was the first occasion on which the faculty heard of the dramatic development. On April 23, at their final meeting, having appointed the trustees of the New School to serve in that capacity for Parsons, the trustees of Parsons resigned.

One important characteristic of the manner of this coupling of the two institutions was its legal nature. Had a formal merger or consolidation of the two institutions been attempted, their state-granted charters would have had to be formally amended by the New York State Board of Regents. This process could have taken some months, time Parsons could ill afford, and

---

[4]*Ibid.*, p. 182.

there would have been no guarantee of its outcome. It was essential that the two institutions be joined speedily. It was also essential to safeguard the assets of the New School from "potential assault by litigants against Parsons School of Design".[5] In addition, in that era of the unionization of faculties of independent institutions, it was important to protect each institution against the effects of faculty unionization in the other. This procedure made it possible for the faculty of one of the institutions to unionize without affecting the other.

The device of combining the two institutions by affiliation was the shrewd invention of lawyers acting for the two institutions. As one of them described it in an interview, affiliation was:

> ... an extremely simple and interesting approach whereby we would have no transfer of assets, we would have no merger, we would have no consolidation agreement; instead, we would follow a procedure under a general letter of intent and agreement, which specifically imposed no legal obligations on either party. The approach used was that we would see to it that the Trustees of Parsons would resign under appropriate circumstances and in such an order, that they would elect new Trustees, who happened to be the Trustees of the New School for Social Research.
>
> So you ended up with a situation finally, whereby the Board of Parsons was the same Board as that of the New School for Social Research. And from a legal standpoint, the separate corporate entities of both corporations, under the Education Law, had not changed at all. From a legal standpoint you can say it was done by the lawyers in such a way that nothing happened.[6]

---

[5]*Ibid.*, p. 241.

[6]Interview quoted by Levy, *Ibid.*, p. 236.

In this manner it was possible to *de facto* merge two institutions without formal state approval, without charter or other legal changes in their corporate structures, and without much consultation of their faculties. At most, the state's role was one of non-participant observer. In the 1970s, this was the only instance where affiliation was used to combine IHEs within New York State, even though the SED staff did recommend the device in various other cases.

The Case of New York University

In the years 1971-73 New York University was financially near collapse. It was rescued only by state emergency legislation. The case casts the state in the role of broker and saviour, negotiating a deal among a set of independent and public institutions and authorizing the sale of NYU's uptown campus as a means of gaining a critically needed infusion of ready capital. The case also illustrates how fast things can change.

In a 16-page brochure, dated May 2, 1969, and addressed to the faculty, students, and staff of New York University, President James Hester announced that the university was about to embark upon "an extremely ambitious new development program - an extraordinary but necessary effort that follows naturally from the development campaign completed just over a year ago".[7] It called for raising $222.5 million in the next five years. Among the many projects outlined as goals of the fund-raising campaign were additional student housing, a new library, and a nuclear engineering building - all at the university's uptown campus at University Heights, in the Bronx. This was the campus that was to be sold four years later to the City University of New York (CUNY) by act of the state legislature.

Only 21 months later, in January, 1971, President Hester was writing the faculty to the effect that:

---

[7]James M. Hester, Memorandum to the faculty, students and staff of New York University: A new stage in the university's development. (New York: New York University, 2 May 1969.)

The University is running serious deficits, and its future viability requires that we eliminate any unnecessary and wasteful expenditures. The Commission on Effective Use of Resources has helped us make substantial savings, but there is strong belief in many quarters that a great deal more could be done if all of us were more economy-minded.[8]

Things had gone sour. Annual deficits had begun to grow - as much as $10 million on a budget of $220 million for 1971-72. Enrolments had begun to decline, partly because of demographic trends and partly because of the bad press New York City was then receiving, causing parents to be reluctant about sending their children to college in the city. Federal grants in aid had failed to rise, as some had hoped. The university's senior administration realized that the situation had become critical, although many faculty members did not realize the seriousness of the situation. Of particular urgency was the fact that local banks had become reluctant to make short-term loans to the university to carry it over periods of low cash flow. A rescue operation was needed.

Early in 1972, the hope was that the university might sell its uptown campus at University Heights, the site of one of its two liberal arts colleges and its school of engineering and science. The money could be used to replenish its unrestricted endowment and to give it working capital. The first plan was for a SUNY-sponsored centre at the Heights. The institution would buy the property and take over the NYU engineering school, also perhaps bringing in the Brooklyn Polytechnic Institute and even Columbia University's school of engineering to create a kind of engineering consortium. The idea foundered for lack of support from SUNY and opposition from CUNY to having a major SUNY institution within New York City (threatening CUNY's free tuition policy and providing competition for City College's school of engineering). Moreover, Brooklyn Polytechnic Institute showed no enthusiasm for the plan, and marshalled opposition to the idea from Stanley Steingut of Brooklyn, the minority leader of the

---

[8]James M. Hester, Memorandum to members of the faculty: need for economy. (New York: New York University, 28 January 1971.)

state assembly. NYU students and faculty members at the Heights campus also voiced their strong opposition to any sale of the Heights. By early 1972 the sale of the Heights campus was publicly acknowledged as the best hope for the university, whose deficit continued to grow.

In February Dean Sidney Borowitz of the University College of Arts and Science at the Heights wrote his faculty a two-page memorandum on the crisis, concluding with these words:

> There is no doubt that the immediate future will be turbulent. I hope that there is enough collegiality and humanity on our campus so that we do not hurt each other too much. I trust that the institutional devices we have developed for communication will be able to stand the strain of the next months. Finally, I pray that we will find a way to resolve our problems with as little trauma as possible - though I fear that there must be some trauma for each of us.[9]

Trauma indeed there was. On February 29, 1972, Hester announced the appointment of a task force "to recommend both short-term and long-term actions that will reduce deficits in ways that sustain the quality of the University's educational programs".[10] As reported on the front page of the New York Times for April 30, the task force aimed to recommend a 50 percent cut in the 600-member undergraduate faculty to adjust to a drop in undergraduate enrolment.[11] But Hester called the report premature. When the task force did issue its report on May 19, it began on this dramatic note:

---

[9]Sidney Borowitz, Memorandum to the faculty. (New York: New York University, University College of Arts and Science, 22 February 1972.)

[10]James M. Hester, Memorandum to members of the New York University community. (New York: New York University, 29 February 1972.)

[11]Laurie Johnston, "N.Y.U. unit asks 50% cut in undergraduate faculty". New York Times, 30 April 1972, p. 1, 29.

Within the next few weeks, New York University must choose which of two precedents it will shatter: it can choose to be the victim of the largest and most spectacular financial collapse in the history of American higher education, or it can choose to surmount by its own resolute actions, the most difficult financial crisis any university has faced and survived.[12]

The report set financial targets for the next three years for each academic and nonacademic unit. It proposed rules, procedures, and reorganization to assure that the targets would be met, and recommended ways of increasing income. The Graduate School of Social Work was to be discontinued (an action later avoided by the success of special fund-raising efforts by the faculty and alumni); the faculty mandatory age of retirement was to be reduced from 68 to 65. Finally it recommended possible termination of tenured as well as untenured faculty members. The termination of tenured faculty never actually occurred, but altogether it was a sober and sobering report.

Meanwhile, early in 1972, negotiations had been going on between NYU and the governor, the state legislature, the state office of the budget, the state university, the city university, Brooklyn Polytechnic Institute, and several other agencies and institutions of higher education. The dream of a metropolitan institute of technology had faded, to be replaced by a politically and economically more feasible solution. The state was clearly alarmed over the dangerous prospect of a bankrupt NYU. On May 24, 1972, the legislature passed legislation to rescue NYU by enabling it to sell the University Heights campus. The following "legislative findings" were set forth in the law signed by the governor:

The legislature finds and declares that the continued viability of the state's system of higher education is threatened by the fiscal crisis facing New York University, the largest private institution

[12] The report of the New York University task force on the financial emergency. (New York: New York University, 19 May 1972.)

of higher education in the state. Emergency action is clearly needed to preserve this outstanding institution and to permit it to continue to serve the educational needs of the people of the state. To provide such emergency action, the legislature has determined that the city university construction fund should acquire and develop the Bronx campus of New York university solely for the Bronx community college, and that appropriate programs and faculty of the New York university school of engineering and science should be merged into the polytechnic institute of Brooklyn.[13]

The sum of $13 million was appropriated as a temporary down payment on the purchase of the Heights campus, and both NYU and Brooklyn Polytechnic Institute were directed to present budgets to the Board of Regents by October 1, 1973, showing how each would achieve a balanced budget by the academic year 1974-75 "without special extraordinary state subsidies".[14]

Negotiations went forward, appraisals of the Heights property were secured from two independent appraisers, the state dormitory authority provided the back-up funds, and the University Heights campus was sold for $61.9 million for the use of Bronx Community College of CUNY. After bonds and other debts associated with the Heights property were paid off and other expenses were met connected with the transfer of the engineering school to Brooklyn Polytechnic Institute (which became the Polytechnic Institute of New York) and the transfer of the liberal arts college from the Heights to the main campus at Washington Square, some $30 million was available as unrestricted endowment for NYU. Stringent economies were made and more efficient financial practices were phased in. The university budget was balanced, and the university financial crisis ended. In 1986, three university presidents

---

[13]Chapter 463, Laws of New York. (New York City University - Heights Campus - Use, 1972.)

[14]*Ibid.*

later, the university launched another fund drive, to raise a billion dollars by the year 2000.

The special law for New York University's liquidation of the Heights campus took considerable negotiating and brokering. Involved were various top personnel of the state and of the university. In all this the Board of Regents and the Commissioner of Education were essentially passive bystanders, giving *pro forma* approval to Chapter 463. The state had seen its largest independent university in danger of bankruptcy and had rescued it.[15]

The Case of Old Westbury

The third case, covering the period 1973-75, is based on the dissertation of Lynn D. Walsh, completed in 1984.[16] It depicts the state in the role of arbitrator and coordinator over the public and independent sectors of higher education in New York State, in contest over whether the State University College at Old Westbury, in Nassau County on Long Island, would be granted permission to institute an undergraduate program in business and management.

After an initial pilot phase, from 1967-71, the State University College at Old Westbury opened in October, 1971, with 570 students as an experimental college with a preponderance of minority students, committed to educating "traditionally bypassed students" in an interdisciplinary mode. From the beginning the college was controversial - not only because of its atypical student body and faculty, but also its unconventional curriculum and administrative practices, and the sometimes deviant public behaviour of both students and faculty. One display of boorish behaviour by students and faculty at a "Dedication Day" ceremony in May, 1973, so turned off

---

[15]S. Borowitz, interview, 15 September 1986; A. Goren, interview, 10 September 1986; and J. O'Mara, interview, 16 September 1986.

[16]Lynn D. Walsh, "A case study of the 1975 decision to amend the master plan of the State University of New York College at Old Westbury to authorize the establishment of programs in business and management", Unpublished doctoral dissertation, New York University, 1984.

members of the college council and SUNY officials that questions were raised as to whether the college should be allowed to continue. It was. But the College's master plan was revised by SUNY central to bring it more into line with the higher education needs of Long Island.

One provision of the revised plan was to make Old Westbury more of an upper division college accommodating the graduates of the three large state university community colleges on Long Island. To develop a college curriculum consistent with the new plan, in the fall of 1973 the college administration proposed a new business and management program within a new division of administrative sciences. As part of the undergraduate program, this proposal was part of the expanded college master plan sent to SUNY central in December, 1973.

Receiving a go-ahead on the master plan the next month, President John Maguire set up an advisory panel for the new administrative science division and instituted a search for a director of the new division. The faculty opposed the master plan because they had not been consulted. They then notified all independent IHEs in the area, warning of the likely effect if the business programs at Old Westbury were developed; it would drain off enrolments from other comparable programs.

Instead, the advisory panel recommended the kind of business and management program that would be attractive to the minority students of Old Westbury. The three regional community colleges vetoed that idea, arguing that their students would not want such a program. The presidents of three of the leading independent IHEs in the area became concerned about competition from Old Westbury's proposed new administrative science program and moved to block it. They met with a key Long Island member of the state Board of Regents and the deputy commissioner for higher education of the SED to express their opposition. One other independent college president later joined the opposition and two more were more ambivalent throughout.

> ... the independent institutions perceived Old Westbury as changing its mission into primarily an upper-division college, which would be attractive to

community college graduates. The original mission, as the independent institutions understood it, had been to educate the educationally and economically depressed citizenry of Long Island ... The problem was not the issue of whether a particular new program would be implemented but the broader issue of the nature of the public college's mission ...

Old Westbury became the focal point for the longstanding philosophical argument about the place of public higher education in New York State. Should public education serve those who could not afford independent higher education or those who were not served at all?[17]

Nevertheless, in February, 1974, President Maguire sent SUNY central a request for registration of seven new programs in three divisions: three of the degree programs were in the division of administrative science. The SUNY Board of Trustees approved them and forwarded them to the Board of Regents for final approval. The SED, however, sent the administrative science program back, saying that a master plan amendment was needed, since Old Westbury had been founded as a college of liberal arts, not including business administration. SUNY central supplied the request for the amendment. The Regents then deferred action on the programs in business and management, pending further study of transfer needs among colleges on Long Island. The Regents also lowered Old Westbury's target enrolment figures for 1980 from 5,000 to 3,200 students.

Maguire continued to develop the business and management program not yet approved by the Regents. He appointed a task force to study it, and included representatives of the Long Island business community, along with representatives of the three local community colleges and of the independent institutions. The task force redesigned the business and management program along traditional lines modelled after the business program of CUNY's Baruch College. This change

---

[17]*Ibid.*, p. 144.

won the support of the three community colleges, and the program was sent to SUNY central for review.

Old Westbury College officials got in touch with officials of the SED and with a member of the Board of Regents to try to convince them of the need for the business and management program. They also had the support of Joseph Margiotta, Nassau County Republican Chairman. The SED requested a survey of Long Island students that, when completed, revealed the need for a business program. Still the heads of local independent IHEs opposed the program. So Old Westbury mobilized a letter-writing campaign by politicians, business leaders, public school administrators and faculty, and representatives of the three community colleges. Local newspapers also gave their support.

The SED continued to question the need for the new business and management program. Old Westbury responded with further data in support of its program, but offered a compromise - that the business and management program be approved for a trial period with a limitation on enrolment. This was to be followed by an evaluation of the effect, if any, that the Old Westbury program was having on independent college enrolments in upper division business programs.

In December, 1974, the state deputy commissioner for higher education met with the Long Island presidents of independent IHEs and the Old Westbury president. The meeting seemed to settle on this compromise, but Old Westbury continued to put pressure on the SED through a letter-writing campaign. And the heads of the larger independent institutions wrote to the SED to express continuing opposition to the new program. In January 1975, the Regents again rejected the new program as not needed.

Maguire then sought further support from Republican Chairman Margiotta (the brother-in-law of one of the high officials of one of the independent institutions). The SUNY associate chancellor for policy and planning proposed to the SED deputy commissioner for higher education a modified trial period for a program of business and management at Old Westbury, restricted in scope and enrolment. A further meeting of heads of the larger independent IHEs revealed their persistent objections.

In January 1975 the SUNY Board of Trustees then asked the Regents to reconsider their action on the Old Westbury program. The chair of the state assembly's committee on higher education (himself from Long Island) then announced there would be committee hearings on the Regents' rejection of the Old Westbury program.

There followed a suggestion from the deputy commissioner for higher education of the SED to the contending independent college presidents proposing the same compromise as had earlier been raised by SUNY central. At a meeting in late January, the institutional heads agreed, and a resolution seemed to be in the air.

The former chair of Old Westbury's college council again obtained support for the new program from Margiotta, who called the vice-chancellor of the Board of Regents (also from Long Island) to urge support of the compromise plan. The then current chair of the college council also saw all the Regents who had voted against the program, informing them "that in his opinion Old Westbury's survival depended upon the business program. He said that Old Westbury could have been turned into a home for the retarded; however, he had argued for its survival".[18]

At a meeting on February 20, 1975, the Board of Regents finally accepted the compromise plan. The struggle was over. A later survey found that the Old Westbury business program had had no impact on the independent college business programs' enrolments. In fact, all such programs had grown. The enrolment restriction was then lifted.

The specific precipitating issue, once resolved, faded away. But the conflict between the public and private sectors of higher education in New York State remained unresolved, only to break out periodically in later years. The SUNY Board of Trustees issued one direct challenge, in the state's highest court, to the authority of the Board of Regents, and lost, as described below in the fifth case study. Through its top governance structure in education (the Board of Regents), the

---

[18]*Ibid.*, p. 181.

state continued to coordinate higher education, but it stayed away from the arbitrator role whenever possible.

The Case of Free Tuition at CUNY

The fourth case, which climaxed in 1976, is based upon the dissertation of Judith S. Glazer, completed in 1981.[19] It shows the state as power wielder and resource provider, as the CUNY Board of Higher Education was finally forced to impose tuition charges for matriculated undergraduate students, thereby terminating its 127-year-old policy of free tuition.

From its opening in 1849, free tuition had been the policy of the "Free Academy", the first municipal college of New York City and the forerunner of the City College of New York. Over the years, "free tuition" in the municipal system of higher education of New York City became political dogma and a rallying cry for political leaders and many supporters of CUNY, even though the actual policy of free tuition was gradually eroded. The policy was supported as the way to provide higher educational opportunities for the middle class of the city, for the immigrants of the late nineteenth and early twentieth century, for the veterans of World War II and for the "minorities" of the mid and late twentieth century. It finally came a cropper because of the city's "fiscal crisis" of 1975-76.

The first breach in the free tuition policy came in 1949 when the Board of Higher Education negotiated an "adjusted" tuition rate, the device used to securing for students the benefits of the "GI Bill of Rights". The veterans did not actually pay tuition; it was just a paper transaction between the two levels of government. The first real break in the free tuition policy came in 1955-59, when three community colleges were established by the Board of Higher Education in which tuition was charged at a rate of approximately one-third the cost of the program, the state and city splitting the remaining two-thirds. "It demonstrated to the state political leaders that when state

---

[19]Judith S. Glazer, "A case study of the decision in 1976 to initiate tuition for matriculated undergraduate students of the City University of New York", Unpublished doctoral dissertation, New York University, 1981.

aid was a factor, policies could be modified pragmatically".[20]
Tuition for graduate work in CUNY was instituted in 1962, in
exchange for state approval of the first publicly supported
doctoral programs. Gradually, in the 1950s and 60s various
non-instructional "fees" were imposed. These were followed by
instructional fees in lieu of tuition and then a combination of
both further wore away the free tuition policy until it became
restricted to full-time undergraduate students matriculated for
the bachelor's degree in CUNY's senior colleges.

In 1961, when the separate senior colleges and community
colleges were combined into the City University of New York,
no long-term agreement was made between the city and the
state over its financing. The creation of CUNY gave New York
State two systems of public higher education, one charging
tuition for undergraduate matriculants for bachelor's degrees
(SUNY), and the other providing free tuition (CUNY).

> This duality could not persist indefinitely as
> governmental involvement increased. Rockefeller
> poured new resources into a friendly SUNY, rather
> than a hostile CUNY. Several former college officials
> acknowledged that CUNY's unwillingness to
> relinquish free tuition in exchange for state largesse
> cost the university much.[21]

> The city's desire to have it both ways - free tuition
> and new construction funded by the state [in 1966] -
> led to the conflict between Albany and the Board of
> Higher Education with the backing of City Hall, that
> was the beginning of the end of free tuition.[22]

The significant expansion of federal aid to higher education in
the form of basic educational opportunity grants (BEOG),

---

[20]*Ibid.*, p. 175.

[21]*Ibid.*, pp. 256-57.

[22]*Ibid.*, p. 264.

instituted in 1972, was another pressure to end the free tuition policy. "CUNY was a heavily undergraduate system, and by not charging matriculated students any tuition, it was denying its students access to new entitlements linked to tuition charges."[23]

It was New York City's fiscal crisis of 1975-76 that brought on the termination of the practice. Beginning around 1968, the city had begun to move operating expenses into the capital budget, thus funding current expenses through the device of long-term bonding. That and other such practices brought a financial crisis to a head in April 1975, when the city, because of its rising budget, heavy debt, and poor credit rating, was closed out of the bond market. In June a municipal assistance corporation (MAC) was formed by the state legislature to help the city meet its financial obligations and avoid going into bankruptcy. MAC was authorized to issue special bonds and notes to the extent of $5.25 billion, backed by the state. Later, in August, the state set up the emergency financial control board (EFCB) to run the city's affairs, superseding both the mayor and the city council.

The attempt to secure federal loans to avert the city's bankruptcy brought CUNY, one of the city's agencies, under examination. The free tuition policy was called into question by the federal government. When a federal loan bill to assist New York City was passed in December 1975, it became a virtual certainty that the free tuition policy would have to go.

Other factors were also crucial to undermining the policy. The open admissions policy, instituted in 1971, had greatly increased the budget for CUNY. The tuition assistance plan (TAP) of New York State, begun in 1974, provided new state revenues to augment operating aid for IHEs throughout the state, but CUNY's free tuition policy kept it from benefitting fully from it. Indeed, the state Board of Regents and the Commissioner of Education criticized CUNY for denying 41 percent of its undergraduate students access to TAP funds by not charging tuition.

---

[23]*Ibid.*, p. 201.

As the fiscal crisis wore on, the Commissioner of Education, in September 1975, urged the chair of the CUNY Board of Higher Education to institute tuition that would equal that of SUNY. Two months later the Board of Regents recommended imposing tuition at CUNY, noting that tuition no longer served as a barrier limiting access to higher education, since state financial aid served to offset it.

But the chair of the CUNY Board of Higher Education was adamant in his opposition to terminating the free tuition policy. And he had the support of Mayor Abraham Beame and Governor Hugh Carey. Carey himself in 1974 had made a campaign pledge of maintaining free tuition to CUNY. As late as September 1975, the New York Times also continued its support of free tuition, arguing that its termination would have an adverse effect upon lower-middle-income students. However, Carey changed his tune in December, acknowledging that those able to pay tuition should do so. By May 1976, the imposition of tuition charges for matriculated undergraduate students was one of ten legislative proposals for rescuing CUNY. On May 27, in the absence of any final legislative action, Chancellor Robert Kibbee closed CUNY until further notice because the institution had run out of funds. On June 1, the Board of Higher Education voted to impose tuition on matriculated resident undergraduates. And Mayor Beame capitulated on June 7, giving public support to imposing tuition. Two days later the state assembly passed the bill, and on June 11, the senate. It was signed the next day by the governor. CUNY now had fiscal parity with SUNY for comparable purposes. It also accepted state responsibility for its governance and funding for three years under an interim arrangement. On June 14 the CUNY Board of Higher Education voted a uniform tuition schedule for 1976-77. Free tuition was dead. The state eventually, in 1982-83, took over full financing of the senior colleges of CUNY, with the city continuing to contribute to the support of the community colleges.

It had been a wrenching experience. Involved from the federal level had been President Gerald Ford and Congress; from the state level Governor Hugh Carey and his staff, the legislature, the division of the budget, the Board of Regents, and the Commissioner of Education; and from the city Mayor Abraham

Beame and his staff, the emergency financial control board and the municipal assistance corporation, the Board of Higher Education and its chancellor, CUNY college presidents, CUNY faculty, alumni groups, students, unions, representatives of the independent IHEs, and the newspapers. The dominant actors, however, were those at the state level, wielding their power of law and their resources of taxes. It took their power and resources, used in a time of extreme fiscal crisis, to overcome the dogma and tradition of the free tuition policy so imbedded in New York City.

The Case of the Court of Appeals Decision

The fifth case reached its climax in 1978 in a decision of the New York State Court of Appeals, the state's highest court. It confirmed the state's role - actually that of the Board of Regents - as regulator and quality controller with respect to programs of the State University of New York. It was an unusual case in that one major governing board in public higher education, the SUNY Board of Trustees, sued what had always been regarded as the state's highest governing board in lower or higher education, the State Board of Regents - and lost. At issue was territoriality.

Following the tremendous expansion in graduate, as well as undergraduate, education in New York State in the 1950s, 60s, and early 70s, the Board of Regents decided to undertake a formal review of the quality of doctoral degree programs in the public and independent institutions of the state. Working through the SED, an elaborate review process was begun in 1973, starting with doctoral programs in the liberal arts subjects.

The process of reviewing each program at each institution involved a self-report based on detailed standards set by the state, a site visit by two or three experts from outside the state, a report prepared by the site visitors, a review of both the self-report and the site visitors' report by a rating committee of experts from outside the state, a review by a statewide council of deans of graduate studies from the major universities of the state, and a final review by the Commissioner of Education. At each review stage there was extensive correspondence with the focal institution, giving it ample opportunity to correct errors of fact and to refute judgments. The possible outcomes were a decision by the Commissioner of Education to approve and reregister the program under review, to place it on probation for three years, pending stated necessary improvements, or to disapprove and deregister the program, terminating all new admissions and ordering the program closed after current matriculants had been given the opportunity to complete their degrees. In short, it was a hard-nosed review, not just a set of commendations and recommendations.

Some 116 programs in ten fields had been reviewed by early 1977. Of these, 26 had been found of insufficient quality to warrant their continuance. Of the 26, 24 were closed without appeal by the sponsoring institution. The remaining two were the doctoral programs in English and History at the State University of New York at Albany. Using these two as test cases, the SUNY Board of Trustees and its Chancellor contested the authority of the Commissioner of Education and the Board of Regents to deregister the programs, arguing that the Commissioner and the Regents had exceeded their authority and really had no authority of program review or of possible discontinuation in the case of the State University.[24]

The SUNY Board of Trustees and Chancellor brought formal suit against the Board of Regents and Commissioner in the State Supreme Court. Losing there and in the next higher court, the Appellate Division, they appealed to the state's top court, the Court of Appeals.

SUNY's case was based on a law of 1961, which gave its Board of Trustees authority to administer the day-to-day operation of the State University, requiring it to submit a master plan every four years as part of the statewide master plan for higher education. SUNY argued that the power of the Regents was limited to supervision and approval of their master plan.

In 1978 the Court held that the 1961 law simply paralleled a 1787 law leaving the day-to-day operation of independent colleges to their own governing boards. It also held that the

---

[24]Edward B. Fiske, State Regents vs. the State U., New York Times, 14 February 1977, p. 30.

preparation of its own master plan did not exempt SUNY from the authority of the Regents. The Court noted that the Regents master plan of 1972 specifically spelled out its plan for program review, including the withdrawal of academically deficient programs. The Court ruled:

> ... section 210 and 215 of the Education Law must be interpreted to empower the Regents to register degree programs as well as the institutions themselves in terms of New York standards. These standards, promulgated as regulations by the Commissioner of Education ... provide the necessary authority for the Commissioner's determination to deny the registration of the English and History doctoral programs offered by the State University of New York at Albany.[25]

The Court went on to caution:

> ... that the power of the Regents is not unbridled. Its function is one of an overseer: a body possessed of broad policy-making attributes. In its broadest sense, the purpose of the Regents is "to encourage and promote education," ... a purpose which must be realized only through the powers granted to the Regents by the Legislature.[26]

The case was a fundamental one. Like two stags fighting for dominance of their turf, the SUNY Board of Trustees and the Board of Regents had locked antlers. At stake was the Regents' historic hegemony over all educational institutions of the state. In this instance their power was found supreme, but it is bound to be challenged again. In a memorandum from the office of the vice-chancellor for university affairs of SUNY, the attorney for SUNY who argued the case, after admitting his great disappointment over the decision, was quoted as saying:

---

[25]Moore v. Regents, State of New York Court of Appeals, 1978.

[26]Ibid.

It should not be taken as an endorsement of
unbridled power in the Department of Education. To
the contrary the decision makes it clear that the rule
of law survives and that nothing need prevent our
stout defense of the University's vital interests in
future time on different facts and circumstances.[27]

Conclusion

In this paper the roles of New York State interacting with
institutions of higher education have been portrayed in five
cases. Nouns and phrases have been used to conceptualize
these roles. In the Parsons case the state was seen as
counselor, explaining to Parsons the procedures to follow if it
had to be bankrupt, and as friendly, but passive, supporter,
largely standing by while institutional lawyers figured out that
"affiliation" far better met the needs of their institutions than
"merger". In the New York University case the state was seen
as broker, working out the deal for NYU to sell its uptown
campus to CUNY and for NYU to spin off its school of
engineering and sciences to the Brooklyn Polytechnic Institute,
and as saviour, providing the $13 million down payment on the
sale of the campus and all of the enabling legislation to
unfreeze NYU's frozen asset of its uptown campus.

In the case of Old Westbury the state was portrayed as
arbitrator, helping, through SUNY central and the SED, to
work out a compromise between Old Westbury and its
neighbouring independent IHEs over a proposed new
undergraduate business program, and as coordinator, trying,
through the Board of Regents, to preserve some rationality in
the distribution of academic programs among the institutions
within a region, whether public or independent. In the case of
the City University of New York, the state was depicted as
power wielder, pressuring the City to put its fiscal house in
order while helping wheedle temporary loans from the federal
government to tide the city over its financial plight, and

---

[27]Richard Gillman, Memorandum to presidents, State University of New
York; chairperson, councils and boards of State University of New York.
(Albany: Office of the Vice Chancellor, University Affairs, State University of
New York, 23 June 1978.)

twisting the arm of the Board of Higher Education to concede the struggle over free tuition, and as resource provider, supplying tax money for student aid and for taking over a greater share of the cost of CUNY.[28]

Finally, in the Court of Appeals case, the state was revealed as regulator, upholding institutions' standards through the court-affirmed power of the Board of Regents, and as quality controller, exercising its power to order discontinuation of doctoral programs found to have insufficient quality.

Ten state roles were thus identified: counselor, supporter, broker, saviour, arbitrator, coordinator, power wielder, resource provider, regulator, and quality controller. Are these a miscellany or do they collectively describe a larger role, a construct that can be called the imperial role, a term not wholly irrelevant to the arrogant way New Yorkers have of designating theirs as the Empire State.

An imperial role is only possible in a state with as highly centralized an educational system as New York. Consistent with such a construct is deciding which institutions shall be established, through the device of chartering, and which shall be permitted to die. Thus, save for the resourcefulness of Parsons and the New School, Parsons might have been permitted to expire - as Bennett, Briarcliff, and Ladycliff colleges were allowed to do at about the same time. In contrast, NYU was seen as important and therefore it must be saved, along with Brooklyn Polytechnic, so the state undertook heroic efforts to save them. Old Westbury stirred up a hornets' nest. The negotiating, mediating and arbitrating skills of SUNY central and the SED were all brought into operation before a compromise could be worked out and the Board of Regents could put the lid on again - after some effective nudging from the chair of the Nassau County Republican Party, an official who had no formal responsibility for the state's educational system.

---

[28] For a further treatment of this case, see Judith S. Glazer, "Terminating Entrenched Policies in Educational Institutions: A Case History of Free Tuition", Review of Higher Education 7 (Winter, 1984), pp. 159-173.

The CUNY free tuition case was a rough and tumble in the end, with all three levels of government in the fray. Again, the state's was the key role, forcing the city and the Board of Higher Education to conform. In another sense, this case could be interpreted as the state being forced to accept some responsibility for the city's crisis, a role that it undertook only reluctantly, that of providing the major support for CUNY. This only developed as a result of the city's fiscal crisis. The Court of Appeals case ruffled the calm of the emperor's court. A power struggle between the two top education "ministers", the SUNY trustees and the Board of Regents, was bound to be disruptive. It took the referee-in-place (the Court of Appeals) to resolve the dispute and restore the court to outward calm.

The point to be made is that the tradition and ethos of New York State virtually forces the state to play the imperial role. The state determines which institutions shall live and which shall be permitted to expire. Like an emperor, the state knocks heads and puts the squeeze on, trying to restore peace when political conflict breaks out. It dispenses or withholds favours and bounty. It regulates and disciplines its minions. In short, these cases reveal that the Empire State really does play an imperial role in higher education.